MARKETING EFFICIENCY IN PUERTO RICO

A Study by the Social Science Research Center

University of Puerto Rico
Rio Piedras, Puerto Rico

MARKETING EFFICIENCY IN PUERTO RICO

by

John Kenneth Galbraith
Richard H. Holton

in collaboration with
Robert E. Branson
Jean Ruth Robinson
Carolyn Shaw Bell

Harvard University Press · Cambridge, Massachusetts · 1955

AS

ACKNOWLEDGMENTS

This study has placed us in the debt of numerous able assistants in Puerto Rico. These included Edwin Andújar, Leo Campbell Street, Peterson Ortíz Terreforte, Benjamin Rivera Ortíz, José M. Cruz Vargas, William Feliciana Ruíz, Fernando Torres, Florencio Vega, Sergio Vélez González, Jaime A. Collazo, Manual Candelario, José Salgado, Luis F. Sierra Pino, and Ramón H. Rodríguez. All of the foregoing were associated with the collection of the original data from store operators of various kinds, and at various stages in the study. Ermida García de Albizu assisted in the tabulation of the results of these interviews. Harry Frank Noriega and Luis Pérez Fiz assisted in collecting the data on which the cost functions of retailers and wholesalers were based. Ada Elsa Izcoa, Román Santos Isaac, Aristalco Calero, and Lydia Vélez García performed various aspects of the research necessary to estimating the cost functions and computing the island food bill. Maximino Vélez Nieves conducted a large number of the interviews of retailers for the purpose of constructing the cost functions and gave invaluable assistance in developing the functions and estimating the food bill savings. Felipe S. Viscasillas, now on the staff of the Office of Research and Statistics of the Department of the Treasury of Puerto Rico, was largely responsible for the planning and carrying out of the survey of food retailers' attitudes.

Professor John D. Black of Harvard University assisted in the initial planning of the study. Robert E. Branson and Carolyn Shaw Bell collaborated in the preparation of Chapters II through V. Chapters VI through IX are the work of Richard H. Holton, and Jean Ruth Robinson conducted the research leading to Chapters X, XI, and XII.

The entire study was financed by the Social Science Research Center of the University of Puerto Rico and particular thanks are due Dr. Millard Hansen, Director of the Center, and his staff. The authors' greatest debt, however, is to the merchants of Puerto Rico, whose heartwarming cooperation made the study possible.

CONTENTS

1. The Approach to Marketing in Puerto Rico   1

2. The Problem in Its Setting   5
     Income Levels and Distribution   5
     Consumption Patterns   9

3. Food Retailing   14
     The Nature of the Field Study   14
     Number and Size of Firms   16
     Types of Operation   19
     Capital Requirements   22
     Buying Practices   23
     Retail Costs and Margins   28

4. Food Wholesaling   36
     The Nature of the Field Study   36
     Management and Employment   37
     Types of Wholesale Operations   39
     Selling Practices   40
     Sources of Supply   44
     Capital Requirements   48
     Labor Utilization   50
     Costs and Margins   54

5. Management Practices and Attitudes   62
     Organization and Entry into Retailing   62
     The Store and the Community   69

6. A Model Food Distribution System   74
     The Concept of the Model   76
     The Alternative Model Systems   80
     Model Retail Firms   81
     The Model Wholesale Firm   83
     Constructing the Model Systems   84

7. The Optimal Retail Unit   86
     The Original Accounting Data   86
     The Projected Cost Analyses   88
     Isolated Rural Stores   90
     Rural Town Stores   93
     Market Town Stores   97
     Metropolitan Stores   100

8. The Optimal Wholesale Unit   105
   The Findings   106

9. The Completed Model   110
   The Present Island Food Bill   110
   The Model Wholesale System   115
   Evaluation of the Savings Estimate   121

10. Non-Food Marketing: Setting and Method   125
   Sources of Information   127
   Sampling Procedure   128

11. Retailing of Non-Food Products   132
   Employment and Employment Functions   135
   Prices and Merchandising Policies   137
   Investment   139
   Retail Costs and Margins   143
   Gross Markups   150
   Credit Policies   150
   Source of Supply   152
   Terms of Purchase   154

12. The Wholesaling of Non-Food Products   157
   The Sample Studied   157
   Size of Firms   160
   Employment and Selling Policies   161
   Investment   164
   Expenses   165
   Information by Lines Handled   169
   Manufacturing Wholesalers   172

13. The Context of Policy   173

14. Measures to Improve the Efficiency of the Marketing System:
   Consumer and Retail Education   177
   Consumer Education   178
   Retailer Education   180

15. Measures to Improve the Efficiency of the Marketing System:
   Direct Steps   185
   Chain Store Operations   185
   Consumer Cooperatives   189
   Central Warehouse and Dock Facilities   191
   Promotion of Price Advertising   192
   Recapitalization of Progressive Firms   193
   Price and Margin Control   193
   Outlawing Exclusive Agents   194
   Control of Entry   196
   Direct Government Intervention   197

   Index   199

TABLES

1. Income distribution of spending units, United States and Puerto Rico, 1950   6
2. Net product of Puerto Rico valued at factor cost, by industrial origin, fiscal years ending June 30, 1940 and June 30, 1951   7
3. Personal consumption expenditures in selected categories, the United States and Puerto Rico, 1950–51   9
4. Selected items of the Puerto Rican food bill   11
5. Retail stores: sales, sales per employee, and sales per customer transaction, by sales class   17
6. Number of retail food stores, by sales class and by percentage of sales on credit   20
7. Number of retail food stores, by sales class and by percentage of sales delivered   21
8. Monthly inventory turnover of retail food stores, by sales class   22
9. Suppliers to retail stores: percentage of sales purchased from and number used, by sales class, by lines handled, and by type of supplier   25
10. Retail gross margins: weighted average, range, and frequency, by sales class   29
11. Average sales, average gross margins, four types of retail food stores, by sales class   30
12. Gross and net margins and operating expense ratios for retail food stores, by sales class (percentage of total sales)   31
13. Number of food wholesalers in sample, and average sales, by sales class   37
14. Average sales per worker, food wholesalers by sales class   37
15. Average sales, range of sales, and salesmen expenditure per month, food wholesalers, according to number of towns served   38
16. Wholesaler sales of five product lines, by location of firm   41
17. Percentage of sales of full-line and limited-line wholesalers, in which products moved through wholesalers' warehouse   42
18. Number of wholesalers, average volume of sales, and range of sales, by per cent of sales delivered   42
19. Number of wholesalers, average volume of sales, and range of sales, according to per cent of sales on credit   43
20. Source of supply for principal products of San Juan wholesalers   45
21. Source of supply for principal products of inland wholesalers   46
22. Source of supply to wholesalers, by sales class   47
23. Inventory turnover, full-line and limited-line wholesalers, by sales class   50

24. Major components of present investment by full-line wholesalers, by sales class — 51
25. Major components of present investment by limited-line wholesalers, by sales class — 52
26. Classification of kind and number of workers employed in full-line wholesale houses, by sales class — 53
27. Classification of kind and number of workers employed in limited-line wholesale houses, by sales class — 53
28. Total sales, gross and net margin, and operating expenses of food wholesalers — 55
29. Sample wholesalers, total sales, and gross profits, by sales class, United States and Puerto Rico, 1949 — 56
30. Expense ratios of food wholesalers selling full line of products — 57
31. Expense ratios of food wholesalers selling limited line of products — 58
32. Percentage markups over cost of goods sold, required by model stores offering no services, credit but no delivery, and credit and delivery, by market area served — 104
33. Computation of island food bill valued at cost to the wholesalers, July 1, 1949 to July 1, 1950 (in dollars) — 111
34. Total operating margins, in dollars, required by retailers in model systems LS, C, and CD, by market area type — 118
35. Number of stores and employment in retail sector of model systems LS, C, and CD, by market area type — 120
36. Distribution of stores in the final working sample, by lines handled and by location — 131
37. Number of stores and total sales in non-food stores, by sales class and by store type — 134
38. Number and percentages of stores, by lines handled and by sales class — 135
39. Average number of employees and sales per employee, by class and by store type — 136
40. Average inventory, total capital, inventory turnover rates and capital turnover rates, by sales class and by store type — 141
41. Average sales, expense ratios, and profit ratios for clothing stores, by sales class — 143
42. Average sales, expense ratios, and profit ratios for shoe stores, by sales class — 143
43. Average sales, expense ratios, and profit ratios for furniture and furnishings stores, by sales class — 144
44. Average sales, expense ratios, and profit ratios for appliance stores, by sales class — 144
45. Average sales, expense ratios, and profit ratios for hardware stores, by sales class — 144
46. Average sales, expense ratios, and profit ratios for drugstores, by sales class — 145
47. Average percentage markups over cost of goods sold for lines handled, by area and volume of sales — 149

48. Distribution of stores according to markups and lines carried   150
49. Percentage of sales for cash or on credit to consumers, by lines handled and by area   151
50. Percentage of sales by source of supply, lines carried, and sales class   153
51. Distribution of wholesalers, by lines handled and by area in census, survey, and sample   159
52. Percentage of firms and yearly volume of sales for wholesalers, by sales class, in Sample, in 1949 Census of Business of Puerto Rico, and in 1948 United States Census of Business   161
53. Number of firms and average volume of sales, by type of wholesaler in Sample, in 1949 Census of Business of Puerto Rico, and in 1948 United States Census of Business   161
54. Average number of employees and average sales per worker, by type of wholesaler   162
55. Average yearly inventory, working capital, and total capital turnover ratios, by type of wholesaler   166
56. Average yearly inventory, working capital, and total capital turnover ratios for wholesalers, by sales class   166
57. Average expenses and profit ratios for wholesalers, by sales class (percentage of total sales)   167
58. Average expenses and profit ratios for wholesalers, by type of wholesaler (percentage of sales)   168
59. Percentage markups over cost of goods sold by wholesalers to various customers, by lines handled   169
60. Percentages of purchases by wholesalers from various sources of supply, by lines carried   170
61. Percentages of purchases on various credit terms, by lines carried   171

FIGURES

1. Percentage markup over cost to retailer required by isolated rural stores offering counter service, no credit, and no delivery   90
2. Percentage markup over cost to retailers required by rural town stores, offering counter service, no credit, and no delivery   93
3. Percentage markup over cost to retailers required by rural town stores, offering counter service, credit, and no delivery   94
4. Percentage markup over cost to retailers required by rural town stores, offering counter service, credit, and delivery   95
5. Percentage markup over cost to retailer required by market town stores, offering no credit, no delivery   96
6. Percentage markup over cost to retailers required by market town stores, offering credit and no delivery   97
7. Percentage markup over cost to retailers required by market town stores offering credit and delivery   99
8. Percentage markup over cost to retailer required by metropolitan stores, offering counter service, no credit, and no delivery   101
9. Percentage markup over cost to retailer required by metropolitan stores, offering counter service, credit, and no delivery   102
10. Percentage markup over cost to retailer required by metropolitan stores, offering counter service, delivery, and credit   103
11. Percentage markup over cost of goods sold required by wholesaler at present and projected sales volumes, assuming no delivery   107

MARKETING EFFICIENCY IN PUERTO RICO

1

THE APPROACH TO MARKETING

IN PUERTO RICO

In this volume we present a comprehensive study of the marketing of food and other important products of everyday use in the Commonwealth of Puerto Rico. In part our purpose is descriptive — for many reasons it is necessary that a community know and understand its economic institutions. The marketing system is an important part of an economy and our first task in this study is to learn more of the consumer marketing system of Puerto Rico for the ends such knowledge may serve.

However, our objective goes beyond such description. Thoughtful Puerto Ricans have long felt that there are serious shortcomings in the way food and other products are distributed to the people of the island and that, in particular, the process is unduly costly and inefficient. The present study was the result of such convictions and the hope that from better knowledge might come reliable indications of how the marketing system could be made to serve the people of the Commonwealth at lower cost. We have gone further to try to compare the present organization of marketing activity with what it might be. And we have also had in mind measures by which the government and people of the Commonwealth could make progress toward a more efficient organization of marketing activity.

A preliminary word is needed on the special objectives, and in some measure also, on the special problems of a study of marketing in Puerto Rico. These goals and problems have general application to the study of marketing in other undeveloped and developing countries.

If manpower or capital is used in marketing when it would yield a higher real return in some other employment, the community is by so much the poorer for this misuse of its resources. A very great deal of our research in marketing in the continental United States proceeds, rightly or wrongly, on the assumption that marketing activity does in fact absorb more than its appropriate share of resources. The utilization of one of these resources in other employments would thus enhance the total real income of the community.

The resource which attracts the greatest attention, in this connection, is labor. Without much doubt, the limits on the productive capacity of the United States are set, more particularly than by any other factor, by the supply of labor and the effectiveness with which that labor is employed. To the extent that labor is employed unnecessarily in marketing we are wasting our scarcest productive agent and denying ourselves production that we might otherwise have.

These are not, however, the standards with which one approaches the marketing system of Puerto Rico. Labor in Puerto Rico is not scarce; on the contrary it is tragically plentiful in relation to the full-time employment opportunities that are normally available. The amount of labor used in marketing, especially in the retailing of food, is exceedingly high as this study will make very clear. But the alternative to such employment is not necessarily a larger contribution to the production and wealth of the Commonwealth; it may only be unemployment or partial employment or even full-time employment at a lower real return than in the marketing system. If it were shown that food could be retailed in Puerto Rico with a third fewer workers than at present and were such an economy of manpower put into effect tomorrow, it is not clear that the labor so released would much increase the output of the island. There is danger that the immediate result would be an increase of about the same number in net unemployment. The reason that the retail food industry of Puerto Rico is overmanned is less that people are drawn into food and other retailing by the normal attraction of wages and profits than that they are propelled into this occupation by the absence of any alternative opportunity for a livelihood.

There is a twofold consequence of this situation which must shape any study of marketing in Puerto Rico. First, and to a far greater extent than in a similar study on the mainland, we may fix our eyes directly on the cost of the marketing system to the consumer. What the consumer pays for an inefficient marketing system and what he would gain from a more efficient marketing system is our fundamental concern. We can be contented, in other words, with the simple, forthright question of what a poor marketing system does to the cost of food, clothing, and other products. The question of what the marketing system denies in useful resources to the rest of the economy is a problem of secondary or minor consequence. To be able to consider marketing efficiency in terms of direct cost to the consumer is a great simplification of our task, and it is further simplified in the case of the great majority of Puerto Rican consumer purchases by the heavy dependence of the island on imported goods. This latter means that the incidence of marketing costs is almost entirely on the consumer — the prices to which Puerto Rican costs and margins are added are made in the markets of the United States or the world at large. Thus, in a study of marketing in Puerto Rico, we can safely set, as our goal, the simple aim of lower costs and margins; and we can be reasonably certain that the benefits therefrom will redound to the consumer.

However, the problem of general efficiency in resource use has its counterpart in Puerto Rico. As just suggested, the overmanning of the Puerto Rican marketing system — and the subdivision of retail business among a large number of very small enterprises which, as we later show, operate at small volume and high cost — is an aspect of the general labor surplus on the island. In one sense the marketing system has become a form of unemployment relief — it returns a small income to people who would not otherwise find a livelihood or certainly not an equally satisfactory one. There is no way in which the marketing system of Puerto Rico can be made more efficient while continuing to employ as many people as at present. It would be easy but wholly improper to say that the good fortune of consumers arising from a less expensive marketing system would outweigh the misfortune of those who would lose their employment or their enterprises in that event. But it is beyond dispute that the utilization, even at small return, of unnecessary manpower in marketing — and the loading of this cost on to the food and clothing bill of a poor community — is a very poor form of unemployment relief. In economic terms it is highly regressive — it imposes on those who are least able to pay the bill the highest share of the cost.

On the other hand, no study of the present sort can be oblivious of the human problems which it raises. Partly in recognition of the role which retail trade plays as a formula for survival, Puerto Rican retailers have developed a live and let live attitude which allows for the business survival of the large number of people found in the industry. Profits that could be made are foregone in order to allow others to make a living. A change in these attitudes or the introduction of new marketing institutions with a different set of attitudes are essential if Puerto Rico is to have a lower cost marketing system. This means the displacement of a substantial proportion of the people now employed in marketing activity on the island. If the decision is taken — and, what may well be more important — if the means are found for reorganizing the marketing system, this must be done in a context where careful and compassionate consideration is given to the employment and well-being of those who are displaced. Such a consideration is not part of the present study: in excluding it, however, we do not minimize its importance. We do conclude that the marketing system of Puerto Rico does indeed impose a heavy burden of cost on the Puerto Rican consumer. We are also of the opinion that by wise and well designed measures, these costs can be reduced. But we believe that any such measures must proceed in harmony with measures designed to provide alternative income and employment for those left unemployed by a reorganized marketing system.

The chapters immediately following picture the food marketing system of the Commonwealth — more particularly the organization of the wholesale and retail trade — as it existed in 1949–50 when the first phase of the present study was initiated. Thereafter, we measure the present organization against a model which we take to represent a reasonable standard of efficiency and which, though no one should suppose it to be immediately attainable, represents, at a minimum, the kind of marketing system which could exist in Puerto Rico. Chapters X through XII deal with certain strengths and weaknesses of the marketing system for clothing, furniture, and other consumer products. In the final chapters of the study we offer our suggestions as to lines of policy which might help the Puerto Rican people to realize their undoubted desire for a more economical marketing system.

2

THE PROBLEM IN ITS SETTING

The way people live has an important bearing on the way goods are marketed. In Puerto Rico the level and distribution of incomes, the sources of supply of goods, and the consumption habits and tastes of the people determine both the nature of the goods consumed and the manner in which these goods are distributed to the people of the island.

Income Levels and Distribution

In Puerto Rico in 1950 the average cash income per spending unit was $898, which may be compared to $3,520 per spending unit in the United States.[1] While this Puerto Rican income figure represents a considerable increase in money income and real income over the level of the previous two decades, consumption by the people of the island is closely limited by the small amount of income available to them. Obviously a large proportion of it must be spent for the prime essentials of life and it is equally obvious that there is no margin for waste.

Not only is the present level of income low, but its distribution is notably unequal. Table 1 compares the distribution of income among all expenditure units in the United States and in Puerto Rico. About one-half of the spending units in the Commonwealth receive less than 15 per cent of the total income. Three-fourths of all the spending units receive less than $1,000 a year; the median income is only $518. On the other hand, people at the upper end of the income scale are strikingly few and wealthy; approximately 25 per cent of the total income goes to less than 5 per cent of the spending units.

[1] Figures from Bureau of Labor Statistics, Puerto Rico Department of Labor; and "1952 Survey of Consumer Finances," *Federal Reserve Bulletin*, September 1952. The spending unit is defined as all persons living in the same dwelling and belonging to the same family who pool their incomes to meet their major expenses. It may be assumed that the differences in non-monetary income — public services, home-grown food, etc. — would be substantially less than the differences in cash income.

Table 1   Income distribution of spending units,
United States and Puerto Rico, 1950

Income (dollars)	Percentage of spending units	
	United States	Puerto Rico
Under 500	} 13	51
500– 999		23
1,000–1,999	17	16
2,000–2,999	19	5
3,000–3,999	19	2
4,000–4,999	12	1
5,000–7,499	14 }	
7,500–9,999	3 }	2
10,000 and over	3 }	
Mean income	$3,520	$898
Median income	$3,000	$518

Sources: *Federal Reserve Bulletin*, August 1951, p. 920, Table 1; Bureau of Labor Statistics, Puerto Rico Department of Labor.

The counterpart of low incomes is low production. The value of the products of the land and factories and of home workers, added to the labor of those who provide services, gives a measure of total economic output. In 1951, this total net product (valued at factor cost) of Puerto Rico was estimated at $747.4 millions, or a per capita average of $336.82. In contrast, the net product (valued at factor cost) in the United States during the same period amounted to $276 billions, or $1,780.64 per person.

The use of resources on the island differs markedly from that on the mainland. In 1951, with the Commonwealth's net product at an all-time high, the four chief contributors were agriculture, retail and wholesale trade, the Federal and the insular governments, and manufacturing and mining, in that order. Agriculture on the island accounts for 22 per cent of the net product, but for only 7 per cent of the United States net product. The difference in industrial development and natural resources between the two economies means that manufacturing and mining contribute only 14 per cent to the total Puerto Rican product, as opposed to 33 per cent in the United States. (See Table 2.)

During the past decade, the island has increased its total production considerably,[2] while various sectors of the economy have shifted in their importance. Agriculture, which formerly accounted for almost one-third of the total income, now accounts for only one-fifth. Though

[2] Allowing for price increases and population growth the increase in per capita real net product is over 50 per cent.

Table 2   Net product of Puerto Rico valued at factor cost, by industrial origin, fiscal years ending June 30, 1940 and June 30, 1951

	1940		1951	
	Amount (in millions of dollars)[a]	Percentage of total[a]	Amount (in millions of dollars)[a]	Percentage of total[a]
All industries, total	227.8	100.0	747.4	100.0
Agriculture	70.5	30.9	164.2	22.0
Sugar cane cultivation	35.8	15.7	70.6	9.5
Other agriculture	34.7	15.2	93.6	12.5
Manufacturing and mining[b]	26.4	11.6	105.7	14.1
Food and kindred products	13.3	5.8	39.4	5.3
Sugar mills and refineries	(9.3)	(4.1)	(27.8)	(3.7)
Beverages	(2.2)	(1.0)	(4.8)	(0.6)
Other foods	(1.8)	(0.8)	(6.8)	(0.9)
Tobacco products	2.4	1.1	3.8	0.5
Apparel and textiles	5.8	2.5	29.3	3.9
Wooden products and furniture	0.6	0.3	3.1	0.4
Printing, publishing and allied trades	0.9	0.4	3.3	0.4
Chemicals and allied products	1.1	0.5	8.3	1.1
Stone, clay and glass products	0.6	0.3	11.0	1.5
Metal and machinery products	1.1	0.5	3.9	0.5
Paper, leather, and miscellaneous manufacturers	0.6	0.3	3.6	0.5
Contract construction	2.6	1.1	23.1	3.1
Transportation	13.5	5.9	36.7	4.9
Motor transportation	9.1	4.0	23.6	3.2
Other transportation services	4.4	1.9	13.0	1.8
Power and gas	1.8	0.8	0.5	0.1
Communications	0.7	0.3	2.0	0.3
Trade	24.3	10.7	160.0	21.4
Government	42.1	18.5	155.0	20.7
Federal	20.6	9.0	51.1	6.8
Insular[b]	21.6	9.5	103.9	13.9
Services	20.5	9.0	65.6	8.8
Finance	3.2	1.4	10.6	1.4
Real estate	21.5	9.4	28.8	3.9
Miscellaneous	4.3	1.9	9.7	1.3
Net international flow of capital returns	−3.6		−14.4	

Source: *Statistical Yearbook, 1950–51* Office of Economic Research, Economic Development Administration, Government of Puerto Rico, San Juan, Puerto Rico.
    [a] Detail will not necessarily add to totals because of rounding.
    [b] The 1940 figures for Insular government include 2.3 million dollars from government owned business enterprises. In 1951 these enterprises were in the private sector of the economy and are therefore included in the industry totals.

manufacturing has expanded sizably, it still provides less than 15 per cent of the total. The government contribution to insular income has increased slightly as a proportion of the total. The outstanding change, however, has taken place in trade (wholesaling and retailing), which expanded almost sixfold during the period and now accounts for 22 per cent of the total. Trade furnishes 14 per cent of the total employment as compared with 7 per cent in 1940. Agricultural employment has declined from 60 per cent to 36 per cent; manufacturing now provides 20 per cent of total employment as against 12 per cent in 1940; government employment, as a per cent of the total, has risen from 1 to 7 per cent over the decade.

The gains in net income, and in various sectors of the economy, have not, however, eliminated a problem of chronic underemployment. In 1940 one out of every six members of the labor force was unemployed; and by 1950 one out of every eight remained out of work. There is some indication, however, that the improvement in the economy has tended to maintain unemployment as an increasing number of women, not previously in the labor force, have begun to seek jobs and to report themselves unemployed.

Because of the age distribution of the population, in particular the relatively large number of children, the civilian labor force amounts to only 35 per cent of the total population. This means that each Puerto Rican worker must provide for two other persons besides himself, while his counterpart in the United States supports only one and one half other people. The number of jobless workers obviously increases the burden on those who do receive incomes.

A further feature of the Puerto Rican employment situation, not reflected in normal employment data, is the widespread underemployment in part-time and low-paying occupations. Almost half of the employed Puerto Ricans work less than thirty-five hours a week. Moreover, total employment, and hence income payments, fluctuate markedly during the year. In the year ending June 30, 1951, employment throughout the year averaged 662,000 persons, but this figure ranged from 587,000 in May to 691,000 in April and March. The "dead season" in the cane industry which extends after the harvest for about six months during the latter part of the year is sharply reflected in employment statistics. Non-agricultural employment also declines during this period, although not so steeply.[3]

[3] Average employment in agriculture during the fiscal year 1951 was 224,000, ranging from 193,000 in December to 253,000 in June. In non-agricultural occupations, employment averaged 438,000 over the same period, with a high of 450,000 in May and June and a low of 418,000 in July.

Consumption Patterns

The low income of the people of Puerto Rico goes far to determine the nature of the goods they consume. Obviously a large proportion of their income must go for food; that spent for other consumer products must be confined to immediate essentials and quality must frequently be sacrificed to low price. In Table 3 consumption expenditures on various types of goods in Puerto Rico are compared

Table 3   Personal consumption expenditures in selected categories, the United States and Puerto Rico, 1950–51

	United States (1950)		Puerto Rico	
	(millions of dollars)	Percentage of total	(thousands of dollars)	Percentage[a] of total
Total expenditures	194,277	100.0	808,731	100.0
Food and tobacco[b]	65,748	33.8	367,784	45.5
Clothing, accessories, and jewelry	23,025	11.9	76,404	9.4
Personal care	2,303	1.2	15,114	1.9
Housing	19,877	10.2	48,312	6.0
Household operations	26,451	13.6	113,521	14.0
Medical care and death expenses	9,463	4.9	32,371	4.0
Personal business	8,741	4.5	19,818	2.5
Transportation	22,526	11.6	67,704	8.4
Recreation	11,330	5.8	30,241	3.7
Private education	1,793	0.9	2,376	0.3
Religious and other nonprofit organizations	1,857	1.0	7,940	1.0
Foreign travel and remittances	1,163	0.6	27,146	3.4

Sources: United States figures adapted from *Survey of Current Business*, August 1951, U.S. Department of Commerce, Washington, D.C.; Puerto Rico figures, preliminary for the fiscal year ending June 30, 1951, adapted from Table 59, pp. 94–5, *Statistical Yearbook, 1950–51*.
[a] Detail will not necessarily add to totals because of rounding.
[b] Includes tobacco and alcoholic beverages.

with those in the United States. Because income is so unequally distributed, even these figures do not give an accurate picture of the typical consumption pattern in Puerto Rico. Many items in the table do not appear in the budget of the average family. Despite the large share of income spent on food, total food consumption remains slightly below the amount calculated as necessary to meet the nutritional needs of the population.

For most Puerto Ricans,[4] the day's activities begin after a break-

[4] The statistical data on diets and consumption in this chapter are obtained from Lydia J. Roberts and Stefani Rosa Luisa, *Patterns of Living in Puerto Rican Families*, University of Puerto Rico, Rio Piedras, Puerto Rico, 1949.

fast of coffee, accompanied in only half the families by bread, cereal, or cold *vianda* — the latter term covers a variety of starchy vegetables. The coffee is strong, black, and heavily sweetened. *Café con leche,* while preferred, depends on milk being available, and almost half the families average less than one cup of milk per person each day. Lunches consist largely of *viandas* or rice and beans; for one-third of the families these foods make up the entire meal; a like number add a little codfish, and the remaining households have other protein foods, vegetables, fruit, and milk. For supper, *viandas* or rice and beans, with no other food, provide meals for three-fourths of the families — a mere 20 per cent enjoy codfish or some other protein as well.

While the staple items in food consumption are all too easily identified, other foods are used in limited quantities. Rice and beans are cooked with lard or salt pork, and with onions, peppers, tomato paste, and other seasoning in *guisados* (stews). A majority of the people eat some fruit daily, though not at meals, and bread, fresh meat, eggs, chicken, and non-starchy vegetables such as *calabaza* (squash), snap beans, eggplant, and salads appear with varying frequency. Seventy per cent of the families average less than two eggs per person weekly — for the price of a single egg a family can purchase enough rice for a meal. Chickens are very rarely used for food. Over 80 per cent of families with a yearly income of less than $500 — and that includes almost half the people of Puerto Rico — reported they seldom or never ate chicken. Other types of meat are likewise costly and little used. Forty per cent of all the families eat meat only on rare occasions if ever.

With such a meager and monotonous diet, little household equipment is needed to prepare and serve food. For the type of cooking found in most households, only a few utensils are indispensable — a bowl, one or two kettles, a coffee-bag and pot, a mortar and pestle, and odd knives, forks, and spoons. Yet many families lack even these simple products, and dishes made at home from gourds or tin cans serve most of the rural families.

Homemade articles also provide many other furnishings. One-third of all urban families and over half the rural families have less than fifteen pieces of furniture — beds, cots, hammocks, a table, bench, stools, or chairs. These latter are often dignified names for old boxes and barrels pressed into service. Used containers also provide the material for shelves and chests and cupboards. Clothing, which is meager for most families, is also frequently made at home, either from discarded materials or purchased yard goods.

The notable difference in consumption in families with different incomes is the extent to which store purchases replace such homemade furnishings. Where there is more money to spend, beds are substituted for hammocks or rough wooden benches, thin mats or springs and mattresses replace the rags used for sleeping, pots and pans and dishes are used instead of gourds, and the typical furniture set of a table and chairs with cane seats and backs appears in place of old crates and homemade tables. Such purchases are almost entirely of imported goods, and the dependence on imported production (chiefly from the United States) is a leading characteristic of Puerto Rican consumption.

The volume of imported food supplies, particularly the staples of rice, beans, tomato sauce, fish, and fat, is impressively large. In 1951 enough rice was imported to provide each person in Puerto Rico with forty-two ounces a week, a figure which checks closely with an estimated average consumption of forty-five ounces per week. Enough vegetable and animal fat (chiefly lard and salt pork) was imported to provide each person with twelve ounces of fat per week, a figure which also corresponds to the average, reported by consumers, of twelve and one half ounces. Imported beans and dry legumes amounted to more than half a pound, per person, out of the average weekly consumption of eighteen ounces.[5] Some 37,000,000 pounds of codfish were imported, to provide an average per capita consumption of 5.2 ounces. Tomato sauce imports amounted to 25,000,000 pounds.

Table 4   Selected items of the Puerto Rican food bill

Rice	$30,000,000
Beans, imported	6,000,000
Beans, domestic	2,500,000
Tomato sauce	3,500,000
Lard	9,000,000
Codfish	8,000,000
Salt pork	3,000,000
Total	$62,000,000

The importance of imported foods is indicated, if somewhat crudely, by multiplying the physical volume of imports by the prices quoted in the Commonwealth Bureau of Labor Statistics Consumers' Price Index. Selected items in the Commonwealth food bill at retail for the year 1949–50 appear in Table 4.

[5] Average consumption figures in Roberts and Stefani, *Patterns of Living*, pp. 368, 386, 371. Figures on rice in Appendix Table 172, on fat in Table 198, and on beans in Table 178. Figures on imported foods from U.S. Department of Commerce, Bureau of the Census, Foreign Trade Division, quoted in Tables 129 and 132, *Annual Book of Statistics of Puerto Rico, Fiscal Year 1949–50,* Economic Development Administration, Office of Economic Research, San Juan, Puerto Rico, pp. 145–207, 278–296.

In 1949, total retail sales of all the grocery stores on the island amounted to approximately $175,000,000.[6] It is obvious, therefore, that these few imported items account for a sizable share of food expenditures.

However, local production — particularly of vegetables, milk, eggs, and pork — provides an important addition to the diet. Much of this supply moves directly into consumption or otherwise bypasses the marketing system. Thus the small amount of rice which is raised on the island is usually consumed by the growers. Eggs, and to a lesser extent milk, are obtained directly from home production. The small farmer who kills a cow, goat, or pig often takes orders for meat from other families before slaughtering the animal. The total amount of food which moves in this fashion cannot be precisely measured, but two examples show the magnitudes involved.

In 1950, milk production on farms was estimated at 164,000,000 quarts. If this production is valued at the retail price of milk sold through stores, some $31,000,000 worth of milk was produced and consumed in the island. Yet total sales of milk at retail amounted to only $2,221,100.[7] On a conservative estimate, therefore, almost fifteen times as much milk was obtained outside the marketing system as through it.

Some crude figures for fresh vegetables are even more striking. Four varieties for which the Bureau of Labor Statistics retail price reporting is available include plantains, bananas, tomatoes, and taniers. These do not exhaust the list of important domestic vegetables, for other varieties are produced in even greater quantities than some of these. If, however, the production of these four items is valued at the retail prices reported by the Bureau of Labor Statistics, the total amount is over $18,000,000. This may be contrasted with the total reported sales of fruit and vegetable stores (which of course handle many other items besides these four and do not, in turn, sell all of the fruit and vegetables that are handled) of less than $3,000,000. The proportion of the total supply of vegetables which moves through ordinary market channels may well be smaller than in the case of milk.

Among non-food products, imported supplies are again dominant.

[6] This estimate was derived from studies made for the present volume, and is described more fully in Chapter IX.

[7] Farm production from Bureau of Agricultural Economics, Department of Agriculture and Commerce. Underestimating is generally expected. The Bureau of Labor Statistics, Department of Labor, reports an average price of 18.8 cents for fresh milk sold in stores. These two figures are on a fiscal year basis. Retail store sales in preliminary figures from Census, covering the calendar year 1949, include sales by milkstands and distributors' routes. A very small amount of milk is sold in other types of stores whose sales are not included in this classification.

Only furniture and clothing are manufactured for sale locally in any volume, and only a portion of the market is so supplied.

Appliances, automobiles, drugs, house furnishings, and all such articles, from the kitchen gadget to the machete in common use, come chiefly from the United States.

In summary, therefore, the function of the marketing system in Puerto Rico is to serve consumers of relatively low incomes with the everyday essentials, of which food is by far the most important. A very large proportion of both the food and non-food products come from abroad, which means that the costs of marketing the goods in Puerto Rico are added to those of ocean carriage to the ports of the island. The combination of incomes barely sufficient to purchase essential products and the long route by which these products come to the people of Puerto Rico mean that marketing costs are of exceptional importance in the welfare of the people of the island. No opportunity for improving the marketing system and lowering its cost can be overlooked.

3

FOOD RETAILING

The outstanding characteristic of Puerto Rican food retailers is their great number and small size, a feature which is of everyday observation and which is affirmed in all the statistics. It is the conclusion which emerges most strongly from the present study of some 470 food stores representative of the most important types of food retailers on the island.

The Nature of the Field Study

Of the 16,746 retail firms listed by the Census of Distribution as selling food, 14,139 are described as grocery stores. The Census describes such a store, known in Puerto Rico as the *colmado*, as primarily engaged in selling processed foods and dry groceries, although fresh meat, vegetables, and fruits may also be carried. It is these stores which are the backbone of the retail marketing system — these are the stores that distribute the imported staple foods throughout the island. It is with these stores, together with the fruit and vegetable markets, that the present study is concerned.

After the grocery stores in importance come four groups of specialized food stores. There are defined, in terms of their principle sales, by the Census as fruit stores and vegetable markets, meat and fish (seafood) markets, milk dealers and milk stands, and miscellaneous food stores. In 1949 there were 1,343 fruit and vegetable stores, 383 meat and fish markets, 22 milk dealers offering home delivery, 170 milk stands, and 469 miscellaneous stores. Except for 8 milk dealers and 9 miscellaneous food stores, none of these outlets had sales exceeding $50,000 a year. The majority of the fruit and vegetable markets and of the candy, nut, and confectionery stores had sales of less than $3,000 a year, while in most of the meat stores sales were between $5,000 and $25,000 a year.

The miscellaneous food group included 11 small bakeries, some house to house distributors of vegetables and fruits, and some *lechoneras.* These last sell roast meat, commonly pork, and are classified as retailers if more than 50 per cent of their sales are for consumption off the premises. Other specialized stores in this category include retailers grinding and roasting coffee for sale.

The stalls in the *mercados* or markets are not all enumerated in the Census. Those rented on a more or less permanent basis — either to farmers who bring bananas, mangoes, or other fresh produce frequently to the market or to retailers who buy from farmers every day — were counted by the Census and most of the very small firms listed as "fruit stands and vegetable markets" in the Census are probably such market stalls. The temporary stands of the farmers who sell intermittently, or of the truckers who fail to dispose of their loads to the usual customers were not enumerated.

Two other types of retail outlets should be mentioned, both peculiar to the Puerto Rican environment. There are the *reposterías,* classified by the Census as manufacturers, which do a sizable volume of retail business, selling ice cream, sandwiches, their own bakery products, soft drinks and coffee, and other light lunch items. (If this latter part of their business is dominant, they may be classified as eating places.) Many of them also sell canned goods, cold meats, and prepared foods, and in this respect they resemble American delicatessens. Secondly, there are *cafetines,* or bars. They sell canned goods, coffee, sugar and other staples as well as rum and beer, but are classified as grocery stores if sales of grocery products amount to 50 per cent of their volume.

There are no data to suggest what proportion of total food supplies move through these last two types of outlets, but two features of their operations should be noted. The *reposterías* and *cafetines* are not subject to the closing hours which affect other types of retailers. Hence food may be purchased on Sundays, holidays, evenings, or while drinking beer or coffee. Conventional retailers, particularly in small villages or towns, may suffer considerably from this advantage of the *cafetines* and *reposterías.* Secondly, because these establishments, despite their considerable volume of food sales, operate as eating places or bars, their operating costs and margins do not necessarily conform to those of food retailers. The type of employee, their working hours and wages, the space used to handle food sales, are all subsidiary to the firm's business of providing refreshments.

Only the conventional food retailers were included in the field study on which this chapter is based. Peddlers, intermittent stall holders, *cafetines, reposterías,* and other stores which might have been enumerated by the Census as grocery stores were excluded. The sample of firms also omitted the smallest stores listed in the Census, specifically some 549 fruit and vegetable dealers and almost 4,000 grocery stores with sales of less than $1,000 a year. These ventures are scarcely commercial operations and, apart from the fact that such minute enterprises exist in large numbers, no analysis of their operations seemed necessary or possible. However, their omission does mean that the sample of firms studied is weighted toward the larger firms, which actually sell most of the food. The 425 groceries in the sample averaged sales of $24,000 yearly. However, 50 per cent of the firms sampled had sales volumes of less than $12,000 yearly. It should be noted that, while Puerto Rico is rightly considered the domain of the small store, a substantial part of the total volume is done by a small number of the larger enterprises. Thus 3 per cent of the firms in the sample accounted for 24 per cent of the total sales. The average sales of this small group were over $100,000 yearly, or four times as great as the average sales of the sample firms as a whole.

The Census lists 1,343 fruit stores and vegetable markets, of which fifty-two, with an average sales volume of $3,630 were selected for the field study. While 40 per cent of the firms enumerated by the Census sold less than $1,000 per year, only 9 such firms were included in the sample, and these were near the top of that sales class. Three firms with sales of $10,000 to $25,000 annually were also chosen for study.

The sample was drawn to include stores in different areas throughout the island. On the basis of one grocery store to each 5,000 people, stores in all the seventy-seven *municipios* in Puerto Rico were sampled, although the final results include firms in only sixty-seven of the *municipios*. Sixty-one of the 425 groceries and 5 of the 52 fruit and vegetable stores are in rural areas. Where more than one store was selected from a given locality an effort was made to represent the various types and sizes of stores there. Because of the nature of the sample the data from the field study cannot be "inflated" to describe the entire retail marketing structure on the island; it does, however, show the important characteristics of food retailing.

Number and Size of Firms

Despite the exclusion of the very small enterprises, the outstanding finding of the study is still the small scale of the typical store. As Table 5 shows, average sales per store are low, average sales per employee are low, and the number of customers served and the dollar amounts involved are strikingly small.

Thus, while a yearly sales volume of $12,000 would appear to be a minimum for the support of even one worker, many smaller stores have two employees. The average sales per employee increases with the volume of sales, but at a decreasing rate. The twelve stores whose

Table 5   Retail stores: sales, sales per employee, and sales per customer transaction, by sales class

Monthly sales (dollars)	Number of stores			Average sales (dollars)		
	Urban	Rural	Total	Per store	Per employee	Per customer transaction
Grocery stores						
Less than 500	73	20	93	296	253.86	0.38
500– 999	87	21	108	686	466.00	0.74
1,000– 1,999	93	17	110	1,334	723.78	0.99
2,000– 3,999	53	1	54	2,692	1,061.09	1.54
4,000– 9,999	46	2	48	5,753	1,484.61	1.77
10,000–40,000	12	0	12	17,583	1,900.90	4.00
Total	364	61	425	—	—	—
Average	—	—	—	2,049	970.33	1.39
Fruit and vegetable stores						
Less than 99	10	1	11	52	48	
100– 299	19	2	21	188	158	
300– 499	13	1	14	387	362	
500– 999	2	1	3	583	350	
1,000–1,999	3	0	3	1,351	676	
Total	47	5	52	—	—	
Average	—	—	—	303	250	

sales range from $10,000 to $100,000 monthly as might be expected, because of their volume, operate more efficiently. Their average monthly sales of $17,500 is sixty times that of the smallest store, and their average sales per employee is $1,900 monthly, or seven and one-half times as great.

Customers typically buy little at a time: the average purchase is less than $2.00 in stores with monthly sales of less than $10,000. Low incomes obviously limit the total food expenditure per family, but the small unit sale reflects frequent transactions as well as small ones. While credit might be expected to allow a family to buy its needs in larger quantities at longer intervals, refrigeration and storage space is scarce in most homes; many housewives also dislike to use leftovers or to prepare food in advance, and prefer newly bought ingredients at each meal. In upper-income areas, stores provide order and delivery services which allow the housewife to buy food several times daily, as her needs occur to her. Consumer habit and preference are clearly reflected in the size of the average transaction.

In larger stores the number of employees and the low sales per employee are also related to the services provided, especially to messenger and delivery service. In smaller stores, employment may be determined less by the needs of customers (who average only twenty to thirty a day) than by the need to provide an occupation for persons connected with the store owner. Thus 93 stores doing less than $500 a month reported 108 workers, including owners and only one paid employee. Among the 103 stores with yearly sales from $7,000 to $9,000 there were only 27 paid employees, 13 of whom were employed by 4 firms. The sales volume of such firms cannot be thought to provide useful work for this number of employees. Rather, the employment reflects the size of the owner's family and the lack of other opportunity in the area. This work force may, nevertheless, furnish a kind of justification for the high prices and margins necessary to support it.

Although a high labor-sales ratio is common among stores with a very low volume of sales, it does not disappear completely at higher sales volumes. Nor do the reasons for it. A store which is expected to support family members even when it is extremely small and unprofitable may be expected to provide more employment as it increases in size.[1]

The smaller firms in the sample do business with a minimum of physical space. Twenty-seven of the grocery stores in the sample occupied less than 100 square feet; 121 firms occupied between 100 and 250 square feet of floor space. In a typical store the equipment consists of a counter and a set of shelves behind the counter, and perhaps an old desk under which there is a strong-box. The stock of the store is piled up haphazardly in every conceivable spot in the store — in front, on top, or under and behind the counter, and on the shelves. Little space is left for the public or clerks to move.

Most of the firms selling less than $500 monthly occupied less than 250 square feet, as did many stores selling up to $1,000 monthly. Stores with 500 to 750 square feet of space had monthly sales ranging from less than $250 to over $10,000. It is evident that a sizable volume of business can be done in limited physical space: over half the stores selling more than $5,000 monthly had less than 750 square feet of space, and one firm with monthly sales of almost $10,000 occupied less than 500 square feet. Only half the firms with sales greater than this figure occupied more than 1,000 square feet of space.

The selling space available to the retailer is rarely planned in

[1] That one function of retailing and wholesaling is to provide more employment than can be justified on economic terms seems to be recognized by many owners and managers. The head of one firm admits that his stores would have done better if he had used a more rigorous and rational personnel policy, instead of yielding to his humanitarian impulses. He is reluctant to weed out inefficient or surplus personnel, preferring to tolerate inefficiency than to leave a man without a job and expose his family to hunger.

relation to operations. The very small outlets may be part of the owner's dwelling or shacks located nearby. Turnover can be substantially increased before larger quarters are required because the average customer transaction is small and inventories are sparse. For twenty or thirty customers a day, little or no space is needed for traffic within the store. For a limited line of goods space is needed for only a few hundred-pound bags, a box of dried fish, and a few other bulk containers.

Types of Operation

Over half the stores were found to carry only staples and canned goods.[2] Sales of these items by such stores accounted for 52 per cent of the total sales of all the firms. While twenty-five other stores carried either fruits and vegetables or meats in addition to these basic foods, only 11 per cent of all the stores were full-line operations (handling staples, canned goods, fruits and vegetables, and meat.) These fifty-four stores, however, accounted for 40 per cent of the total sales. The specialty stores, selling only meat, only canned goods, or only fruits and vegetables, were few in number and their total sales were small.

The sales volumes of the different types of stores cover a wide range. Monthly sales of the outlets with from 90 to 100 per cent of sales in staples ranged from less than $250 to over $7,000. Stores carrying canned goods, cereals, and staples appeared in every sales volume class up to $15,000 monthly, although most of them grossed between $1,000 and $2,000 monthly. This latter type of store is the most common in both rural and urban areas. Few stores of any size carry the specialty lines of fresh produce or meat; those that do, usually firms selling between $1,000 and $2,000 monthly, are commonly found in urban locations. In the country, consumers buy meat, fruit, and vegetables directly from producers.

The fifty-four full-line stores — those with sales of staples, canned goods and cereals, fruits and vegetables, and meats — ranged in sales volume from $800 to $40,000 monthly. Half of them grossed less than

[2] A store was considered to handle canned goods only if these foods amounted to 15 per cent of total store sales. Fruits and vegetables were counted as products offered if these sales amounted to 10 per cent of total sales, and the same rule was followed for meat. The stores classified as selling staples were those where sales of staples amounted to 25 per cent of the total sales. If a store sold any amount of all four types of products, it was defined as a full-line outlet. Staples were defined as all foods, other than canned goods and cereal products, which do not require refrigeration. This definition includes rice, dried beans and peas, lard, dried fish, coffee, sugar, salt pork, cured ham, onions, and so forth. Canned goods are self-explanatory, except that canned powdered milk and canned meats were included, along with bottled items. Cereals include macaroni and spaghetti, crackers, cereals, and other grain products. Fruits and vegetables include all these foods except onions and potatoes. Meat was confined to fresh meat requiring immediate sale or refrigeration.

$4,500 per month, but ten did over $10,000. None of these stores was located in a rural area.

In the continental United States, where cash-and-carry stores are common, credit where offered by retailers can be considered a special service. The alternative of cheaper cash purchase is readily available. The credit offered by Puerto Rican retailers is, in contrast, an intrinsic and nearly universal feature of the marketing system.

Aside from the 6 stores for which information was lacking, 94 per cent of the stores made some credit sales, and more than half did over 60 per cent of their total volume of business on credit. In every sales volume class, as shown in Table 6, most firms sold from 40 to

Table 6   Number of retail food stores, by sales class and by percentage
of sales on credit

Monthly sales (dollars)	Per cent on credit					Total
	0	5–39	40–79	80–100	N. A.	
			Number of stores			
Less than 500	8	17	49	13	6	93
500– 999	4	31	62	11		108
1,000– 1,999	3	14	71	22		110
2,000– 3,999	4	6	33	11		54
4,000– 9,999	2	11	30	5		48
10,000–40,000	1	1	8	2		12
Total	22	80	253	64	6	425

80 per cent of their total volume on credit. A breakdown by the location of stores shows that credit sales are about equally prevalent in rural and in urban areas. A slightly higher proportion of rural stores make from 75 to 100 per cent of all their sales on credit than is the case with urban stores.

A rough designation of the income area where the store was located suggests that credit sales are by no means confined to low income areas. Thirty-two per cent of the stores located in urban high-income areas did between 75 and 100 per cent of their business on credit, as did 24 per cent of the stores located in average-income urban areas, and 31 per cent of those in lower income urban areas. Only 17 of the 364 urban stores offered no credit as opposed to 5 of the 61 rural stores.

Credit extended to upper-income consumers involves extensive services. Such customers use telephones or messengers to place orders, have their purchases delivered, and are at liberty to return merchandise. The middle- or upper-income Puerto Rican housewife is unwilling to perform the chores of marketing, particularly when these require her to carry bundles. Again, credit makes the individual transaction small and requires the large number of employees previously noted. The more efficient retail stores usually limit the amount of credit extended to any individual customer, and some retailers make loans to consumers apart from the store accounts.

Delivery, on the other hand, is much less common than extension of credit. (See Table 7.) None of the rural stores studied offered

Table 7 Number of retail food stores, by sales class and by percentage of sales delivered

Monthly sales (dollars)	Per cent delivered						Total
	0	5–19	20–39	40–59	60–79	80–100	
	Number of stores						
Less than 500	93	0	0	0	0	0	93
500– 999	101	3	2	1	1	0	108
1,000– 1,999	87	11	6	3	2	1	110
2,000– 3,999	34	3	3	5	7	2	54
4,000– 9,999	23	3	4	5	7	6	48
10,000–40,000	0	1	0	0	8	3	12
Total	338	21	15	14	25	12	425

delivery; these small enterprises are widely scattered over the country-side and are within walking distance of their clientele. Only one quarter of the urban stores delivered orders. More of the stores located in upper-income areas offered delivery service than did those in the average- and lower-income areas, and delivered sales form a larger share of total sales for stores located in the upper-income areas.

Delivery service is not closely correlated with the volume of sales: the twelve firms which deliver from 80 to 100 per cent of their sales, range in volume from one at $1,200 sales monthly to one at $25,000. However, most of the smaller stores which offer delivery, deliver less than one half their sales volume, while most of those doing over $3,000 monthly deliver over half of their total sales. Better delivery service was mentioned by retailers as one method by which they sought to maintain or develop their busines in 41 out of 421 instances, and these ranged, again, from the smallest sale class to the largest.

There were 18 strictly cash-and-carry stores among the 425 firms studied. Four cash stores made deliveries, and two of these delivered between 70 and 79 per cent of their total sales.

Capital Requirements

Many of the characteristics of Puerto Rican retailing so far discussed — the heavy concentration on canned goods and staples, the small sales per employee and per customer, and the atomistic nature of food retailing in general — are reflected in the current assets of the stores studied.

Table 8   Monthly inventory turnover of retail food stores, by sales class

Monthly sales (dollars)	Monthly sales total (dollars)	Inventory total (dollars)	Monthly inventory turnover (percentage)
Less than 500	27,544	27,205	1.012
500– 999	74,094	66,484	1.114
1,000– 1,999	146,746	134,360	1.092
2,000– 3,999	145,369	137,175	1.059
4,000– 9,999	266,116	250,824	1.061
10,000–40,000	211,000	222,900	.947
Total	870,869	838,948	
Average	—	—	1.038

Table 8 shows the total inventory and sales for firms in each sales class in the sample. These figures are of limited reliability, particularly for the small volume firms, and accordingly a subsample of retailers were asked for more detailed information. These show that inventories vary over an extremely wide range. Small volume outlets (those with sales of under $500 monthly) have inventories ranging in value from $25 to $1,200. These stores, of course, sell only staples and canned goods. Larger stores handling these products also manage with relatively small inventories — some stores selling over $5,000 monthly had inventories valued at as low as $1,000. On the other hand, inventories valued at $5,000 were found in cases where monthly sales fell below $4,000. The full-line stores, of course, averaged higher inventory figures than other types of stores in the same sales volume class, but even these stores had inventory figures scattered over a wide range. Thus, in twenty-two full-line stores selling between $4,000 and $10,000 monthly, inventory valuation ranged from $1,800 to $12,000.

The value of equipment was substantially greater for full-line stores than for the other types. This is owing not only to the fresh and refrigerated produce carried by the full-line stores, but also to the delivery service which is frequently offered by this type of outlet. The average value of equipment for stores selling canned goods and staples was less than $2,000 for every sales class up to those selling $10,000 monthly. The full-line stores, on the other hand, averaged an equipment investment of $2,000 when sales were as low as $1,000 a month, and the average value of equipment for the other sales classes ranged from $2,350 to $12,750.

These data on assets suggest that the investment required for retailing is relatively modest. The initial investment of the firms in the sample supports this observation. The average initial investment of eighty-six stores with a sales volume of less than $500 monthly was $372 per store. About twice this amount was invested, on the average, by stores in the next largest sales class (from $500 to $1,000 monthly), and stores selling from $1,000 to $2,000 a month averaged $1,365 for their original investment. Only the stores selling over $10,000 monthly averaged an original investment of as much as $10,000.

The typical retailer opens an outlet with very little capital, though he subsequently adds substantially to his investment. In every sales class, the average present investment amounts to at least 150 per cent of the original investment, and in the medium-sized stores investment has doubled. These averages, moreover, include some firms with very large increases in investment.

When the retailers in the sample were asked why they opened food stores, 24 per cent gave as their reason that food retailing was an easy business to operate, and these included firms with present volumes ranging from less than $500 to over $20,000 per month. Less than half had previous experience; the proportion of urban store managers with previous experience was slightly higher than that in rural areas.

Buying Practices

That congestion in retailing is paralleled by a similar situation in wholesaling is well illustrated by the data on buying methods of retailers. Eight types of suppliers were investigated in the field study. These included agents and brokers (who are nearly always also wholesalers) for staples, cereals, canned goods, and meats; central wholesalers (located in the metropolitan areas of San Juan, Ponce, and Mayaguez); intermediate wholesalers (located in some other city but not in the retailer's locality); local wholesalers in the same town with the retailer; retail-wholesalers; truckers of fresh fruits and vegetables; and for meats, local slaughterhouses or the retailer's own slaughter. The types of suppliers used by any given retailer depended, of course, on the lines of foods carried by the store.

In determining the number of suppliers who served the retailers, a rough distinction was made between "few" and "many" wholesalers. A retailer was considered to buy from few wholesalers if three or less supplied the store in any one line of goods. Thus, a full-line store purchasing from twelve wholesalers would be counted as one having "few" suppliers. Conversely, the store was said to purchase from many wholesalers when more than three suppliers existed for each line of products. It was possible, of course, that a firm could be served by one wholesaler in each of several lines, so that the number of suppliers recorded for each line of products might exceed the total number of suppliers to the given firm.

In most cases, those stores which fell into the category of having "many" wholesalers reported far more than three or four wholesalers for each line of products. For example, one store with a sales volume of just over $30,000 per year, purchased canned goods from eight different firms and bought staples from seven. Another firm with annual sales of $72,000 was served by eight wholesalers in two lines. A fairly large firm, selling about $150,000 yearly, purchased canned goods from eight wholesalers and staples from eight wholesalers.

With this fairly broad definition of "few" wholesalers, the number of retailers who purchase a line of goods from three or fewer wholesalers is strikingly small. Only 127 firms out of a total of 422 were served by "few" wholesalers. There is a strong tendency for smaller stores, and those located in rural areas, to depend upon fewer rather than many wholesalers. One quarter of all stores purchasing from a few wholesalers are rural stores, and over one half are urban stores with a volume of less than $1,000 monthly.

The reasons given by the retailers for their buying practices followed no clear pattern. Some retailers noted a price advantage in buying from few wholesalers; others found the same advantage in patronizing many. It must be assumed that the type of buying method depends less upon deliberate economic calculations than upon opportunity and habit. Urban firms with large sales volume use many wholesalers merely because there are more wholesalers in urban areas. Because larger firms handle a varied stock of food products, they can be attractive customers to a larger number of suppliers. The smaller firms and most of the rural stores might be profitable accounts for one or two wholesalers, but not for a larger number. Small rural firms are also supplied by retail-wholesalers to a greater extent than the larger urban stores, and this too is a function of location and the type of wholesaling available.

The types of wholesalers commonly used show how long the distribution channel is between the original handler and the consumer. As indicated in Table 9, direct purchases from the manufacturer or producer are rare. The table also shows the relative importance of the different types of wholesalers who supply retail firms.

While over half of the total sales volume of canned goods, cereals,

Table 9a Suppliers to retail stores: percentage of sales purchased from and number used, by sales class, by lines handled, and by type of supplier

Monthly sales (dollars)	Number of stores	Monthly sales (dollars)	Canned goods, cereals, and staples									
			Agent or broker		Central wholesaler		Intermediate wholesaler		Local wholesaler		Retail wholesaler	
			Per cent of sales	Number used	Per cent of sales	Number used	Per cent of sales	Number used	Per cent of sales	Number used	Per cent of sales	Number used
Less than 500	89	28,925	—	—	35	168	13	69	34	130	18	70
500– 999	98	65,173	—	—	36	304	15	82	34	178	16	84
1,000– 1,999	109	138,245	8	9	47	564	14	91	24	167	14	93
2,000– 3,999	49	122,914	6	39	49	277	13	67	28	108	5	24
4,000– 9,999	41	200,841	7	53	65	332	4	20	20	66	4	14
10,000–40,000	9	120,600	31	25	63	97	1	2	4	7	—	—
Total	395	676,698	—	126	—	1,742	—	331	—	658	—	285
Average	—	—	9	—	54	—	9	—	21	—	7	—

Table 9b Suppliers to retail stores: percentage of sales purchased from and number used, by sales class, by lines handled, and by type of supplier

| Monthly sales (dollars) | Number of stores | Monthly sales (dollars) | Fruits and vegetables and meats | | | | | |
| | | | Central wholesaler[a] | | Local wholesaler[b] | | Producer[c] | |
			Per cent of sales	Number used	Per cent of sales	Number used	Per cent of sales	Number used
Less than 500	27	1,057	4	1	70	16	25	12
500– 999	22	5,067	31	5	12	17	57	9
1,000– 1,999	36	5,009	10	4	68	56	22	13
2,000– 3,999	26	11,653	15	17	66	46	19	15
4,000– 9,999	32	29,884	40	38	38	67	22	10
10,000–40,000	11	55,737	50	27	48	47	2	1
Total	154	108,407	—	92	—	249	—	60
Average	—	—	40	—	47	—	13	—

a Includes agents for meats.
b Includes truckers selling fruits and vegetables and retail-wholesalers.
c Includes slaughter by local house or by the retailer.

and staples are obtained from central wholesalers (those located in San Juan, Ponce, and Mayaguez) the local wholesaler contributes a sizable proportion of supplies even for firms doing up to $10,000 monthly. Only the largest firms use agents and brokers to any extent, while the medium sized firms are supplied by all of the various wholesale outlets.

The route for fruits and vegetables and meats is equally roundabout. Purchases direct from the producer or trucker or from the local slaughterer amount to only one quarter or less of total sales in most sales classes. Local wholesalers including retail-wholesalers are far more important in these lines than in the canned goods and staples, for almost half of the total sales of fresh produce and meats are supplied by wholesalers in the same town as the retailers giving the data.

These general conclusions can be verified in more detail. Over half the firms doing less than $1,000 monthly relied upon local wholesalers and retail-wholesalers for more than 50 per cent of their supplies of canned goods, cereals, and staples. Central wholesalers supplied some needs of the small stores, however, and most of the outlets with sales between $1,000 and $20,000 obtained the bulk of their supplies from this source. Only three of the four full-line stores selling over $20,000 a month secured 50 per cent or more of their supplies from agents and brokers.

The local wholesaler not only accounts for most of the retail sales of fruits and vegetables, but supplies most of the stores selling these items. Forty-six per cent of all the stores purchase at least half of their fruits and vegetables from such suppliers. Truckers, on the other hand, supply more than half the stock for most of the stores selling less than $2,000 monthly, whereas the very large firms, doing over $20,000 per month, buy most of their fresh produce from wholesalers in the central market. There is a similar pattern for meat. Local slaughter, including that of the retailer, provides 50 per cent or more of the meat for stores selling less than $2,000 a month. Agent wholesalers, however, are the chief source of supply for firms doing over $4,000 a month, although local wholesalers remain important for firms up to the largest sales class. This situation obviously reflects the types of meat handled: the large-volume stores sell frozen and other imported meats, while the medium sized and smaller stores rely more heavily on local production. In this line the retail-wholesaler is relatively unimportant; because of the lack of refrigerated transportation equipment, supplies tend to move more directly either from the importer or the local slaughterer.

Retail Costs and Margins

The data from the sample of 470 grocery stores lead to reasonably firm conclusions on food retailing in Puerto Rico: that stores are numerous, extremely small in terms of sales volume, physical space and inventory; that relatively few customers are served in small individual transactions; that credit sales form an overwhelming proportion of the total in all stores while delivery is a service offered mostly by urban high-volume stores; that the ratio of labor to sales is high and the number of suppliers servicing these outlets is also extremely high. There remains the question of the cost of providing the retail service. To gain more precise information on the effects of the foregoing characteristics upon costs and on the efficiency with which various types of retail stores operate, a subsample of 229 grocery stores was drawn from which more detailed information on margins was obtained.

By product line, the subsample contains about half the stores selling staples or staples and canned goods, the most common combination of items. Full-line stores account for 17 per cent of the total number, compared to 13 per cent of the larger sample. The subsample is also weighted in favor of the larger firms (those grossing over $12,000 yearly), because more precise information could be obtained from such firms, a consideration which outweighed the advantages of a more strictly representative sample. In the original sample, average monthly sales were $2,049, and 70 per cent of the stores had smaller sales. In the subsample, average monthly sales were $2,698 and only 65 per cent of the firms did less than $2,000. Rural and urban stores were represented in the same proportions as in the original sample. In addition to the data which has been previously discussed, information was obtained from these stores on cost of goods sold and operating expenses. Table 10 summarizes the information on gross margin by stores according to sales volume; Table 11 gives the same information by stores according to products carried and sales volume.

The range of gross margins is in many ways more significant than the weighted average gross margin in each class. While the low volume retailers are concentrated toward the lower end of the range of gross margins, there are two firms with less than $500 monthly sales and five with sales between $500 and $1,000 where gross margins are 38 per cent of sales. The 15 per cent gross margin noted in five sales classes was represented by only one firm in each instance, so that the distribution of firms by individual gross margins from 16 per cent to 34 per cent includes the significant portion of the total range.

While Table 10 shows no decline in gross margins at higher volumes

Table 10   Retail gross margins: weighted average, range, and frequency,
by sales class

Monthly sales (dollars)	Number of stores	Gross margin, average (per cent)	Gross margins, range (per cent)	Number of stores[b] with gross margin		
				from 16–21 per cent	from 22–27 per cent	from 28–34 per cent
Less than 500	35	21.25	15–39	8	13	10
500– 999	44	25.63	15–38	17	10	10
1,000– 1,999	68	25.00	15–38	26	20	16
2,000– 3,999	39	21.59	15–39	18	10	8
4,000– 9,999	33	22.71	15–37	16	10	2
10,000–40,000	10	23.35	17–38	7	2	0
Total	229	—	—	92	65	46
Average		23.11[a]				

[a] Total gross profit for all firms as a percentage of total sales.
[b] Totals less than 229 because some stores' markups were outside the range considered here.

of sales, such a trend can be seen when the stores are grouped according to products sold, in Table 11. It then appears that the larger volume stores of each type have lower margins than smaller stores of the same type. The exception are the retailers handling fresh produce, where the gross margin not only increases with sales volume, but exceeds the margins of any other type of store. On the other hand, the firms selling staples only are very few in number, and the average margin in at least one class may not be statistically valid.

The other two types of stores, those handling staples and canned goods and the full-line retailers, are represented by enough cases in each sales volume class to make the average gross margin more significant. Gross margins for the first type decline steadily, from 25 per cent at sales of less than $500 a month to slightly over 20 per cent at sales between $4,000 and $10,000 monthly. Gross margins for the second type decline from 26 per cent at monthly sales of less than $2,000 to 23 per cent at monthly sales between $10,000 and $40,000. If the one retailer in this latter class whose margin is 38 per cent be removed, the group average falls substantially to a margin of only 19 per cent.[3]

[3] The store here excluded is, however, of interest. Its operations are probably typical of high-volume stores located in particular high income areas. The store in question had average sales per employee of $2,500, as opposed to the average for the sales class as a whole of $1,900; removing this firm lowers the average sales per employee to $1,800. Only 5 per cent of its total sales are made on credit although three-quarters of its sales are delivered. Where other high-cost firms have made high prices normal, a firm which lowers its costs can maintain an impressively high margin as does this one.

Table 11 Average sales, average gross margins, four types of retail food stores,
by sales class

Monthly sales (dollars)	Staples			Staples and canned goods		
	Number of stores	Average monthly sales (dollars)	Average gross margin (per cent)	Number of stores	Average monthly sales (dollars)	Average gross margin (per cent)
Less than 500	3	265	19.37	23	421	25.34
500– 999	5	590	26	34	692	23
1,000– 1,999	5	1,596	25.91	49	1,295	23.36
2,000– 3,999	3	3,309	30	25	2,629	21.23
4,000– 9,999	5	5,589	22.14	10	5,225	20.67
10,000–40,000	——			——		
Total	21	—	—	141	—	—
Average	—	2,270	24	—	2,052	22

Monthly sales (dollars)	Staples and/or canned goods, plus fruits and vegetables			Full line		
Less than 500	8	272	27.17			
500– 999	3	603	24.59			
1,000– 1,999	7	1,244	29.32	7	1,400	26.43
2,000– 3,999	1	2,900	31.03	8	2,488	25.55
4,000– 9,999	—	—	—	16	5,565	25.15
10,000–40,000	—	—	—	10	18,900	23.35
Total	19	—	—	41	—	—
Average	—	1,255	29	—	7,088	24

It is evident that margins can decline substantially with higher sales volume.

However, this may not happen. Table 12 shows operating costs and net margins as a per cent of sales for firms in different sales classes. Total expenses for stores doing less than $1,000 monthly average about 13.5 per cent of sales, with a decline of only 3 per cent for stores doing up to $4,000 monthly. After this sales volume is reached, operating expenses drop to around 8 per cent of sales, but the gross margin remains high, with a consequent increase in the net margin as a per cent of sales. For all the firms, net margin averages 14.6 per cent of sales, with a range from 7.5 per cent to 15.3 per cent. This net return is not to be identified with net profits, for it includes all returns to the owner-managers, whose salaries were not computed separately.

The absolute net returns, per store and per owner-manager, are extremely meager in most cases. The final column in Table 12 is a

Table 12   Gross and net margins and operating expense ratios for retail food stores, by sales class (percentage of total sales)

	Monthly sales (dollars)						
	Less than 500	500 to 999	1,000 to 1,999	2,000 to 3,999	4,000 to 9,999	10,000 to 40,000	Average
Number of stores	35	44	68	39	33	10	
Monthly total of sales (dollars)	12,844	29,435	89,926	104,058	180,226	189,000	
Monthly average net margin per store[a] (dollars)	27.67	82.35	176.15	296.17	781.53	2,884.10	386.03
Gross margin	21.25	25.63	25.00	21.59	22.71	23.35	23.11
Net margin[a]	7.54	12.31	12.32	11.10	14.31	15.26	14.6
Total expenses	13.71	13.32	11.68	10.49	8.4	8.09	9.51
Rent and utilities	5.55	3.89	2.61	1.91	1.45	1.57	1.78
Taxes	0.50	0.65	0.33	0.21	0.17	0.30	0.27
Equipment expense	.90	1.04	.95	.76	.55	.50	.66
Supplies	.10	1.39	1.22	.71	.50	.45	.68
Insurance		0.02	0.08	.05	.09	.08	.07
Stock loss	0.90	.88	.63	.51	.42	.20	.43
Selling costs	4.30	3.30	2.46	2.09	1.43	1.24	1.79
Buying cost	0.44	0.92	0.66	0.65	0.65	0.34	0.56
Labor	.43	1.50	2.78	3.58	3.14	3.40	3.12

[a] Net margins include the wages of the owner(s) who commonly work in the store. The actual returns to the owner also include that portion of food taken for his personal use and included, in this analysis, in the cost of goods sold.

computation of the average net margin per store, and it is this sum which the owner-manager receives for his time and labor, his capital and his venture. A reference to the Census of Distribution shows how small the return is for most retailers. According to the Census, 87 per cent of the firms classified as groceries did less than $10,000 of business per year. The average monthly return for these firms would be less than $175 per month, based on the margins shown in the sample. For well over half of all the stores enumerated by the Census, the return would average only $28 a month. It is such returns that, in the absence of alternative employment, people look to retailing to provide. And such returns, plus some food obtained at wholesale prices, are sufficient to maintain the large number of retail food stores in business.

On the other hand, it is clearly apparent that large volume retailers can derive generous profits from their businesses. The average net returns shown in the last two rows of Table 12 show the gains which are made by a few in a market where prices remain high. While these returns, like the lower ones, include the wages of management, and as noted Puerto Rican retailers are both owners and managers, the average return is still substantial. It amounts to $781.63 for stores selling from $4,000 to $9,000 monthly, and to $2,884.10 for the largest group of stores.

Thus the high gross margins which are typical of food retailers of all sizes provide the small retailer with little return over the costs of doing business; they allow high profits in larger stores where costs decline markedly as a per cent of sales. This is especially evident in two important types of stores, those handling canned goods and staples, and those carrying a full line of products.

The outlets specializing in staples have, of course, lower operating costs than any other type. Since their space requirements are smaller, their rent, utilities, and equipment are all less costly. Stock loss is smaller, for while staples deteriorate they are not as subject to pilferage as are canned and packaged goods, and the selling cost is low since few such stores offer delivery service. Their clientele is also stable and advertising is rare. Such stores, however, typically operate at a low volume of business, which makes operating costs high as a percentage of sales. While expenses for nine stores selling less than $1,500 monthly ranged from 14 to 17 per cent, operating costs for nine stores selling from $1,500 to $5,000 monthly were only 9 per cent of sales. Three such stores, with monthly sales volumes between $5,000 and $7,500, showed operating costs amounting to 5 per cent of sales.

A similar pattern of operating costs, showing a sharp decline at higher sales volume appears in the stores handling canned goods as well as staples. (This combination of products is far more frequently found than stores carrying staples only.) Expenses were 17 per cent of sales for stores handling canned goods and staples at monthly volumes of less than $500. As sales increase, the ratio drops to 9 per cent at a monthly volume of $2,000. Stores selling between $4,000 and $10,000 monthly averaged operating expenses of 7 to 8 per cent of sales.

The limited line stores here discussed are of primary importance in Puerto Rico, given the present pattern of incomes and consumption. Full-line stores can be expected to operate successfully only in metropolitan areas or large towns. It is extremely significant, therefore, that stores specializing in the few basic items — rice, beans, lard, tomato sauce, canned milk — can still attain sufficient volume to bring their operating expenses to the minimal levels noted above. The gross and net margins that are typical of the stores selling staples and canned goods cannot be compared with any figures for the United States since their equivalents in type and volume of operations do not exist on the mainland.

For full-line stores, on the other hand, a comparison with mainland food retailers is more appropriate. *The Progressive Grocer* for 1951[4] gives an average gross margin of 15 to 16 per cent of sales for independent food retailers. The average gross margin of 24 per cent of sales for the Puerto Rican full-line grocers is thus more than 50 per cent above the margin on the mainland. This comparison, however, is subject to qualifications. In the first place, the 15 to 16 per cent gross margin quoted for the mainland is based upon a survey of successful independent retailers. The greatest number of these firms had annual sales of $100,000 to $300,000, which is well above the volume of all but a few of the retailers in the Puerto Rican sample. The lowest gross margin for a group of stores on the island is the 19 per cent for the stores selling from $10,000 to $40,000 monthly, obtained by an average of all stores but the one outlet which took a 38 per cent margin on sales. Actually, none of these stores exceeded $100,000 in yearly volume. The higher Puerto Rican average gross margin represents, in part, the absence of stores with sales volumes comparable to the mainland operations.

Secondly, the average percentage for the United States represents independent stores offering both self-service and full service. Gross margins in self-service independent stores are estimated to be as low as 11 per cent and 12 per cent on sales, while other independents offering extensive services have gross margins as high as 20 per cent. The sample of Puerto Rican firms also includes both self-service and full-service stores, but the latter are far more common in the market as a whole. The self-service store in Puerto Rico is a recent innovation, and its adoption has very often had little effect upon the costs of doing business.[5]

The problems of the self-service store in Puerto Rico are revealed by a comparison of their operations with full-service stores. Five full-line retail stores, ranging in sales volume from $10,000 to $20,000 a month, which offer partial self-service, were compared to four full-service stores, whose sales range from $15,000 to $25,000 monthly. The total sales of the first group amounted to $74,000 monthly; of the second group, to $75,000 monthly. In making the comparison, it must be noted first that self-service stores in Puerto Rico require a considerable

---

[4] *Facts in Food and Grocery Distribution as of January 1951*, published by *The Progressive Grocer*, p. 9.

[5] This is particularly owing to the fact that consumers have not accepted, in full, the practices of self-service stores. One retailer operating on a semi-self-service basis feels that an extension of such sales would benefit both consumers and the store manager, who would be relieved of telephone orders, assigning employees to dispatch the orders, and receiving goods returned by customers. He has repeatedly urged housewives of his acquaintance to come shopping for themselves, and has told them the many advantages of such a procedure, but he has had little success.

amount of service. There are no prepackaged meat counters in any of
the stores classified as self-service. Fruits and vegetables and some bulk
produce are also dispensed by clerks in self-service stores. The self-
service stores in Puerto Rico were also all fairly new. Of the five stores
offering self-service, three began operations only one or two years
prior to the field study, and the other two, while both established retail stores, had introduced self-service but recently. On the other hand
the four full-service stores, with one exception, had from ten to twenty
years of experience. Consequently, the difficulties of introducing any
new way of doing business, as well as the actual differences in operating
methods, may be reflected in the experience of the self-service stores.

The self-service stores used labor much more efficiently than the
full-service stores. Average sales per employee were $1,974 for the
latter group, and $2,470 for the self-service stores. On the other hand,
the twenty-nine employees of the five self-service stores were much
more highly paid than the thirty-five employees of the other four stores,
so that labor cost was considerably higher in the self-service stores. The
total payroll amounted to 3.4 per cent of sales in the latter group, and
only 2.5 per cent of sales for the full-service stores. Owners' salaries
were not included in labor costs for either group of stores, and the
self-service firms, as a group, had two unpaid employees compared
with three unpaid employees in the other stores.

Along with higher labor costs in the self-service stores go higher
equipment costs, requiring heavier depreciation — estimated at six
times that for the non-service stores — and also larger repair expenses.
The total value of equipment owned by the full-service stores was
slightly over $30,000; equipment in the self-service stores was valued
at $57,000. The fact that the self-service stores began this type of
operation since the war may have increased their equipment expense —
costs of shelving, refrigeration space, customers' baskets — all reflect
the higher prices of the period. On the other hand, these costs represent
only a partial substitution of capital for labor in the self-service store,
and the delivery service offered by both types of stores accounts for a
substantial part of the equipment. The four full-service stores owned, in
aggregate, three trucks and ten bicycles, with which they delivered 83
per cent of their total sales. The five self-service stores, however,
owned five trucks and seven bicycles among them, while just over 70
per cent of their total sales were delivered. Consequently, the heavier
equipment expenses cannot be attributed entirely to self-service operations. Depreciation expense for the full-service stores amounted to 4.6
per cent of the value of equipment, and to 9.5 per cent of the self-
service stores equipment value. Along with higher depreciation costs
go larger repair bills for the stores which have introduced self-service.
Monthly repair expense for the latter totaled $850 as opposed to $575

for the full-service store. Consequently, the total equipment expense in self-service stores amounted to 0.728 per cent of sales, whereas in the service stores such expense amounted to 0.349 per cent of sales.

The turnover rate is much lower for the self-service stores; inventory divided into cost of goods sold gives an annual figure of 7.24 for the self-service stores and 23.5 for the service stores.

Both the inventory and equipment valuation figures used in this comparison are based on rough estimates, with no consistent guide as to the basis for valuation. Furthermore, since the newer stores may be expected to use somewhat more up-to-date methods of accounting, this would result in an understatement of expense figures for the full-service stores. Nonetheless, the comparison between the two types of stores suggest that costs are not greatly lowered by the introduction of self-service operations. Since delivery service is not greatly reduced, a substantial part of the labor cost remains. The additional equipment imposes a real addition to total costs. Consequently, while the gross margin taken by the full-service stores of 20.28 per cent is larger than that obtained by the self-service stores (18.47 per cent), the expense ratio of the latter group is 9.2 per cent as opposed to only 7.2 per cent for the full-service stores. The result is, of course, a considerable difference in net profits, which amount to 13 per cent for the full-service stores and 9.2 per cent for the self-service stores.

The gross margins for these two types of stores do not differ by as much as do gross margins for similar stores on the mainland, where self-service independents gross about 15 per cent and full-service stores as much as 20 per cent.[6] More important than comparisons between types of retail operations or between Puerto Rican and mainland stores are the contrasts to be found within Puerto Rican retailing itself. The fact that some efficient stores can maintain an operating expense ratio of 5 to 8 per cent of sales (as compared with 16 to 20 per cent for others) is striking. And it is also significant that the low ratios appear at relatively small volumes of sales, from $4,000 monthly upwards, and in the type of store, selling canned goods and staples, which dominates the food retailing business. These figures show that substantial economies are possible within the present framework of retail operation. Unfortunately the public does not now benefit from the efficiency of which the best retailers on the island are capable.

[6] *Facts in Food,* p. 9.

4

FOOD WHOLESALING

Since the bulk of Puerto Rican food supplies are imported and reach consumers through a large number of small retailers, the position of the food wholesaler is one of strategic importance. In relation to the physical volume of foodstuffs handled and to its limited variety, the number of wholesalers, like the number of retailers, is strikingly large.

The Nature of the Field Study

In 1949 there were 434 firms classified by the Census as merchant wholesalers of dry groceries and food specialties. These reported sales of $179,700,000, or an average volume of $414,217 yearly. Comparable United States firms in 1948 had, on the average, a volume of $654,293 yearly. There were also in Puerto Rico, 150 firms classified as agents and brokers, an unknown number of whom handled food products.[1] Many firms act as both wholesalers and brokers. Between one-third and one-half of the firms were covered in the present study (also made in 1949–50) but with an average annual volume of $689,136 these accounted for two-thirds of total wholesale sales. Many of the smaller wholesalers listed in the Census were also retailers, and these firms were studied separately.

The small scale of wholesale operations is readily apparent when firms are classified by sales volume. In a sample of wholesalers studied, 71 per cent of the firms accounted for only 27 per cent of the sales. At the other extreme, eleven firms in the sample, selling over $2,500,000 yearly, accounted for one-quarter of the total sales of the sample firms.[2] Table 13 shows, for the 171 firms studied, the number and average monthly sales in different sales classes.

[1] A study made in 1940 listed 82 firms handling food out of a total of 222 agents and brokers.

[2] Similarly, one-quarter of the firms listed in the Census, with average yearly sales of less than $100,000, accounted for less than 5 per cent of total wholesale sales, while the sales of 84 firms, grossing over $500,000 yearly, amounted to two-thirds of the total.

Table 13 Number of food wholesalers in sample, and average sales, by sales class

Monthly sales (dollars)	Number of wholesalers	Average sales per firm
Less than 10,000	20	$ 6,218
10,000– 19,999	34	14,247
20,000– 29,999	38	23,200
30,000– 49,999	30	37,067
50,000– 99,999	24	68,875
100,000–199,999	14	126,071
200,000–299,999	6	233,333
300,000–499,999	3	395,999
500,000–750,000	2	604,167
Total	171	—
Average sales for all firms	—	57,427

Management and Employment

Wholesaling in Puerto Rico, like retailing, is to a considerable extent an owner-operated business,[3] and figures in Table 14 show employment

Table 14 Average sales per worker, food wholesalers by sales class

Monthly sales (dollars)	Number of wholesalers	Total workers	Average sales per worker (dollars)
Less than 10,000	20	72	1,728
10,000– 19,999	34	155	3,119
20,000– 29,999	38	211	4,185
30,000– 49,999	30	216	5,157
50,000– 99,999	24	255	6,491
100,000–199,999	14	242	7,310
200,000–299,999	6	105	13,341
300,000–499,999	3	150	7,941
500,000–750,000	2	61	19,809
Total	171	1,467	
Average sales per worker, all firms	—	—	6,700

and sales per worker for both paid and unpaid employees. The average sales per worker increases steadily with the size of the firm, up to a monthly sales volume of $300,000. In firms of this size, monthly sales

[3] Information was not obtained from all the sample firms, but some 250 owners were reported for 150 of the firms, and these included only 14 "silent" partners.

per worker were $13,341, or seven times the average for the smallest firms. Only five firms with sales above $300,000 were included in the sample. One of these is primarily a brokerage firm, with fourteen employees and annual sales of $8,000,000 and is therefore scarcely typical of wholesale operations in general. The average sales per worker for the other four firms were $8,834 monthly, or substantially less than the figure for firms in the $300,000 monthly sales class.

Most of the larger wholesale firms are located in the port cities. According to the Census, 135 wholesalers did business in 1949 in the San Juan area, and 70 others were in Ponce and Mayaguez; the remaining 229 firms were scattered throughout thirty of the island's *municipios*. The sample studied included 109 firms in the port cities and 62 located elsewhere.

Each wholesaler serves a fairly limited geographical area. As shown in Table 15, only seventeen firms handling dry groceries sold to

Table 15   Average sales, range of sales, and salesmen expenditure per month, food wholesalers, according to number of towns served

Number of towns served	Number of whole-salers[a]	Sales per month (dollars)		Salesmen dollar expenditure per month average	Per cent of sales
		Average	Range		
1	8	18,487	8,667– 33,560	51	0.3
2–3	34	23,015	5,000–125,000	142	.6
4–6	39	36,087	8,350–108,000	276	.8
7–10	30	59,013	8,000–208,333	756	1.3
11–15	11	71,848	20,000–166,333	529	0.7
16–20	6	81,666	21,833–250,000	889	1.1
21–30	5	55,967	7,500–130,000	419	0.7
31–50	6	115,025	20,000–242,520	1,133	1.0
51–60	2	343,750	20,833–666,667	978	0.3
77	17	137,169	8,333–541,666	1,860	1.4
Total	—	—	—	—	
Average of 158 firms		59,354		584	1.0

[a] Excludes fruit and vegetable wholesalers.

customers in seventy-seven towns, which would represent all the *municipios* on the island together with Vieques and Culebra. However, the sales of these firms represented almost one-fourth of the total sales of the sample firms. One hundred and three firms, or 71 per cent of the number sampled had customers in ten towns or less; these were chiefly smaller firms, none selling over $100,000 monthly. The total sales of this group amounted to almost half the sales of the entire sample. The number of towns served was not strictly a function of size, however, for some firms selling less than $10,000 monthly were found serving from twenty to twenty-seven towns. But of the eleven larger firms (those with monthly sales volumes of $200,000 or more), only one served fewer than thirty towns.

Generally, more workers were employed by firms serving a wide area, but this was not true in every case. Of two firms grossing less than $10,000 monthly, with customers in seventy-seven towns, one had three workers, the other had nine. Two firms selling over $250,000 monthly each employed nineteen workers, although one had customers in only twenty towns and one served seventy-seven. These erratic relationships were repeated in the figures for salesmen's expenditures, which did not increase steadily with the number of towns served, nor with the volume of sales. Salesmen's salaries and travel expenses, which are shown in average terms in Table 15, amounted to 1.3 per cent of sales for wholesalers serving ten towns and to only 1.4 per cent of sales for firms covering the entire island. The lowest expenditure, 0.3 per cent of sales, was reported both by firms selling merely within their own locality and by others selling to fifty or sixty towns.

The average salesmen's expenditure in dollars represents in each case a considerable range. Many firms, including those with customers throughout half the island, reported no salesmen expenditure at all, since selling was merely one task of the working owners. Salesmen expenditure of over $2,500 monthly was reported by firms serving ten towns or less, while none of the firms selling to twenty to sixty towns spent more than $1,948 monthly in this way.

These relationships suggest that the characteristics associated with large sales volume may be found at every level of sales. It cannot be assumed, however, that small firms, particularly those lacking a specialized sales staff, serve a wide geographical area as efficiently as large firms. For the most part the small wholesaler exists to supply small retail firms within a fairly limited area.

Types of Wholesale Operations

The nature of wholesaling differs with the location of firms and the lines of goods which they carry.

The wholesalers studied carried food and supplies in various combinations. More than half the firms — which for purposes of analysis are termed full-line wholesalers — handled canned goods, cereals, and staples. (Since the sample was deliberately weighted in favor of the larger wholesaler, it exaggerates the apparent number of such full-line firms.) Of the remaining seventy firms, half carried limited lines — either canned goods and staples or cereals and staples. The rest specialized in meats, fruits and vegetables, dairy products, or such non-food articles as soap, matches, twine or rope, machetes, and tobacco.

Virtually all of the limited-line wholesalers were found in San Juan; firms located in the other port cities or inland carried a full line of goods. The thirteen specialist wholesalers, handling fruits and vegetables, or meats, or dairy products, were all very small. Half of the sample firms selling less than $10,000 monthly were of this type.

The distribution of all sales by product line reflects the consumption pattern of the island. Monthly sales of all wholesalers totaled slightly over $8,000,000, and 70 per cent of this was of staple goods — rice, beans, dried peas, lard, dry salt pork, codfish, coffee, sugar, potatoes, and onions. Canned goods were next in importance, accounting for 19 per cent of total sales. These include canned and dried milk and tomato paste — two products which are widely used throughout the island, as well as the canned fruits, vegetables, juices, soups, and meats which are luxuries afforded only by the higher income classes. Sales of cereals amounted to only 4 per cent of total sales, dairy and poultry products to 3½ per cent. Locally produced foods in both these categories are distributed largely outside the wholesale market, while imported packaged cereals, cheeses, and poultry products form a minor part of total consumption. The same facts explain the small proportion — 3½ per cent — which meat sales bore to the total.

These proportions hold roughly for wholesalers throughout the island (see Table 16), except for San Juan where luxury foodstuffs were sold in slightly greater volume. Many imported canned goods are handled exclusively by San Juan agents, and the limited-line firms in San Juan often carry more cereals or canned goods than wholesalers located elsewhere. In Ponce and Mayaguez, local production and imports from neighboring countries lead to a relatively high proportion of meat sales by wholesalers in these cities.

Selling Practices

Because of the large number of small wholesale firms, inter-wholesale sales are common. The 140 wholesale grocers in the sample reported one-third as many wholesaler customers as retailer customers. Only in the case of meat and fresh produce, both perishable items, is wholesaling largely confined to one level.

Two types of firms sold most frequently to wholesalers — the limited-line firms, particularly those with small total sales, and the full-line wholesalers selling over $300,000 monthly. Exclusive agencies are often granted to limited-line firms — those who specialize in canned goods or cereals for instance — and these in turn supply other wholesale houses. The large full-line wholesaler, on the other hand, supplies the needs of wholesale firms whose small volume does not justify direct purchase or import. The number of customers varied with sales volume only at wide intervals. Full-line wholesalers doing less than $30,000 monthly averaged about eight retailer customers while firms grossing from $30,000 to $200,000 averaged about twenty retailer customers.

Table 16 Wholesaler sales of five product lines, by location of firm

Firms in	Total monthly sales	Staples	Canned goods	Cereals	Dairy products and fresh produce	Meats
San Juan						
Amount	$5,702,676	$3,924,476	$1,186,098	$199,652	$211,087	$181,363
Percentage of sales	100.0	68.0	21.0	3.5	3.7	3.2
Ponce and Mayaguez						
Amount	$1,277,725	$906,084	$165,036	$93,318	$46,903	$66,386
Percentage of sales	100.0	71.0	13.0	7.3	3.7	5.2
Interior towns						
Amount	$1,255,710	$930,426	$224,153	$49,110	$29,861	$22,160
Percentage of sales	100.0	74.0	17.0	3.9	2.4	1.8
Total	$8,236,111	$5,760,986	$1,575,287	$342,080	$287,851	$269,909
Average percentage	100.0	70.0	19.0	4.0	3.5	3.3

Institutional buyers — hotels, restaurants, and other large buyers — were not important customers of food wholesalers. While the 1949 Census reported 85 hotels and 774 eating places, only seven hotels grossed more than $100,000 yearly, and only a few more restaurants attained this volume of sales. The majority of tiny *cafetines* or eating places buy their needs from retail-wholesalers or retailers located in the vicinity. Institutional customers were most frequent among the food wholesalers of medium size — those with monthly sales volumes of $30,000 to $200,000 — although the two largest firms, doing over $500,000 monthly, reported some twenty customers of this type. It should be noted that the largest hotels and restaurants are able to purchase many of their supplies directly from the mainland.

Where wholesale firms act as agents or brokers, the goods are commonly delivered directly from the dock to the final buyer. As shown in

Table 17   Percentage of sales of full-line and limited-line wholesalers,
in which products moved through wholesaler's warehouse

Monthly sales (dollars)	Full-line wholesalers			Limited-line wholesalers		
	Number	Average	Range	Number	Average	Range
Less than 10,000	9	100	100–100	1	100	—
10,000– 19,999	25	98	50–100	7	81	20–100
20,000– 29,999	23	99	80–100	7	83	40–100
30,000– 49,999	26	98	75–100	2	75	50–100
50,000– 99,999	19	95	75–100	5	74	40–100
100,000–199,999	5	97	85–100	7	57	20–100
200,000–299,999	2	72	45–100	3	63	20–100
300,000–499,999	1	28	—	2	30	20–40
500,000–750,000	1	95	—	1	—	—
Total	111			35		

Table 17, the percentage of sales from warehouses was smallest for limited-line firms, particularly the larger houses which serve in the role of agent. Even among the full-line wholesalers, however, were some whose warehouse sales were less than three fourths of the total.

The delivery services offered by the firm depend partly on the proportion of sales from warehouses and partly on the customers' location and ability to pick up supplies. Very few firms deliver outside the

Table 18   Number of wholesalers, average volume of sales, and range of sales,
by per cent of sales delivered

Per cent of sales delivered	Number of whole-salers[a]	Per cent of whole-salers	Volume of sales per month (dollars)		
			Total	Average	Range
0	40	25	2,444,704	61,118	5,000–666,667
1–10	7	4	657,120	93,874	10,000–162,500
11–20	9	6	614,298	68,255	16,666–208,300
21–30	8	5	465,106	58,138	8,667–242,520
31–40	1	1	80,000	—	—
41–50	15	9	1,149,532	76,635	6,000–541,666
51–60	5	3	107,000	21,400	8,000– 42,000
61–70	4	2	153,930	38,482	20,000– 64,000
71–80	11	7	510,544	46,413	8,333–241,660
81–90	16	10	765,951	47,872	9,000–125,000
91–99	8	5	438,583	54,823	8,350–250,000
100	37	23	1,982,732	53,587	9,000–441,667

[a] Excludes fruit and vegetable wholesalers.

immediate locality. Table 18 shows the various delivery practices of different firms. One-fourth of the firms delivered 100 per cent of their sales and about as many delivered none. Both groups included very small and very large wholesalers. The remaining firms were fairly evenly divided with as many delivering over half their sales as those who deliver less than half.

Provision of credit by wholesalers is a nearly universal practice. Five wholesalers in the sample did an entirely cash business, the rest all extended some credit. (See Table 19.) Eighty per cent of the whole-

Table 19   Number of wholesalers, average volume of sales, and range of sales, according to per cent of sales on credit

Per cent of sales on credit	Number of whole- salers[a]	Per cent of whole- salers	Volume of sales per month (dollars)		
			Total	Average	Range
0	5	3	143,000	28,600	8,000– 55,000
1–10	3	2	742,667	247,556	25,000–666,667
11–20	4	2	40,000	10,000	10,000– 20,000
21–30	1	1	33,029	—	—
31–40	3	2	95,833	31,944	9,000– 49,833
41–50	11	7	297,000	27,000	15,000– 55,000
51–60	3	2	247,766	82,589	23,166–125,000
61–70	3	2	66,393	22,131	8,333– 33,560
71–80	28	17	1,245,618	44,486	8,350–208,330
81–90	45	28	1,944,811	43,218	5,000–250,000
91–99	31	19	2,204,635	71,117	6,000–541,660
100	25	15	2,676,573	107,063	9,000–441,667

[a] Excludes fruit and vegetable wholesalers.

salers sold over two-thirds of their total volume on credit, and twenty-five firms had a 100 per cent credit business. Like delivery service, this feature bears little relation to sales volume. The largest firm made fewer than 10 per cent of its sales on credit; the smallest firm sold between 80 and 90 per cent of its total volume on credit, and the third largest firm made all of its sales on credit.

The credit and delivery services offered account for some variation in price quotations. Seventy-four per cent of the full-line wholesalers and 49 per cent of the limited-line firms offered cash discounts, while one-third of the firms varied the price depending upon delivery. Half of the latter group varied the price with the distance of delivery. Quantity discounts on some items were offered by 72 per cent of the full-line wholesalers and almost half of the limited-line wholesalers. Aside from these variations among the firms themselves, the buyer faces further differences in a single wholesale house. Few firms have a fixed policy with respect to any of the discounts. Prices are often determined by haggling with individual customers, as are the terms of sale, and these latter do not apply consistently to any general types of sales or class of customers.

Sources of Supply

Three buying methods are used by wholesale firms. These are direct purchase from the manufacturers, either local or mainland firms; direct shipment to the wholesaler, who places orders with a local agent and takes delivery of the shipment at the dock; and purchase from other wholesalers.

The buying method employed depends chiefly on the location of the Puerto Rican wholesaler. Firms in San Juan obtained half of their supplies by direct purchase, but firms outside the three major ports acquired less than 1 per cent of their purchases directly. But the typical source of supply also depends on the product involved as well as the sales volume of the wholesale buyer. Tables 20 and 21 show, for wholesalers located in San Juan and elsewhere, the proportion of total sales of each product line obtained from the different types of suppliers. Table 22 compares buying methods among firms of various sizes.

For the island as a whole, more supplies were obtained by ordering through agents than by any other procedure. Even in San Juan, where wholesale firms are larger, and where the limited-line firms are located, over 45 per cent of the two principal products — staples and canned goods — were bought in this way. Elsewhere, of course, the wholesalers are even more dependent on other firms to act as importers. Direct shipment (with purchase through agents) accounted for 75 to 90 per cent of supplies to inland wholesalers, with the exception of cereals, half of which come from local manufacturers.

The local producers of cereal products supply chiefly macaroni, spaghetti, biscuits, and crackers. As a proportion of sales, local supplies of cereals were much more important to the interior than to San Juan wholesalers, although the dollar volume involved was slightly less. Cereals are, comparatively, a luxury and hence are sold in smaller quantities in the poorer inland areas. The San Juan wholesalers, also, sell a high proportion of imported cereals.

Wholesalers buy cereal products and canned goods more frequently than staples from agents. The latter type of food is usually sold in bulk, while United States canners and cereal manufacturers, who are concerned with brand names and product lines, employ selective distribution. The small volume of meat and dairy product purchases are

Table 20 Source of supply for principal products of San Juan wholesalers

Product	Number of firms selling product	Total monthly sales (dollars)	Direct purchases		Direct shipment		Exclusive agents		Intermediate wholesaler[a]		Local manufacturer	
			Amount (dollars)	Per cent	Amount (dollars)	Per cent	Amount (dollars)	Per cent	Amount (dollars)	Per cent	Amount (dollars)	Per cent
Canned goods	86	1,181,597	602,718	51.1	400,257	34	138,907	11.8	36,715	3.1		
Cereals	66	195,068	103,263	52.9	135,834	18.4	22,909	11.7	4,231	2.2	28,831	14.8
Staples	83	3,589,752	1,703,261	47.4	1,427,850	39.8	220,675	6.2	237,966	6.6		
Meats	44	159,678	103,628	62.2	22,397	17.6	33,653	20.2				
Dairy and poultry products	62	199,122	140,663	70.6	28,222	14.2	27,647	13.9	2,140	1.1	450	0.2

a Wholesale firms located outside the San Juan area.

Table 21 Source of supply for principal products of inland wholesalers

Product	Number of firms selling product	Total sales (dollars)	Direct purchases		Direct shipment		Exclusive agent		Central[a] wholesaler		Intermediate wholesaler		Local manufacturer	
			Amount (dollars)	Per cent of total	Amount (dollars)	Per cent of total	Amount (dollars)	Per cent of total	Amount (dollars)	Per cent of total	Amount (dollars)	Per cent of total	Amount (dollars)	Per cent of total
Canned goods	35	224,153	2,000	0.9	156,063	69.6	24,561	11.0	41,529	18.5				
Cereals	34	49,110	108	.2	13,117	26.7	10,110	20.6					25,775	52.5
Staples	33	930,426	1,164	.1	555,926	60.4	129,959	14.1	226,107	24.6	7,520	0.8		
Meats	33	22,160			17,823	80.4	4,337	19.6						
Dairy and poultry products	31	29,861	1,971	6.6	15,156	50.8	12,518	41.9			216	0.7		

a Wholesale firms located in the port cities of San Juan, Ponce, and Mayaguez.
b Wholesale firms located in Puerto Rico outside the port cities, but not in the locality of the reporting firm.

Table 22 Source of supply to wholesalers, by sales class[a]

Monthly sales (dollars)	Number of firms	Total sales (dollars)	Direct purchase		Direct shipment		Exclusive agent		Wholesaler		Local manufacturer	
			Amount (dollars)	Per cent	Amount (dollars)	Per cent	Amount (dollars)	Per cent	Amount (dollars)	Per cent	Amount (dollars)	Per cent
Less than 10,000	13	87,623	5,071	5.8	20,405	23.3	13,056	14.8	37,557	42.8	11,273	12.8
10,000– 19,999	33	384,994	88,033	22.8	151,507	39.2	65,934	17.1	72,479	18.8	7,041	1.8
20,000– 29,999	37	902,384	120,222	13.3	424,001	47.0	143,207	15.9	197,631	21.8	17,323	1.9
30,000– 49,999	30	873,331	52,657	5.9	501,347	56.7	158,511	17.9	144,930	16.3	15,886	1.8
50,000– 99,999	24	1,263,374	143,174	11.3	913,801	72.5	161,322	12.8	25,305	2.0	19,772	1.5
100,000–199,999	14	1,269,165	462,666	36.4	606,734	47.8	124,673	9.8	56,122	4.3	18,970	1.4
200,000–299,999	6	1,124,246	810,932	72.3	264,879	23.6	45,831	4.1	2,604	0.2		
300,000–499,999	3	748,126	471,200	62.9	272,509	36.4	4,417	0.7				
500,000–750,000	2	1,120,833	1,071,000		49,833							
Total	162	7,774,076	3,224,955	41.5	3,205,016	41.2	716,951	9.2	536,628	6.9	90,265	1.1

[a] Excludes wholesalers handling fruit and vegetables only, and fruit and vegetables sales of all other wholesalers.

even more concentrated in exclusive agents, and few brands of packaged meats, bacon, eggs, and cheese are sold on the island.

The larger the wholesale firm, the greater the likelihood that it will buy directly from abroad. Firms selling less than $10,000 monthly obtain almost half their supplies from other wholesalers and over 15 per cent of the total is purchased in this way by wholesalers doing up to $50,000 monthly. This is true not only for inland firms, but for those located in San Juan. Some purchases are made from other wholesalers by firms selling as much as $200,000 monthly, although only a fraction of total supplies come from this source. The volume of purchases through agents, with direct shipment from the manufacturer, increases with size of firm since the larger concerns are able to take delivery of sizable quantities at the docks. Direct purchase from manufacturers, however, without the use of an agent, accounts for less than one-third of all supplies for firms selling less than $100,000 monthly. Not until twice this volume is reached do firms buy more than half of their foods directly from manufacturers.

Most of the firms use all the buying methods described. To some extent this reflects the differing importance of the product lines carried. Any wholesaler carrying a full line of canned goods, for example, might be able to purchase some brands directly but would be forced to deal with exclusive agents to secure others. Where sales of a particular brand or product are relatively small, it might not be possible or worthwhile to deal directly with the manufacturer. As a general rule, therefore, it is the limited-line wholesalers who buy more directly and from fewer suppliers.

There is a substantial turnover in the business. When firms are distributed by years in business the largest group in the sample was found to have been operating from only six to ten years, and 54 per cent of all the firms were less than ten years old. Some new firms have built up sizable sales volumes, while others remain at the lowest level ($10,000 monthly or less) reported. The ten firms with sales exceeding $200,000 monthly have all been in business from ten to forty years. Firms over forty years old ranged in sales volume from $10,000 to $175,000 monthly, which may represent a decline from previous higher sales. These figures suggest a relation between business success and the energies of the single proprietor, who builds up the enterprise during his working life.

Capital Requirements

As might be expected from the foregoing, capital investment in Puerto Rican wholesaling varied considerably among individual firms. The initial capital requirements for all firms averaged $23,000, and many firms began with a much smaller investment. The average present investment of all firms was $91,000, or over three times the original capital. However, a considerable range is involved. One firm began twelve years ago with an initial investment of $6,000. Its 1949 sales volume was $8,000,000 annually, with an investment of over $800,000. Some firms, on the other hand, had as little as $10,000 currently invested.

The range of investment when firms are grouped according to sales volume is striking. The average ratio of sales to investment was .57 for full-line wholesalers and .52 for limited-line firms. Among the full-line wholesalers, the average sales investment ratio ranged from .36 at sales of less than $10,000 monthly to .70 at $200,000 monthly sales. Over this sales volume the ratio declined again to .38 at sales of $500,000 monthly, although the largest firm showed a ratio of .62. But these averages are computed from wide ranges within each class, for example, the investments of firms selling between $50,000 and $100,000 monthly ranged from $46,000 to $173,000. For limited-line firms there was no consistent relationship between sales volume and sales investment ratio. Only thirty-three firms of this type were studied, so the absence of a pattern may result from the small number of cases. These limited data, however, show even wider variations in current investment than for full-line firms. Seven limited-line wholesalers, selling between $100,000 and $200,000 monthly, reported an average present investment of $244,420, but one of these firms had $70,000 and one $580,000 currently invested.

The extreme variations noted are partly derived from the manner in which the figures are reported, since the firms' estimates of current assets were accepted at face value. Different valuation methods may have caused considerable variation, particularly for those firms owning a sizable amount of equipment.

The difference in functions performed by the firms is, however, the major cause of variations in investment. A large part of wholesale sales may represent merely the services of brokers, with little physical handling. (See Table 17.) Furthermore, much of the capital required for wholesale distribution may be hired rather than owned by the firm. The shipping lines furnish free storage on the wharves for a five-day period, enabling supplies to move directly from the docks to wholesale customers. Rental of warehouse space, either adjacent to the docks or in one of the three wholesale market centers, is a common practice among San Juan wholesalers.

A substantial amount of transportation is also hired by wholesalers. None of the firms selling over $200,000 monthly owned more than one truck, and payments to independent truckers, for the group as a whole, amounted to over 50 per cent of the total trucking expense. Small firms

more frequently used their own trucks for delivery while hiring independent truckers' to bring in their own supplies. The ratio of trucking expense to sales declines with the volume of sales, from 2.3 per cent
for the ten smallest firms to .5 per cent for firms selling over $200,000
monthly. To some extent this ratio reflects the location of the larger
firms in San Juan, where receiving expense is small. But it also indicates
that the independent truckers, which are heavily used by the large
firms, provide transportation services more cheaply than the wholesalers themselves.

The rate at which goods are moved through the wholesale market —
from ships to shippers' storage to outside truckers' delivery equipment
to customers — is shown by the inventory ratio. Table 23 shows the

Table 23   Inventory turnover, full-line and limited-line wholesalers, by sales class

Monthly sales (dollars)	Full-line wholesalers	Limited-line wholesalers
Less than 10,000	8.7	50.1
10,000– 19,999	12.6	15.6
20,000– 29,999	13.2	13.2
30,000– 49,999	16.3	44.8
50,000– 99,999	20.6	18.3
100,000–199,999	18.9	17.9
200,000–299,999	17.1	32.3
300,000–499,999	11.2	10.0
500,000–750,000	27.1	—
Average	16.4	16.3

total annual sales divided by total inventory for firms in the several
sales classes. The larger firms, and those handling a limited line of
goods, ship more of their sales directly from the docks, and, consequently, operate with a smaller inventory. The difference in function
among firms of the same sales volume, which has been noted previously, accounts for the erratic ratios of limited-line firms.

Although their different operations require quite different types and
amounts of capital, most of the firms have one common characteristic,
that of extending credit. The volume of accounts receivable therefore
accounted for over half the present investment, and particularly for
the larger firms was the single most important figure in the asset statement. Tables 24 and 25 show the components of present investment by
firms grouped according to sales volume.

Labor Utilization

Labor utilization by wholesalers varies in much the same manner
as the use of capital. Tables 26 and 27 show the type of workers em-

Table 24 Major components of present investment by full-line wholesalers, by sales class

Monthly sales (dollars)	Number of wholesalers	Total present investment	Inventory	Accounts receivable (dollars)	Delivery trucks	Sales trucks	Sales cars	Other equipment
Less than 10,000	9	196,282	98,000	79,876	5,873	—	6,700	5,833
10,000– 19,999	25	726,791	335,000	291,719	45,200	3,000	25,015	26,857
20,000– 29,999	23	953,908	485,751	399,100	27,240	2,300	21,700	17,817
30,000– 49,999	26	1,545,886	710,212	680,859	30,250	7,200	35,146	22,219
50,000– 99,999	19	1,838,900	744,000	970,000	24,100	16,600	41,700	42,500
100,000–199,999	5	894,700	400,000	440,000	10,500	1,200	13,000	30,000
200,000–299,999	2	983,640	350,000	500,000	10,000	—	18,640	105,000
300,000–499,999	1	1,177,000	475,000	685,000	—	—	10,000	7,000
500,000–750,000	1	883,773	239,672	600,821	2,322	—	8,958	32,000
Total	111	9,200,880[a]	3,837,635	4,647,375	155,485	30,300	180,859	289,226

[a] Total exceeds component breakdown since detail investment not available in some cases.

Table 25 Major components of present investment by limited-line wholesalers, by sales class

Monthly sales (dollars)	Number of wholesalers	Total present investment	Inventory	Accounts receivable	Delivery trucks (dollars)	Sales trucks	Sales cars	Other equipment
Less than 10,000	1	9,012	2,000	5,000	2,000	—	—	12
10,000– 19,999	7	183,800	83,300	68,000	9,000	—	8,800	14,700
20,000– 29,999	7	244,165	146,000	72,700	15,500	—	3,000	5,000
30,000– 49,999	2	48,000	20,000	22,000	—	—	3,500	2,500
50,000– 99,999	4	538,745	244,142	265,786	2,000	—	17,722	9,095
100,000–199,999	7	1,710,938	561,842	989,618	10,331	108,000	—	1,800
200,000–299,999	3	887,000	257,000	600,000	—	—	18,000	12,000
300,000–499,999	2	2,098,684	900,000	1,012,684	—	4,000	27,000	155,000
500,000–750,000	1[a]	44,800	15,000	20,000	—	—	4,200	5,600
Total	34	5,765,144[b]	2,229,284	3,055,788	38,831	112,000	82,222	205,707

[a] This wholesaler engaged primarily in a brokerage business.
[b] Total exceeds component breakdown since detail investment not available in some cases.

Table 26 Classification of kind and number of workers employed in full-line wholesale houses, by sales class

Monthly sales (dollars)	Number of wholesalers	Owners[a]		Number employed[a]				
		Working	Not working	Office Staff[b]	Salesmen	Warehouse workers	Truck drivers	Truck helpers
Less than 10,000	9	13.00	—	3.03	2.00	9.00	2.00	2.16
10,000– 19,999	25	45.25	1	10.33	12.00	28.16	10.50	11.00
20,000– 29,999	23	30.00	1	20.16	14.00	27.50	10.50	12.00
30,000– 49,999	26	41.00	—	29.00	34.00	40.75	18.00	19.00
50,000– 99,999	19	36.00	3	30.00	41.84	50.25	14.66	13.00
100,000–199,999	5	9.00	—	23.00	10.00	10.50	8.00	10.00
200,000–299,999	2	3.00	3	9.00	14.00	5.00	2.00	1.00
300,000–499,999	1	7.00	—	14.00	9.00	.69	—	—
500,000–750,000	1	2.00	—	15.00	6.00	17.00	4.00	3.00

[a] Number of workers expressed in full-time equivalents.
[b] Includes accountants employed on part-time basis.

Table 27 Classification of kind and number of workers employed in limited-line wholesale houses, by sales class

Monthly sales (dollars)	Number of wholesalers	Owners		Number employed				
		Working	Not working	Office staff[a]	Salesmen	Warehouse workers	Truck drivers	Truck helpers
Less than 10,000	1	1	—	—	—	1.00	1	1
10,000– 19,999	7[b]	12	—	5.00	7	3.00	3	—
20,000– 29,999	7	7	—	8.50	10	7.67	3	5
30,000– 49,999	2	2	—	3	8	—	—	—
50,000– 99,999	4	6	4	7	12	7.00	1	1
100,000–199,999	7	14	2	36	20	12.00	35[c]	6
200,000–299,999	3	8	—	9	16	13.00	—	—
300,000–499,999	2	11	—	50	31	17.00	3	5
500,000–750,000	1	3	—	4	5	2.00	—	—

[a] Includes accountants employed on a part-time basis.
[b] Information not available for one of these wholesalers.
[c] One wholesaler accounted for thirty-one truck drivers in this group.

ployed by wholesalers grouped according to sales volumes. The large number of working owners, who usually perform all kinds of tasks, reduces the need for specialized help. Not until a sales volume of $100,000 monthly was reached did a clear cut division of labor take place, and the number of working owners become smaller than the number of employees in any one category. As firms increase in size, the office staff grows, and more of the working owners' knowledge of the business is derived from bookkeeping and other systematic procedures. The salesmen's functions also outgrow the capacities of the owners, and at least one specialized salesman was employed by all firms grossing over $30,000 monthly. The small numbers of warehouse workers employed by the limited line and large full-line wholesalers reflect the tendency of such firms to move a smaller proportion of their sales through warehouses. Similarly, since outside trucking is used extensively by the large firms, fewer truck drivers and helpers were employed.

Costs and Margins

The major objective in studying wholesaling operations in Puerto Rico is to see how these functions are translated into money costs and prices borne by retailers and, ultimately, by Puerto Rican consumers. To this end, sixty-four wholesale firms were selected for a more detailed investigation of gross margins, operating costs, and net profit. This group differed from the larger sample by including more of the larger full-line wholesalers, located in San Juan.

The average gross margin for all firms taken together was 14 per cent. Details of sales, gross and net margin, are given in Table 28, for firms classified by product line and sales volume. In every sales class but one, the average gross margin of the full-line firms exceeded that of limited-line firms by 1.2 to 7.4 percentage points. The average gross margin for full-line wholesalers was 15.5 per cent of sales; that for limited-line firms was 11.8 per cent. No marked difference in operating costs seemed to exist between the two types of firms. Consequently, the net profit received by full-line wholesalers averaged 11.8 per cent of sales as against 8.7 per cent for the limited-line firms.

Net profits, in this table, include all returns to the owners, comprising wages for their labor, return on capital investment, and entrepreneurial profit. Since there are few non-working owners, the percentage of net profit may be calculated in terms of the dollar returns to active managers. The smallest firms, earning from 5 to 9 per cent profit on their sales, may pay only $200 to $300 monthly to their owners. (However, the owner of one firm selling less than $10,000 had a monthly return of $1,500, which is a not inconsiderable reward for combined labor, capital, and management.) At the other extreme were two firms grossing over $200,000 monthly, with net profit margins of 7 and 12 per cent. The first provided a monthly return of $27,000 to the four working owners; the second secured almost $29,000 monthly to its five active owners. Even a smaller firm, selling only $55,000 monthly, netted $6,000 a month to three working owners. In view of the small initial capital required, and the possibility of expanding sales without adding much capital, the returns which exist in most cases represent a strong inducement to enter the field.

Because net profit is calculated to include all returns to the owner,

Table 28 Total sales, gross and net margin, and operating expenses of food wholesalers

Monthly sales (dollars)	Number of firms		Total sales (dollars)		Per cent of sales					
					Gross profit		Total expenses		Net profit	
	Full-line	Limited-line	Full-line	Limited-line	Full-line	Limited-line	Full-line	Limited-line	Full-line	Limited-line
Less than 10,000	4	1	34,700	8,350	14.7	16.2	8.1	10.6	6.6	5.6
10,000– 19,999	14	1	190,532	16,333	15.0	13.8	6.0	3.9	9.0	9.9
20,000– 29,999	11	3	247,400	69,499	16.8	17.3	4.7	4.2	12.1	13.1
30,000– 49,999	10	1	393,212	33,029	16.2	10.8	3.3	2.5	12.9	7.3
50,000– 99,999	9	2	605,885	152,250	15.2	7.8	3.1	2.6	12.1	5.2
100,000–199,999	2	3	296,333	387,500	17.0	12.5	2.9	3.7	14.1	8.8
200,000–299,999	—	1	—	241,666	—	14.5	—	2.0	—	12.5
300,000–499,999	—	1	—	392,825	—	10.0	—	3.1	—	6.9
500,000–750,000	1	—	541,666	—	13.9	—	3.5	—	10.4	—
Total	51	13	2,309,728	1,301,452						
Average for all stores					15.5	11.8	3.7	3.1	11.8	8.7

a simple comparison with firms operating in the United States is not strictly valid. Table 29, however, compares sales and gross margins for three sizes of firms in Puerto Rico and in the United States. The smallest firms in the United States, those grossing less than $500,000 annually, have average sales which are considerably larger than Puerto Rican firms in the same sales class, reflecting the presence of many smaller firms on the island. Among the larger firms, average sales in the United States and Puerto Rico are more nearly equal.

Table 29 Sample wholesalers, total sales, and gross profits, by sales class, United States and Puerto Rico, 1949

Annual sales volume	Number of firms	Total annual sales (dollars)	Average annual sales per firm (dollars)	Gross margin (per cent of sales)
Under $500,000				
United States	28	10,730,424	383,229	9.103
Puerto Rico	43	9,108,960	211,836	18.328
$500,000 to 1,000,000				
United States	56	43,017,516	768,170	8.163
Puerto Rico	14	10,279,224	734,230	13.524
$1,000,000 to 2,000,000				
United States	88	120,467,016	1,368,943	8.983
Puerto Rico	5	8,205,996	1,641,199	14.098

Source: United States figures adapted from John R. Bromell, *Survey of Wholesale Grocers' Profit and Loss Figures*, United States Wholesale Grocers' Association, Inc., Washington, D.C. (n.d.).

Gross margins on the mainland are from one-half to two-thirds those in Puerto Rico, but a large part of the difference reflects the presence of working owners in the Puerto Rican firms. Thus, for four United States firms selling less than $500,000, total wages and salaries amounted to 6.890 per cent of sales, whereas wages and salaries for Puerto Rican firms of approximately the same size ranged between .64 and 1.84 per cent of sales. Were the owners of Puerto Rican firms to be compensated by salaries, this figure would, of course, be much higher, and the net return reduced accordingly.

Owing to differences in computation, other operating costs of the United States firms are not comparable to those of firms in Puerto Rico. Tables 30 and 31 show the detailed operating costs as per cent of sales for full-line and limited-line wholesalers on the island. Total expenses are here shown to range between 2.92 and 8.00 per cent of sales for the full-line wholesalers, as opposed to an average expense ratio for United States firms of 7.826 per cent of sales.

This survey shows the gross profit percentages for wholesalers to be

Table 30 Expense ratios of food wholesalers selling full line of products

Monthly sales (dollars)	Number of whole-salers	Sales per month (dollars)	Total expenses per month (dollars)	Per cent of sales										
				Total	Rent and utilities	Taxes	Equipment cost	Supplies	Insurance	Stock loss	Selling cost	Sales car expense	Buying cost	Labor costs
Less than 10,000	4	34,700	2,776	8.00	.95	.34	.05	.13	.12	.15	1.32	.46	1.49	2.99
10,000– 19,999	14	190,532	11,295	5.93	.93	.26	.11	.08	.06	.14	1.26	.43	.63	2.03
20,000– 29,999	11	247,400	11,592	4.69	.51	.14	.04	.10	.04	.16	.91	.18	1.00	1.61
30,000– 49,999	10	393,212	12,986	3.30	.30	.15	.04	.05	.06	.06	.66	.23	.54	1.21
50,000– 99,999	9	605,885	18,690	3.08	.36	.17	.04	.05	.04	.07	.56	.16	.59	1.04
100,000–199,999	2	296,333	8,642	2.92	.22	.17	.12	.08	.20	.04	.22	.15	.51	1.21
200,000–299,999	—		—											
300,000–499,999	—		—											
500,000–750,000	1	541,666	19,063	3.52	.10	.20	.10	.03	.08	.05	.83	.09	.52	1.52

Table 31 Expense ratios of food wholesalers selling limited line of products

Monthly sales (dollars)	Number of wholesalers	Total sales per month (dollars)	Total expenses per month (dollars)	Per cent of sales										
				Total	Rent and utilities	Taxes	Equipment cost	Supplies	Insurance	Stock loss	Selling cost	Sales car expense	Buying cost	Labor costs
Less than 10,000	1	8,350	886	10.61	.31	—	a	.15	—	1.00	3.36	—	2.47	3.32
10,000– 19,999	1	16,333	625	3.83	.60	.03	.02	.10	.04	.77	.83	—	.92	.52
20,000– 29,999	3	69,499	2,918	4.20	.77	.03	.03	.04	.04	.07	.58	—	.67	1.97
30,000– 49,999	1	33,029	1,177	3.56	.36	.07	.02	.10	.03	.19	.14	.51	.30	1.84
50,000– 99,999	2	152,250	3,848	2.53	.38	.32	.02	.03	.04	.02	.27	.21	.60	.64
100,000–199,999	3	387,500	14,237	3.67	.13	.25	.07	.13	.07	.06	.74	.13	.27	1.82
200,000–299,999	1	241,666	4,804	1.99	.10	.16	.02	.02	.02	.01	.21	.18	.52	.75
300,000–499,999	1	392,825	12,293	3.13	.20	.43	.03	.05	.04	.01	.91	.11	.16	1.19
500,000–750,000	—		—											

a Less than .01 per cent.

considerably higher than have two previous surveys of food wholesalers conducted in recent years. One of these, published by the Junta de Salario Mínimo, found the average gross profit to be 6.25 per cent compared with the present survey's findings of 15.5 per cent for full-line wholesalers and 11.8 per cent for limited-line wholesalers.[4] An unpublished survey conducted by the Economic Stabilization Administration on the island showed the markups over cost on thirty-five food items to range from 5 to 12 per cent. Local wholesalers believe the lower margins to be much more realistic in the light of their own experiences. It is appropriate, therefore, to review briefly the methods of the three studies and to evaluate the reliability of the various estimates.

The average gross margin of 6.25 per cent of sales reported by the Junta de Salario Mínimo was based on a study of forty-three food wholesalers. The study actually covered wholesalers of all types of goods, food and non-food. From a universe of 1,303 firms a 25 per cent sample (326 firms) was drawn at random, which sample was then adjusted by dropping some firms and adding others so that the geographical scatter would be reduced somewhat in the interest of economy in conducting the survey. For various reasons, 9 of the resulting 326 firms were not interviewed. In the remaining cases, employers and employees were interviewed with the object of completing five questionnaires dealing with the nature of the business (lines of goods handled, sources of supply, etc.) and with wages, hours, and working conditions. Financial data necessary to complete the balance sheet and the profit and loss statement were also solicited. When possible, copies of the financial statements were obtained.

At least two comments on the validity of the gross profit findings seem warranted. First, data for profit and loss statements were obtained from only 60 of the 317 firms interviewed, or about one out of every five. Forty-three of the 60 firms were food wholesalers.[5] Secondly, some downward bias in gross margins and upward bias in expenses is surely present, since the firms knew the findings would affect the minimum wage law.

The Economic Stabilization Agency conducted a survey of wholesalers' margins on thirty-five food items after the outbreak of the hostilities in Korea as a first step toward establishing maximum margins. The reported margins were discussed by a panel of advisors drawn from the food wholesalers and retailers and were compared with the margins permitted under the OPA regulations of World War II.

---

[4] *Estudio Estadístico del Comercio al por Mayor en Puerto Rico,* Junta de Salario Mínimo, Gobierno de Puerto Rico, San Juan, 1949.

[5] The Junta's study is puzzling in that it is stated (page 10) that "in each case" the data necessary for the preparation of the financial statements were obtained, yet Appendices T and U (pages 75 and 76) report on only sixty firms.

This procedure resulted in a list of what might be called "negotiated" percentage markups over cost for the thirty-five items.[6] The percentage markups on this list ranged from 5 per cent to 12 per cent over cost, or 4.75 per cent to 10.7 per cent of sales.

The ESA markups are difficult to evaluate. The survey was conducted by mailed questionnaire, a method subject to certain obvious objections.[7] The markups were probably overstated on the questionnaire since the respondents were aware of the purpose of the survey. The final list of markups is not intended to represent average markups; they may rather approximate maximum markups. The OPA markups constituted a ceiling for the ESA margins, but how did the OPA markups compare with the average? Supposedly the wholesalers represented on the ESA food advisory panel regarded at least most of the thirty-five markups as satisfactory to the trade, but was their impression of satisfactory markups accurate? And finally, were these ESA markups adhered to by wholesalers at the time the present survey was being made?

One can conclude that while the Junta de Salario Mínimo study undoubtedly contains a fairly significant downward bias, the ESA markups probably do not. These two studies point to a wholesale margin in the vicinity of 7 to 9 per cent. Yet a review of the methodology of the present survey shows little cause for doubting the results, namely, gross margins of 11.8 per cent of sales for limited-line firms and 15.5 per cent for full-line firms.[8]

There is apparently little or no bias in the gross margin arising from the sampling technique employed. Each retailer interviewed was asked the names and addresses of his suppliers. The resulting unduplicated list of 543 firms (wholesalers and retail-wholesalers) compared with 598 wholesale firms listed by the General Supplies Administration, so virtually a census was available. For the general information (that is, other than expense information) all the wholesalers (retail-wholesalers excluded) in San Juan, plus about half of those outside the metropolitan area, were covered. This group constituted the universe from which the subsample of sixty-seven wholesale firms was drawn for the expenses information. Hence the San Juan wholesalers were oversampled. This may mean that the large firms are overrepresented, but Table 28 indicates that the average gross profit margin was probably

[6] The OPA markups were an upper limit on these markups because of the agreement that in no instance should the ESA markup exceed that allowed under OPA.

[7] Of the 250 wholesalers to whom the questionnaire was sent, 106, or 42 per cent, responded.

[8] There is no question raised as to the probable validity of the expense ratios reported by this study. Only the net profit margin, defined here to include owners' salaries, is in doubt, and hence the question basically turns on whether the gross margin reported by this survey is too large.

affected but little by this, since the margins did not vary significantly by size.

Expenses schedules were completed for each of the firms by means of interviews with the owners or managers. In some interviews the data were taken directly from the firm's books. The firm was not asked directly what percentage gross margin it operated on. Rather the sales data, cost of goods sold data, and all operating expense information were collected so that a complete profit and loss statement could be drawn up and the percentage gross margin was computed therefrom.

All schedules were carefully checked for completeness and consistency. Firms reporting unusually high or unusually low gross profit margins were interviewed again. In several cases firms reporting cost of goods sold and sales figures which showed gross margins in excess of 15 per cent, when checked, verified that the margin was correct

Thus there seems little reason to doubt the validity of the present survey unless the respondents did not report accurately. And if they did not, it seems unlikely that they should report figures giving too high, rather than too low, a gross profit margin. It is important to realize that the high average margin is not the result of a few firms or of one sales class. Table 28 shows the high margins to appear in all sales classes.

In view of these conflicting results, it would seem prudent to consider the gross profit percentages of 15.5 per cent and 11.8 per cent to be slightly overstated. It would seem unlikely, however, for these margins to be overstated by more than 1 or 2 per cent.

5

MANAGEMENT PRACTICES AND ATTITUDES

The data obtained from the field studies of food retailers and whole-salers present a clear picture of the scale of operations in food market-ing. However, in addition to such economic factors, distribution in Puerto Rico is also deeply influenced by the attitudes of the men who manage the firms, and their ways of doing business.

To learn of such attitudes and the nature of management generally, a series of interviews were conducted with retailers and wholesalers of some experience in both food and non-food lines. Twenty grocery firms and fifteen firms selling hardware, drugs, and yard goods were visited, and the interviewers talked at length with owners and managers. While the same points were covered in each interview, the respondents were encouraged to talk freely about business in general. In their own histories, in their comments on business policies and practices, and their plans for the future, a significant common pattern of management attitudes and methods emerges.

Organization and Entry into Retailing

The formal partnership or corporation is rare among Puerto Rican wholesalers and retailers. Most of the firms, especially those with the typically minute sales volume, are single proprietorships, and such proprietory operations are characteristic even of the larger firms.

The organization of retail enterprise reflects the comparative ease of entry into this business and the numerous reasons impelling Puerto Ricans to turn to it as a prospective means of livelihood. The selling of goods which everyone needs and with which everyone is familiar is a task which may be easily performed by nearly everyone. The over-head costs of a shop in the home, a roadside shack, a stall in the market, or a pushcart, are negligible. Much of the working capital can be obtained through credit from the supplier. The seller, therefore, regards even the smallest return as sufficient compensation for his time and labor. He views his small enterprise as an alternative to idleness or the seasonal drudgery of the cane fields. In many communities "one of the means by which local workers feel they might be able to win their permanent economic emancipation from the cane is the acquisition of a small retail business." [1]

An independent business is also frequently the goal of employees in existing stores. Many retailers, operating both small and large businesses were once clerks or assistants in another shop. Their ambition to open a store of their own is paralleled by that of many of their employees today.[2]

In the characteristic small firm, the owner-manager maintains complete control of all operations. Ordinarily he does so with a minimum of record keeping. He is likely to have neither basic accounting statements or the more elaborate control systems associated with decentralized operations. One successful retailer, who has expanded his business many fold over his original $40 investment expressed a common attitude as follows: "I have books because the government forces me to do so, otherwise I wouldn't have any. I don't need them to know the economic conditions of the business." Stock control or purchasing control are also all but unknown even in stores selling as much as $100,000 yearly. Physical inventories are taken yearly if at all, and book inventories are the exception. Many retailers reorder stock only when they sell the last item, or when the wholesaler's representative reminds them of their need for replacements. On occasion several partners in a firm may purchase the same item, with consequent overstocking. Yearly income accounts and statements of condition are becoming more common, but the validity of these statements in the absence of detailed record keeping is open to question.[3]

[1] Sidney W. Mintz, "Canamelar: The Contemporary Culture of a Rural Puerto Rican Proletariat," unpublished MS at the Social Science Research Center, University of Puerto Rico, submitted in partial fulfillment for Ph.D. at Columbia University, 1951, ch. 5, p. 15. In this study, Mintz goes on to emphasize that while a small business or some other means of escaping from work in the cane is a universal ambition, even the few dollars of capital needed to begin are beyond the reach of most. Two of the stores in the community studied by Mintz were established by means of lottery winnings.

[2] One established firm, the oldest in a fairly large city, has regularly employed assistants with some professional training. "They begin to work with us very enthusiastically, but after a year or so they want to get independent. They want to buy the store they are running and that is not our purpose." Consequently, out of ten or twelve new stores in this line in the area, six are owned by former employees of the retailer quoted.

[3] While each of the field studies reported in later chapters of this work includes an evaluation of the data collected, it may be pointed out here that these business conditions inevitably rendered most statistics subject to error. The personnel who were responsible for the Census are extremely dubious as to the validity of sales data. The staff of the field surveys in the marketing project report case after case of firms giving estimated, rather than recorded figures on sales volume and cost of operations. This is obviously more of a problem with small sellers than with larger firms, and with certain figures, chiefly those on inventories, credit losses, value of assets and depreciation accounts, and stock losses.

It would be easy to exaggerate the effects of this informality. The owner-manager, working in the store, acquires an intimate knowledge of its condition and is highly sensitive to changes for better or worse. He has learned to think about his business without analyzing figures. This intimate acquaintance with the business is characteristic of most Puerto Rican entrepreneurs.

There is little or no specialization of management effort in the typical store. The owner purchases and receives goods, clerks in the store, makes deliveries, takes orders, and pays bills. It follows that the successful businessmen work extremely hard and for long hours. Owners regularly insist that authority or responsibility cannot be delegated and in doing so cite the low caliber of their employees, who are treated with a mixture of suspicion and generous paternalism. Here are characteristic employer attitudes:

> Employees are selected on the basis of appearance and character, and disposition to learn, without any regard to previous experience. We train them on the job. They have to be watched continuously.

> The worst kind of people flow into the grocery business. They are dishonest, shiftless, unreliable. There is not one employee who can be relied upon to open up the branch store on time every morning. They do it for the first few days, and then begin to open up late or not at all because they are "sick" (really because they have been drinking the night before) or one thing or the other.

> I treat my employees as if they were my sons and daughters. I chat with them, but always keeping the distance that distinguishes everyone's position in the business. I distrust any employee who believes he knows more than I. Such employees do no good to your business and you should get rid of them. They are ignoramuses.

> I try to make of my business force a big family. I pay good salaries, treat them well, help them out if they have any problem, give them advice like a father instead of scolding them when they do wrong.

Judging from the remarks of many retailers, however, the personal pride in his business may lead the owner-manager to exaggerate the shortage of trained personnel. Not only is one-man operation typical of Puerto Rican wholesaling and retailing firms, but many entrepreneurs are convinced that such control is essential, and that no one can do the job as well as the owner. As a result little authority is delegated:

> The progress of this business is based on the personal attention of the owner. It is not the same if I am looking after the business as if someone else is doing it for me.

> This business [drugs] requires the personal attention of the owner because many people seek and trust the opinion and counsel of the pharmacist. To many of them the drugstore is like the doctor's office. They walk in

asking for the person in charge, explain their symptoms to him, and wait for their prescription.

This is a business that requires the personal attention of its owner.

Even with the most advanced checking schemes, the business requires very strenuous supervisory effort from its manager.

The existence of many small firms may thus be the result of two interacting forces, the refusal of owners to delegate responsibility — traceable partly to a disbelief in the ability of others and partly to the difficulties of finding suitable employees — and the desire of ambitious employees to advance. The aspiring clerk or assistant, if he is to realize his ambitions, must go into business for himself, and this is well recognized in the trade. A typical case history is that of two brothers employed by the same dealer to manage two branch stores. As managers, their salaries were $15 weekly; when they requested a pay increase it was denied. They then left to open their own store, which is now doing more business than that of their former employer. This and similar personnel policies come in for general criticism:

The trouble with most grocers is that when they have a vacancy they get a man just to "fill that hole" without any concern for his ability to grow.

The trouble with most store owners is that they pay very low wages and "wring the juice" out of the clerks. That is why only the people who cannot get work elsewhere are willing to work as grocery clerks and only for a short while.

Salaries are low because you can't get good people, and good people are not attracted because salaries are low. The only chance of getting good personnel is training them yourself. It is a tremendous effort to train personnel and to get subordinates to use business methods effectively.

As a rule the promising employees, once you train them, quit to open up their own stores. That is why owners are not very concerned with hiring people of superior ability who could be developed into managers. Returns in the trade are high enough to afford fairly high salaries to be paid to managers of branches, but people always think they can do even better by themselves.

Personnel policies bear importantly on the possibilities of aggressive merchandising and expansion by successful retailers. Present operations are generally enlarged or expanded only when other members of the family are available to share the work. The typical larger firm is managed by several brothers, by a man and his wife, by relatives by marriage, and only occasionally by unrelated partners or by a hierarchy of hired employees:

When I was young it was not difficult to get good help in the business. Mothers brought their sons to my father asking to have them trained. Many of the young men who were employees later quit to open up their own stores. Today I have been looking for some employees to assist in managerial tasks, but with no success. I am now training my only daughter to do the office work and my wife to do the over-all managerial duties.

My branch store is across the street. The main purpose in opening it was to give my brothers a way to make a living. They manage the store, but I keep a close supervision on the business.

(Three brothers who are joint managers). The distribution of our duties and responsibilities in the management of the business has been a very important factor. Harmony among the partners of the firm is something that should be kept by all means.

I have tried to induce my sons and nephews to join me in the business, but they prefer to work for somebody else in a "clean" job.

I have no incentive to expand. I am fifty years old and all my children are educated and married and settled. None of them will take over the business.

A further deterrent to expansion is the lack of capital for retail enterprise in light of the risks involved. While trade has provided exceedingly handsome returns on investment to some firms, many others are regularly on the edge of bankruptcy. A general attitude that retailing is risky was reported by a number of retailers:

It takes a lot of capital to open a store. Only people who are already in the business as owners or, more likely, as experienced employees, are willing to sink their capital in the grocery business. Outsiders do not want to invest in this field, which does not offer very attractive returns. Most grocery firms are bankrupt or on the verge of bankruptcy.

Those who want to expand must count on their own resources. People with liquid funds not in the business already are not prone to lend their funds to grocers or to enter into a partnership with grocers. The grocery business has a reputation for being risky.

Shortage of capital is a barrier to expansion. It is hard to get money for risky ventures, banks grant loans in such a case only against a good collateral. There are many wealthy families in ———— with thousands of dollars idle in the banks who are only out to speculate in real estate, but would not sink a penny on risky ventures.

However, even those firms who claim that they can obtain outside capital rarely wish to do so, because of the threat to their independent operations. Once again, the belief in one-man control is paramount:

I am very reluctant to take in "silent" partners. They get used to a certain level of profits and if at any time things happen which prevent the business from reaching this level, they become disappointed. Since they are not in close contact with the business, their first guess is that the active partner is cheating.

I have received numerous offers from people who wish to become silent partners. I would accept an offer of this sort if the partner were willing to assume the duties of management. I feel that the parties making these offers want to make easy money on the basis of my own experience and effort.

Also, I do wish to preserve my independence. I am extremely proud of my achievements, and I do not wish to share either my work or my profits with anybody else.

I would not mind taking on a partner in order to increase the capital if I could find a good man. On the other hand, I have struggled quite a lot all alone to keep my business afloat, and I would not like to share it with somebody else. The experience of other people who have gone into partnership makes me a little wary of the idea.

I have never considered having a branch store. I believe in partnerships with my relatives, but not with people outside my family.

The problem of reciprocal trust between partners weighs heavily in the decision to expand a business by taking in outside capital. Some retailers reported bitter experiences with partners, many of which ended in a disastrous split of the firm, and such cases are common knowledge among the trade. Very few partnerships seem to be based upon legal contract, and hence the personal relations between the partners is of central importance.

One final characteristic of the Puerto Rican store owner must be noted, and this is a nearly universal attitude of live and let live. The practical manifestation of this attitude is a non-aggressive attitude on prices and a tendency toward sharing of whatever business is available. Various factors contribute to this attitude, some of which have already been presented — the fact that managers work long and hard, the lack of suitable personnel to handle expanded operations, the absence of family members who will be interested in taking over an expanded enterprise, and the general knowledge that the distributive trades are overcrowded are all important. In many cases live and let live is the easiest approach to managing a business:

It is true that many grocers do not expand because they are old and want to take it easy. Most establishments in the island are started by former employees, who, after working ten or twenty years to get experience and save money, have to work ten or twenty more years to build up their business. By the time they are firmly established they are fifty or sixty. In this circumstance, if they can get a comfortable living without much exertion, they are satisfied.

I do not lower my prices as much as possible, because I am already getting more business than I can handle. One of these days, I will get so "tired" with the business that I will just sell out and retire.

I have no incentive to expand. I can make a comfortable living without "killing myself much" in my present situation. I would not own a chain organization if it were given to me.

I would like to expand this business to a certain limit, but going further than this would mean working very hard. I would like to have more business, but not wear myself out.

Anyone who would reduce prices and expand their sales volume would do very well financially in the grocery business. But I am not interested in this possibility. Doing business at a large scale volume involves too much work. I would have to take care of a larger business, with more store space to watch, a bigger working force to handle, more customers to deal with. They would be different customers, too, the *hoi polloi*. I would need two detectives around every gondola. I am quite contented with the way things are shaping up and am not too sure I want additional business responsibilities. As it is, my business takes up quite a bit of my time. I would be interested in adopting techniques which would enable me to expand without too much additional personal effort, but I have been too busy to give it much thought.

There may be something to the notion that grocers are quite contented with achieving a level of income which will enable them to educate their children and retire in comfort, and let things go at that. Grocery stores require a lot of attention from the owner, and once you are getting a good income additional returns cost more in terms of added exertion than it is worth.

I am in business just to make a living for myself and my two aging parents and, thank God, I am doing fairly well. I don't care if I never get rich in this store; once you have enough to live on you should be contented.

As long as the store gives me a decent living without doing hard work, that is all I need.

There is also, however, a prevailing attitude concerning proper behavior in business — a notion that some practices are ethical and others (including price competition) are not. Back of this concept is often the idea that the retail market is definitely limited, that an expansion of sales volume for one store means losses for some other store. The net result is an agreement not to spoil the market. While in many cases such an agreement is implicit in the retailers' recognition of their situation, the understanding may on occasion be explicit:

I have no competitors because I have business agreements so that we can sell the same lines at more or less the same prices. I am not interested either in expanding this business nor in opening branches, because the customers are limited and the volume of business would be the same whether I have branches or not.

I do not keep track of my competitors' prices. I price my articles according to a standard markup system. Of course, that also varies with the kind of article and the kind of customer.

In this neighborhood, the store owners do not believe in competition, but in harmony and fellowship. My store and _____'s are like one. We share a common clientele, and send each other customers when one of us is too busy, or does not have an item requested. We borrow goods from each other, if one of us is momentarily short. _____'s clerk comes over to help me, when he is not too busy at his employer's place. Prices are the same at both stores, although we never consult each other expressly on this point.

We believe in the principle of "live and let live." At times we go out of our way to avoid ill will from competitors. We sell some goods wholesale to competing stores and to peddlers. Once we softened up the selling activity of the _____ agent for our ice cream, when an old man complained that we were taking over his small local ice cream market. We did this until the man decided to shift over to the grocery business.

I do not go out of my way to get customers. In fact, I consider it unethical to try deliberately to take away customers from competitors.

Our relation with other competitors is cordial. There is one competitor who is resorting to "uncommercial" (to put it mildly) competition. He sets his price below the level required to stay in business. We frown on this sort of thing because we take the long run view.

In some cases, the fear of spoiling the market is complicated by the wholesale connections of certain retailers:

I am reluctant to compete on a price basis because I would be competing with the stores who are customers of my father's wholesale business.

It is not wise of us to lower our retail prices because we are the ones who supply many of the small stores in this area, and if we lowered our retail prices it would be resented and they would stop doing business with us. Besides, the retail store is the most profitable part of the business.

The general conclusions to be drawn from these comments are already evident: retailing and wholesaling in Puerto Rico are highly personal enterprises. They are one-man firms, or family firms under the control of, with few exceptions, a single manager. The continuous and detailed supervision of the owner is substituted for the relatively formal personnel policies and administrative procedures of larger mainland stores. Partly to protect themselves and others from overexertion and failure, and partly because they believe that the market is limited, a live-and-let-live attitude toward competition is adopted by most entrepreneurs.

The Store and the Community

The identification of the store with the personality of its owner is important to consumers. In all areas a close personal relationship with the store owner is of significance to patrons. Rural consumers are especially dependent on the small isolated grocery stores. Here people are too poor to buy supplies in large quantities, or to make the regular trip into town which such purchases would require. The country *colmado* therefore stocks soap, machetes, drugs, and even dry goods. However, purchase of many other non-food items is sufficiently rare that it warrants the additional effort of a trip to a nearby town.

Aside from the dependence on whatever store is within walking distance of the family, the Puerto Rican consumer is further tied to his grocery because of the almost universal use of credit. Credit is such an integral part of purchasing in Puerto Rico that it cannot be thought of, like the charge accounts or installment sales in the United States, as a method of payment. Frequently it is a rigorous necessity; where it is not, it may be completely habitual. The customer buys on credit, the retailers also purchase on credit, and credit transactions bulk large in wholesale trade. Most retailers and wholesalers believe that credit is costly, that it is a nuisance, but because cash purchases are beyond the resources of either consumers or tradesmen, that it is also inescapable:

> Cash-and-carry stores cannot get very far in Puerto Rico. Many of the ones now in operation are doing well only because they are "skimming the cream."
>
> You cannot sell unless you sell on credit. There is a man here who tried a cash-and-carry system. He had to switch to credit and has now more accounts receivable than I.
>
> Maybe if all grocers went on a cash basis simultaneously you could abolish credit. But, of course, you cannot do that when everybody has hundreds of thousands of dollars "in the streets." The cost reduction of buying from wholesalers on a cash basis would not amount to much.
>
> We have set up a credit system which is turning out to be very profitable. It is my opinion that this business [appliances] has to be carried on a credit sales basis. Rich customers are not good customers. Most of them when they make a purchase ask for a reduction in price or take over sixty days to make the payments.

Credit sales are a higher proportion of the total in food stores than in non-food outlets, and there are more stores on a strictly cash basis in the non-food lines. However, credit transactions have been developed, particularly in the appliance and home furnishings field, to accommodate consumers with low incomes. The grocer nonetheless is the primary source of credit:

> If somebody is ill in the family and the doctor's bill amounts to a lot, you call the grocer and tell him you won't pay him that month's bill now, but that you will pay it by installments later. The grocer is human and he understands. If he did not extend you credit, you would have to borrow the money to pay the doctor's bill from somebody else.

The druggist comes next in importance:

> People like to have credit always in their drugstore, so that if any emergency comes up, they don't have to worry if they have no money.

But much of the credit can be considered habitual, and for higher-income consumers it is a corollary of services which range from convenience to extravagance:

For many people buying on credit is just a habit. They have an income high enough and steady enough to purchase on a cash basis. In fact, some of my credit customers have thousands of dollars idle in the banks. But it would not occur to them to buy with cash.

Once you have been doing business with a grocer for a period of time, there are a lot of things you can do and get away with. The grocer will let you postpone payment of your bill from one month to the next, he will give you prompt delivery service even if you live in the far end of town, and phone in orders three times a day instead of consolidating all your needs in one order. Why, sometimes a lady calls up just to order the half-pound of codfish for her supper she forgot to order in the morning. The delivery of the goods in such a case costs me about as much as the merchandise itself.

The retailer in a small community enjoys considerable prestige, partly because he has reached a goal held by many — the independent business. The store also often serves as a meeting place or clearing-house for news in the community, and the owner's advice is sought in connection with many problems. The retailer's power to give and with-hold credit reinforces his position of leadership, but this is far from absolute. The retailer knows that his customers are used to receiving credit, and that other outlets able to serve his clients can spring up overnight when they do not already exist. As a result, retailers extend credit freely, although sometimes with a crude attempt to vary the line of credit according to the trustworthiness of the individual. While excessive accounts receivable have forced some firms to fail, an aggressive collection policy, which might get bills paid, would also lose customers. For the most part, retailers report that all customers want to settle their accounts and fail to do so only in an emergency. This mutual trust between store and consumer is a mark of a successful business: the retailer is proud of his honest dealing and reliability, the low-income customer who buys on credit is a good risk who eventually pays his bills.

Good personal relations play an important part in the sales policy of most retail stores. Managers stress the need for building up such relationships, and look for personnel who are "jovial," "friendly," or "able to chat with people":

The individual customer should be treated as an old friend and an important client. No matter what the status of the person is, we always try to be familiar with him. If a plumber walks into the store we attend to him personally, treat him as an old friend, talk to him about baseball or some of his other interests. If a farmer comes in and is not too eager to buy I take over and start talking about agriculture and the difficult problems that farmers have in making a living. You have to identify yourself with your customers, show them the best merchandise and make them feel flattered, make them think they are important. We give the same service to all our customers, whether they buy a five-cent article or purchase one hundred dollars' worth of goods.

What has given me the best business results is to be on friendly terms with my customers.

Another thing is that the customers don't like to be continuously watched. I make them feel free to go around looking at everything. If there is one who takes away or steals or robs anything, it is not a matter to worry about. In one way or another I have been paid for it. Maybe the same person comes in some day later and makes a good purchase. He is then paying for what he took before. If that doesn't happen other customers have already paid for it.

What insures the return of a customer to a drugstore is fast service. If the customer wants a medicine in a hurry and it is out of stock I will phone all the local drugstores and send a messenger for the item. If it cannot be found in this town I order it from San Juan. All this is done in front of the customer to show our interest in his particular case.

I also give the people what I would like if I were able to have it. As you know, it is very hot in ———— almost all day long, so I ordered an air conditioning set up when I built this new building. It is comfortable and people like it very much. This innovation has helped me to increase sales.

Emphasis on personal relations, coupled with the live-and-let-live approach noted previously often leads the retailer to rate regular patronage above a high turnover from a larger number of buyers. The retailers interviewed repeatedly stressed this point while adding that they depend upon a satisfied clientele to maintain their volume of business:

I do not go out of my way to get new customers; I have my regular, steady, time-tested clientele. Occasionally, some regular customers bring their friends or relatives into the clientele.

When I opened my new store, I contacted personal friends and newcomers to town to seek their patronage. Satisfied customers in turn bring along their friends.

It may be inferred from all this that retailing in Puerto Rico is much more than the impersonal transfer of goods from the producer to the consumer at the lowest possible price. Price competition is infrequent. While the non-price considerations, including credit, friendly relations with one's retailer, advice from one's druggist, and so on, form a large body of "services" rendered along with the distribution of goods, it is still open to question whether these services provide an effective substitute for the economies to the consumer from more energetic price competition. A further word on this is in order.

The Puerto Rican marketing system might be thought to offer a classic case of what economists refer to as monopolistic competition. Each market contains a number of firms, each offering a slightly differentiated product. Price competition is virtually non-existent. The sellers believe that they are confronted by demand curves which are inelastic — that a lower price would not increase total sales sufficiently to enhance or even maintain their margin of profit. The signs of non-price competition exist in the varying services offered by different stores. However, because of the live-and-let-live approach to business typical of most entrepreneurs, analysis in terms of monopolistic competition, or any type of competition, may be inappropriate. It is doubtful whether owners seek to maximize profits, either by price or non-price competition, in the usual sense. They may be thought of as maximizing profits if one includes in marginal costs the subjective costs of becoming unpopular with competitors.

Where profit maximization is not a goal, although the more efficient firms may earn substantial returns, the less efficient outlets are not weeded out of the market structure. The succeeding chapters undertake, after a fuller examination of wholesaling and retailing firms, to measure the costs of maintaining these relatively efficient firms.

6

A MODEL FOOD DISTRIBUTION SYSTEM

The preceding survey of wholesalers and retailers has shown small scale operations and high costs to be the most striking features of the food marketing structure of Puerto Rico. The sales of the median retail store among the sample firms were less than $12,000 per year, and this figure would have been appreciably lower had the *cafetines* which sell groceries and the peddlers selling chiefly fruits and vegetables been included in the survey. Fifty-four per cent of the wholesale firms and 81 per cent of the retail-wholesale firms studied reported sales of less than $30,000 per month, so even the wholesale structure is marked by a predominance of relatively small firms. Comparing data from the 1948 U.S. Census of Business with the 1949 Census of Business for Puerto Rico shows that the average retail food store sales on the mainland are more than ten times as great as in Puerto Rico. Average sales for merchant wholesalers handling primarily foods are almost twice as great in the continental United States as in Puerto Rico.

High markups at both the retail and wholesale levels accompany this small scale of operations. The average gross margin at retail was found to be about 23.5 per cent, the average net margin about 12 per cent. At wholesale, the average gross margin is 14 per cent while the average net margin stands at approximately 10 per cent. These compare with mainland gross margins of about 9.0 per cent at wholesale and 15 to 16 per cent at retail.[1] Both the retail and wholesale net margins for Puerto Rico, however, include the owners' salaries.

For the policy-makers of Puerto Rico, the foregoing statistical description of food marketing is essential in that it provides the concrete basic data on the existing situation. That these data scarcely do more than corroborate the widely held opinion that Puerto Rican re-

[1] John R. Bromell, *Survey of Wholesale Grocers' Profit and Loss Figures*, United States Wholesale Grocers' Association, Inc., Washington. D.C., p. 11.

tail and wholesale margins are high does not detract from their value. But such information, even though detailed, falls far short of meeting the policy-maker's need for material on which to base his decisions. The information presented thus far has indicated that wholesale and retail gross margins are very high, by mainland standards. It is tempting to conclude that the food distribution costs in Puerto Rico should be as low as on the mainland. Yet it has already been emphasized that the services performed by the distribution system in Puerto Rico differ markedly from those performed on the mainland and so it would be a grave error to accept mainland margins as the ideal for which Puerto Rico should strive. It is conceivable that the existing margins on the island might be as low as possible, given the Puerto Rican context; that operating costs are high, due to credit costs, consumer demand for locational convenience, and the high return paid to the scarce entrepreneurial talent. On the other hand, one might argue that Puerto Rican margins could be lower than those on the mainland because of lower labor, equipment, building, and utility costs, fewer lines of goods to handle, and so on.

In other words, although it is now known what distribution costs are in Puerto Rico, the realistically achievable distribution costs, given the Puerto Rican economic and cultural environment, have not been identified. The preceding chapters have revealed *what is;* the next five chapters are addressed to the question of what *should be.*

Intelligent policy-making demands a clear conception of the goal, otherwise serious errors may result. Many variables in the problem may be attacked, such as credit costs, net profits, size of store, delivery costs, owner attitudes, consumer attitudes, and so on. Some of these variables may now be as near an optimum as is possible for Puerto Rico whereas others may be subject to great improvement. It is important that the people of Puerto Rico know which aspects of the present distribution system might lend themselves most readily to change.

Furthermore, careful thought must be given to the various methods of changing the more malleable characteristics of the system if rationalization is to proceed with minimum friction consistent with the desired rate of improvement.

Finally, the policy-maker needs the goal clearly defined in terms of the social cost incurred and benefits derived from rationalization. Otherwise it is impossible to judge whether the rationalization scheme is desirable as a whole.

While recognizing the necessity of a well defined goal, it should not be inferred that it is attainable on short notice. Social and economic changes of the type necessary in the present problem to be permanent usually cannot be rapid. Rather the purpose of developing the model is to assure that future change is in the right direction and to accelerate, if possible, the desirable changes which will undoubtedly occur eventually in Puerto Rico as the island develops.

To establish a bench mark for policy decisions, it is necessary to construct rather carefully what amounts to a model food distribution system. It is then possible to see what kinds of business units would be required in such a model system, to estimate the total cost of operating such a system, and to see clearly the costs and shortcomings of the marketing system now in existence.

The Concept of the Model

As a practical matter it is necessary to design not a single model or ideal system but a number of alternatives to the present system. No single decision can be made on the services to be offered to consumers by retailers and, for somewhat different reasons, there are differing possible relationships between wholesalers and retailers. A useful goal for marketing policy in Puerto Rico must encompass these several possibilities.

In other respects, the models constructed in this section are pragmatic in the sense that they fit the context of present day Puerto Rico. They take incomes and consumer tastes as they now are. They assume the present state of transportation — which means that all islanders must be within walking distance of at least one food store. The store must stock the types of foods used by its customers. This latter requirement means that we must distinguish between different market areas on the island. Thus the type of merchandise sold in the metropolitan food stores differs markedly from that handled by the rural town and isolated rural stores. Because of the differences in income, the diets of the metropolitan consumers are, on the whole, considerably more varied than the diets of the rural consumers. The rural consumer buys only a few staple items from food stores whereas the more well-to-do customer in the larger towns and cities buys a considerably higher proportion of canned goods, meats, and dairy products. Besides handling a smaller variety of foods than the metropolitan firms, the rural stores sell primarily in bulk whereas the retailers in the larger towns and cities sell a greater proportion of canned and packaged goods. The typical rural store has several bins into which the owner empties hundred-pound sacks of rice, beans, flour, cornmeal, and so on, which he then packages at the time of sale.

Not only the type of foods handled but also the pattern of services offered by retailers differs between the rural and urban areas. Credit is offered by the great majority of food stores in Puerto Rico as the preceding chapters have indicated. However, delivery service is rare in the smaller towns and rural areas. Self-service stores are also virtually unknown in the smaller towns, partly because staple goods are not pre-packaged. Retailers' buying practices also differ from place to place on the island; as noted in Chapter III it is more common for the retailers in the larger towns to buy direct from the mainland or from metropolitan wholesalers whereas the retailers in the smaller towns more commonly buy from intermediate wholesalers.

A further outstanding difference between the city store and rural store operations lies, of course, in the volume of sales. This difference arises not only from the varying population density among the market areas but also from the disparity in personal incomes. Finally, a differentiation of market areas is necessary because labor and building costs are considerably lower outside the metropolitan areas. As one example, the legal minimum wage for grocery clerks in greater San Juan is twelve dollars per week but only eight dollars per week in rural towns.

To deal with these variations in operating conditions four market area categories were established for purposes of this study. The first of these, the *metropolitan* market area, includes greater San Juan (including Santurce and Rio Piedras), and the urban sections of Ponce and Mayaguez. The *market town* market areas are the urban portions of the municipalities of Fajardo, Humacao, Caguas, Guayama, Manatí, Arecibo, and Aguadilla, all of which have populations exceeding 10,000 persons. The *rural town* market areas comprise the urban sectors of all other towns on the island. All the non-urban sectors of the island are considered *isolated rural* market areas.

The retail firms are model firms within the model system in three different senses. First of all, it is assumed that the retail firm will offer the types and lines of goods that are common in the area served. For this reason it is assumed that the metropolitan stores will all be full-line stores. This is deemed advisable because computations based on data obtained in the field study indicate that slightly more than 12 per cent of total metropolitan store sales consisted of meat sales and 6.1 per cent consisted of produce sales. The market town stores of the model are also assumed to be full-line outlets; the survey has shown that almost 10 per cent of the total market town sales were represented by meat and just under 4 per cent by produce. (The produce percentages would be even higher for the metropolitan and market town stores were the fruit and vegetable stand sales included.) The rural stores, on the other hand, do not commonly offer a full line of foods. Only 2½ per cent of the total rural food store sales were meat sales and .7 per cent were produce sales. As has been indicated in earlier chapters, produce and meat typically do not reach the rural consumer through food stores but rather direct from the producer.

Constructing the model under the assumption that all market town and metropolitan stores should be full-line establishments presumes that meat and produce can be distributed more efficiently through full-line stores than by other means. There is a strong a priori argument for this. Meat distributed through full-line groceries rather than through meat markets carries a lower building cost overhead charge per pound. The utility expense per pound will be less for large, full-line stores than for small, specialty meat markets because the graduated electricity rate structure will lower the marginal cost of operating refrigeration equipment. Labor cost per pound of meat sold should be less for full-line stores because of better utilization of labor. Full-line stores mean that fewer stores are necessary in the model, hence the level of managerial talent should be higher than if many stores are operating. Finally, full-line stores lend themselves more handily to integration than do specialized food outlets.

The argument that produce can be distributed more efficiently in the market town and metropolitan areas through full-line stores rather than through specialized stores is not as clear as in the case of meat. For produce, the alternative distribution method is through peddlers and fruit and vegetable stands. Unlike meat these do not involve high fixed charges. Stock loss on fresh produce may also be greater for the full-line stores than for peddlers because the latter can vary the price so as to clear inventories each day if necessary. Furthermore, the labor cost of distributing produce by peddlers and by produce stands may be extremely low because the peddler or proprietor is not assured a minimum wage. However, the labor cost of distributing produce in a self-service market should be comparable to the labor cost of distributing produce through peddlers.

The strongest case for the assumption that meat and produce can be most efficiently distributed through full-line stores in the metropolitan and market towns turns on efficiency that can be realized only through integrated wholesale-retail operations and the fact that the marginal cost of distributing meat and produce through an integrated marketing system is almost certainly less than through other channels. While there is no final proof of these points, the experience of the corporate food chains on the mainland points strongly in this direction.

Because of the low volume of meat and produce sold by rural stores, such firms are assumed in the model to offer so little meat and produce as to require no special refrigeration. Under such circumstances the additional or marginal cost of selling a dollar's worth of meat or produce is likely to be little different from the marginal cost of selling a dollar's worth of other foods.

The models are constructed under the assumption that the rural stores will continue to sell primarily bulk goods whereas the market town and metropolitan stores will sell a greater proportion of packaged goods.

The firms not only represent the model type for their area, but they are also assumed to do the most economical volume of business. In other words, each store in the model is assumed to operate at such volume as will render minimum margins profitable. In terms of economic theory the model firms are assumed to operate at or near the low points of their long-run cost curves. However, in order to meet the requirement that all consumers be within walking distance of a food store, it is necessary that in some of the sparsely settled rural areas the stores operate at less than optimum volume.

Finally, the stores in the model are assumed to have a better than average quality of management. The estimated operating costs of the model stores are based on separate intensive cost analyses of what appear to be the more efficient firms now in operation on the island. In other words the quality of management that is assumed does exist. Were the model considered a goal, it would be legitimate to suppose that managers would be recruited or trained up to the level of achievement now reached by the firms subjected to the cost analysis.

The wholesale firms which compose the model distribution system are also model firms. They are all assumed to be located in the metropolitan (port) cities of San Juan, Ponce, and Mayaguez. The entire retail food system of the island could in fact be serviced from these points (the island is only one hundred miles long and thirty-five miles wide). Such a wholesale system would obviate the present practice of routing a considerable proportion of food imports through intermediate wholesalers. The wholesale firms in the model are also assumed to offer a full line of merchandise (although not necessarily fresh produce) since such firms are more adaptable to integration. Finally, as in the case of the retail stores, costs are based on the performance of wholesale firms of better than average efficiency for Puerto Rico.

Certain additional comments about the concept of the model are in order. No allowances are made for increases in per capita incomes and food expenditures nor for the possibility that management might be improved beyond the level achieved by the more efficient operators at present. In the alternative models, estimates are made of the dollar savings that would be possible were consumers persuaded to forego delivery services and were it possible for them to dispense with credit. Beyond this, no changes in the Puerto Rican distribution system are assumed.

The models presented in this section are not to be viewed as achievable in the foreseeable future. It must be emphasized again that the purpose of constructing the models is to establish a bench mark by which the efficiency or inefficiency of the present system can be measured.

The Alternative Model Systems

We turn now to a number of questions concerning specific characteristics of the model food distribution system. Answers to these questions bear directly on the cost of marketing services in the system we are erecting as a standard. The critical questions are: (1) Should credit and delivery service to consumers be provided by retailers, as in the present marketing system or should these functions be shifted to the consumer for purposes of the model? (2) Should credit be extended by wholesalers to retailers or should the model consist only of self-financing retailers? (3) Should the model assume complete rationalization and disregard the need for competition among retailers or should competition be assumed? And finally, (4) should the model assume wholesalers and retailers to be independent of each other or should vertical integration be assumed?

All of these possibilities are relevant. It is also important to know which promise the greatest economies. Accordingly, alternative models, constructed under different combinations of the above assumptions, would be of maximum value to the policy makers. We have undertaken therefore to identify and design the various alternative food marketing model systems which would be workable in Puerto Rico. The alternative systems, their working designations, and their assumptions are as follows: Model LS (limited service) assumes that the retailers offer neither credit nor delivery to their customers and that the retailers are not integrated with wholesalers. Model LS also ignores the question of competition. It is essentially an engineering concept of a model food distribution system.

Model C is constructed on the same assumptions as Model LS except that credit is presumed to be offered by the retailers to their customers.

Model CD assumes credit and delivery are both offered by retailers; otherwise the assumptions are the same as in Model LS.

Model Retail Firms

The characteristics of the model retail firms are based on intensive studies of existing real firms. The panel of retail firms subjected to this analysis was selected in the following manner. First the sub-sample of firms from which the detailed cost and margin data discussed in Chapter III had been obtained was reviewed and those stores reporting ratios of operating expenses to cost of goods sold of 10 per cent or less were listed. There were fifty-six such firms, distributed more or less evenly over the island. Each of these stores was visited and the owner was interviewed. Some of these stores had gone out of business since the data was collected; others had changed from food store to *cafetín*. The owners still operating food stores were interviewed informally. In the course of the conversation each man was asked by what methods he had attempted in recent years to increase his sales, how he had tried to lower his operating costs, where he bought his inventory and what methods of reducing his buying costs he had attempted, and what steps he had taken to reduce his credit losses. These questions were sufficient to generate a discussion of general business methods and problems of the store owner. The conversations easily distinguished the more aggressive and intelligent store owners from the more passive type. In the course of interviews it was discovered that some firms showed low operating expenses (as a ratio to cost of goods sold) in the data because, for example, imputed wages to unpaid employees were not recognized as an expense. Such stores were dropped unless they appeared, on the basis of the interview only, to be managed efficiently. Eliminating from the list of fifty-six stores those which have disappeared from the scene, those which have left the grocery business for other types of enterprise, and those which appeared to be poorly managed resulted in under-representation in the revised list for the market towns. The market towns which were not represented were then visited and the prominent store owners in the town were interviewed. By this time approximately forty store owners had been visited and interviewed; by then it was rather easy to identify the more efficient stores on the basis of the interview alone. Such factors as an excessive number of employees or of expensive equipment, inefficient clerks and delivery service methods, and a lackadaisical attitude on the part of the owner become apparent rather quickly. Therefore, on the basis of the interview only, some stores in the market towns were added to the list. The final list of twenty-nine stores consisted, therefore, not only of stores included in the original survey but also a few which were not.

If, in the course of each interview, it became obvious that the store was satisfactory for cost analysis, the owner's cooperation on the project was solicited. There was not a single refusal by a retail store owner asked to cooperate.

The final list of firms subjected to the cost analysis consisted of four isolated rural stores, seven rural town stores, eight market town stores and ten metropolitan stores.

For each of the panel retailers an income statement and a balance sheet were drawn up at the time of the first interview after the panel stores were chosen. The income statement described the physical factors used: for example, the size and type of building, number and functions of employees. The original cost analysis, based on the balance sheet and income statement data, listed all out-of-pocket costs as reported by the retailer, and by a standardized procedure in-pocket costs were also estimated. All equipment was valued at depreciated replacement cost regardless of the valuation on the firm's books and a common depreciation method was used for all firms. Buildings were appraised by the method used by the Commonwealth government's new Scientific Assessment program for the property tax. A 10 per cent return on the owner's investment was recorded as an expense. This standardized procedure of estimating real operating costs, described in detail in Chapter VII, assured that identical firms would show identical operating costs.

On completion of the original cost analysis, the retailer was interviewed a second time. He was asked what changes in physical units of input would be necessary to support a volume of business one and one-half times as great as his present volume, twice as great, and three times as great, assuming the proportion of credit and delivery sales remained constant. The increase in operating costs could then be identified and cost analyses for the projected volumes of sales drawn up. Finally, credit and delivery costs were determined for the present and projected volumes of business.

The procedure just outlined resulted in several sets of cost analyses for each firm. The original cost analysis set forth the real operating costs (in-pocket as well as out-of-pocket) for the firm as operating at the time of the survey. For a retailer offering credit and delivery, eleven additional cost analyses were completed. One set of three projected cost analyses assumed credit and delivery to be offered at sales volumes 50 per cent, 100 per cent and 200 per cent greater than the sales volume of the original cost analysis. A second set of four projected cost analyses presented the operating costs at the present and projected sales volumes assuming only credit to be offered. A third and final set assumed cash-and-carry operations.

Projected cost analyses assuming a particular service to be offered were not completed where firms did not extend that service to consumers at present. Under such circumstances the costs of the service would have been completely hypothetical for that retailer.

The operating costs, when expressed as a percentage of the cost of goods sold (which was assumed to increase proportionally with sales) under the various assumed conditions, rendered a series of mark-ups which could be plotted against the cost of goods sold so as to describe a crude cost curve. On the basis of the cost curves of the panel stores for each of the four types of market areas, the optimal volume and the mark-up that would be required at that volume could be determined.

The Model Wholesale Firm

For the reasons discussed earlier, only full-line metropolitan wholesale firms were chosen for cost analysis. The sample of wholesalers which had previously been subjected to detailed study (Chapter IV) was reviewed and fourteen full-line metropolitan firms reporting a ratio of expenses to cost of goods sold of 5 per cent or less were selected. These wholesalers were visited and interviewed in the same manner as were the retailers. One wholesaler did not wish to cooperate, another operated two retail outlets in conjunction with his wholesale business and did not keep separate accounting records, a third was in the process of liquidation and a fourth had already gone out of business. Other full-line metropolitan wholesalers were then visited and interviewed in order to choose firms to fill out the panel list. By this process a panel of thirteen wholesale firms was chosen, distributed among the three metropolitan cities in approximately the same ratio as the firms in the large sample discussed in Chapter IV. Their monthly sales volumes ranged from $16,000 to over $500,000.

The wholesalers' operating costs were analyzed by the same method used for the retailers. The original balance sheet and original income statement were completed in the first interview. On the basis of these the original cost analysis was completed, recognizing as operating costs all the economic costs of operation, both in-pocket and out-of-pocket. As with the retailers, a common depreciation expense policy was applied and a 10 per cent interest return on invested capital was allowed.

In a second interview after the original cost analysis was completed the wholesalers were asked what additional input factors would be required were their business volumes to increase by 50 per cent, by 100 per cent, and by 200 per cent. The additional costs which would be incurred by such increases were computed. The markups required at the several higher volumes were then derived. Credit and delivery costs were identified.

From the firm cost curves based on the cost analyses, the optimal volume and required markup of the model wholesale firm were determined assuming credit but not delivery service to be offered by the wholesaler. The reason for this treatment in contrast with the retailer analysis is explained in Chapter VIII.

Constructing the Model Systems

The final step in establishing the model or bench mark system of distribution was to combine the model firms into a distribution system for the island as a whole. The operating costs of the model were then estimated and compared with the cost of the present system. To do this, the value of the island's food at different stages in the present (that is, 1949–50) distribution channel were estimated — these estimates covered the value of food at the time the original wholesalers bought it, the value when sold to the retailers, and finally the value to the consumer.[2] Certain of these values are required for the construction of the model system as well as for estimating the possible savings over present distribution.

To construct the model distribution system, the value of the wholesalers' original purchases, in other words, all wholesalers' purchases except those from other wholesalers, were first divided by the volume of the model wholesaler to arrive at the approximate number of wholesalers needed in the model. The model wholesaler markup (assuming credit but no delivery) was then applied to the value of the wholesalers' original purchases to estimate the cost of supporting the model wholesale system under the assumption that the wholesalers would pay for no delivery service.

The sum of the wholesalers' original purchases and the cost of operating the model wholesale system gave the value of the food purchased, in the model, by retailers from wholesalers. To this total were added retailers' purchases direct from the producer, such as those of local meat and produce. This total value of retailers' purchases was then distributed among the seventy-five *municipios,* and between the rural and urban sections of each, in the same proportions as the sales of grocery stores, meat and fish markets, and fruit and vegetable stands were distributed as shown by the 1949 Census of Business for Puerto Rico.

The cost of trucking each *municipio* food supply from the nearest port city was then added to the retailers' purchases to arrive at the total value of the food by the time it reached the retailers.

---

[2] Again it is well to emphasize that this study is concerned only with the distribution of that part of the island's food which is sold through food retailers, excepting milk dealers, milk stands, bakeries, candy stores, and other specialized food shops.

Total sales, valued at cost to the retailer in the model, were computed for each of the four market areas (metropolitan, market town, rural town, and isolated rural) from the above listing. The cost of operating the model retail system assuming, say, that neither credit nor delivery were offered by retailers, could then be calculated by applying to the total sales of each market area the limited service markup required by the model store for each type of market area, and summing the four products.[3]

The number of model stores required to service the island was computed by dividing the sales of the rural and urban sections of each *municipio* by the volume of the model store for that particular type of market area. The resulting number was compared with that required to insure that all customers were within walking distance of a store. In all cases the number of optimum volume stores exceeded the number necessary to leave all consumers within walking distance of a store.

The markups required by model retailers if credit only and if credit and delivery are offered were applied to the sales for each market area in the same manner as just described, to determine the cost of operating the retail sector of Model C and Model CD. Finally, a rough estimate of the savings resulting from more economical retailer-wholesaler credit relationships was derived. The results of these calculations are set forth in the following chapters.

[3] The detailed presentation of this calculation in Chapter IX adjusts the model store markups, which are based on February–May 1952 prices, for the price change since 1949 and for the difference between the actual value of retailers' purchases in 1949–50 and the model value of the same physical quantity of goods.

7

THE OPTIMAL RETAIL UNIT

With the foregoing outline of objectives and procedure in mind, it is now possible to proceed to the more detailed task of identifying the conditions under which the individual retail outlet in Puerto Rico would operate at optimal efficiency. Since the results of this exercise are as valid only as the methods by which they are arrived at, it will be necessary to ask the reader to bear with a rather careful outline of these methods. It is perhaps worth stating once more our over-all goal, which is to see what kinds and numbers of retail and wholesale units doing what volume of business would effectively serve the people of Puerto Rico and what the costs of this service would be in contrast with those of the present food distribution system.

The Original Accounting Data

The first task was to establish a clear picture of investment, income, and costs of the firms studied before projecting any changes that might be expected to lead toward greater efficiency.

The individual asset and liability accounts of each of the firms used as a point of departure for constructing the model retail outlets were first listed in balance-sheet form. The buildings and equipment were valued at replacement cost less depreciation, regardless of the valuation on the firm's books. Prior to undertaking the cost analysis of the retailers, information on the replacement value of all grocery store equipment was gathered from equipment dealers in San Juan. Buildings were appraised by the Commonwealth's Scientific Assessment method.

The original income statement of the firms was based upon information taken from the profit and loss statement of the individual firm when such statements were available for the last fiscal year. These were available however, only in a small minority of cases.

If the retailer did not have an adequate profit and loss statement, the original income statement was completed from other available data such as sales and expense records. Such original income statements were based upon at least five months' records. The only exceptions to this rule were two of the small rural stores, which had almost no information on sales or cost of goods sold. In such cases an inventory of the store was listed on the same day that the retailer began keeping a very simplified set of books provided for the purposes of this project. Daily sales, expenses, and payments for goods received were recorded over a period of about six weeks. At the end of this time the retailer was revisited, the inventory taken a second time, the record kept by the retailer over the intervening weeks was picked up, and the cost of goods sold and the sales for the period computed. Thus a fairly accurate profit and loss statement was completed for these small firms.

If the in-pocket operating costs were not recognized by the firm, they were not entered on the original income statement. These statements were therefore incomplete as profit and loss statements but they contained all of the data necessary, when coupled with the original balance sheet, to complete the original cost analysis.

The original cost analysis statement listed all of the real costs of operation and described such physical inputs as the size of the building, the number of employees and their function, the individual pieces of equipment, and so on. This cost analysis, which was completed at the research headquarters, was based upon the information contained in the original balance sheet and the original income statement. Throughout the cost analysis procedure, operating costs were estimated on the high side in all doubtful instances in order to avoid overstating the possible savings of the model distribution system.

Certain principles applied in the original cost analysis should be examined with care. As a rule, all of the out-of-pocket costs were recognized on the original cost analysis as reported by the firm. There were exceptions, however. Insurance expense, for instance, was standardized. Each firm was considered as insured against the same risks — specifically each was assumed to carry customer risk insurance, fire insurance on inventory and equipment, and delivery equipment insurance. The property tax expense was computed according to the Scientific Assessment method even in cases where the retailers had not yet paid a property tax bill computed by the new system.

In-pocket costs were estimated by various procedures. Depreciation expense for buildings was based on the valuation and length of life tables of the Scientific Assessment program. Equipment depreciation rates were determined principally from the U.S. Bureau of Internal Revenue estimates, altered in some instances by the estimates provided by San Juan grocery equipment dealers.[1] The wages of unpaid employees were imputed; the owner was asked what wage he would have to pay if a paid clerk were substituted for the unpaid employee. The stock loss expense ratios reported in the larger sample (see Chapter III) were tabulated by sales class and lines of goods handled. Stock losses of the firms here analyzed were computed therefrom.

The amount of the owner's investment was calculated by difference. From the sum of the firm's assets (valuing the fixed assets at depreciated replacement cost) was subtracted the capital provided in the form of accounts payable and loans. On the resulting amount, that is, the owner's equity, a 10 per cent interest return was recognized as an expense. Ten per cent appears high by mainland standards, but interviews with merchants in the San Juan area indicated that it is appropriate for Puerto Rico. It is supported by the fact that some retailers are paying 9 per cent to their banks for short-term inventory loans.

A special procedure was devised for determining the owner's salary for both the original and projected cost analyses. The owner of each of the retail firms studied was asked at the time of the first interview what salary he would pay himself in view of the earning capacity of the business and his weekly withdrawals of cash and of goods. These responses were then plotted against the monthly volume of sales. It was apparent that the salaries increase at a decreasing rate as the volume of sales increases and that the owners of stores selling approximately the same quantity of goods each month expect higher salaries if they are located in metropolitan areas or market towns than if they are located in the smaller towns or in the country. Considering each market area separately, standardized owners' salaries for use in the cost analysis, were derived, based on the curvilinear relationship between sales volume and reported owners' salaries. Thus the original and the projected cost analyses for firms serving the same market area and reporting the same sales volume show identical owners' salaries.

The Projected Cost Analyses

After the completion of the original cost analysis, each retailer was visited a second time and was asked what increases in the physical input factors would be necessary to support a 50 per cent increase in sales volume. On the basis of the owner's response to this question a projected cost analysis was computed, taking into account the increase in the physical factors and the increase in the other expenses which would result from an increase in sales. For instance, the credit loss

---

[1] See *Bulletin "F," Income Tax Depreciation and Obsolescence, Estimated Useful Lives and Depreciation Rates,* U.S. Treasury Department, Bureau of Internal Revenue.

was assumed to remain a constant per cent of sales. If the owner said that an increase in the size of the building would be necessary to support a higher volume of sales, not only was the rent or the building depreciation expense changed, but also the property tax expense, the building insurance expense, the repairs and maintenance expense, and the interest on the owner's investment if the building was owned. As just noted, the owner's weekly salary at the projected sales volumes was based on a standardized salary scale.

Computation of the interest expense on the projected cost analysis required an estimate of the changes in the capital asset and liability accounts. Stores operating on a cash basis with their customers were assumed to need cash accounts equal to their accounts payable, and the latter were increased correspondingly as the sales volume. If the store was selling on credit then the cash account was increased sufficiently to maintain a current ratio of two to one. The accounts receivable were assumed to increase in the same ratio as credit sales. The inventory-turnover rate was assumed to remain constant except in cases where the owner considered it possible for him to increase the rate of turnover significantly. Care was taken to insure that the change in inventory was consistent with the change in building size.

These procedures enabled the calculation of the capital requirements at the expanded sales volume. When an increase in capital was required it was assumed that this would be provided by the owner; the interest expense for the additional capital was therefore 10 per cent. This illustrates the liberal estimate of operating expenses because if the owner were to borrow the additional capital his total annual interest expense would increase by less than 10 per cent of the increase in capital.

By this same general method, a further projected cost analysis was completed assuming increase in sales of 100 per cent; a third projected cost analysis was completed assuming an increase of 200 per cent in the sales volume. No increase in advertising expense or any other "business-getting" cost was allowed in the projected cost analyses.

For stores offering credit and delivery service, eight additional projected cost analyses were completed. Four of these itemized the operating expenses of the firm at the present volume, one and one-half times the present volume, two and three times the present volume, assuming that credit, but not delivery, were offered. (It was presumed that dispensing with delivery service would have no effect on sales.) Four more projected cost analyses were carried out, assuming cash and carry operations.

In cases where the firm offered only one of the two services of credit and delivery operating costs were analyzed at the four sales volumes assuming that the present service was offered and assuming it was dropped. For cash-and-carry firms, only the original and three projected cost analysis with increased volume were prepared. To estimate the increases in operating cost which might result from providing a service not currently offered by the store would have been an unduly speculative enterprise.

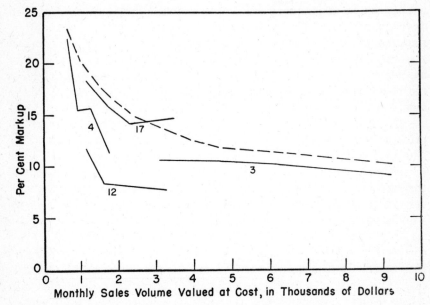

Figure 1   Percentage markup over cost to retailer required by isolated rural stores offering counter service, no credit, and no delivery.

The owners' estimates of the changes in the input factors with changes in volume and services were accepted without question, except where the resulting ratio of input factors to sales seemed either unreasonably high or low compared with the experience of the retailers interviewed in the process of selecting the panel stores. The cost analysis of each store was handled by only one interviewer, and only two interviewers were used in the entire retail store survey. In this way it is believed that differences in estimating procedure were kept to a minimum.

Isolated Rural Stores

In Figure 1 are shown the markups or margins required by isolated rural stores at various sales volumes, measured in terms of cost of goods sold, assuming that counter-service is combined with cash-and-carry operations.[2] (Throughout this chapter, all sales volumes are in terms of cost of goods sold unless otherwise noted.) The general pattern is a curve falling at a decreasing rate but never entering a phase of increasing costs. In view of this and the fact that the plotted points do not describe a single continuous curve, a procedure for deriving such a curve must be devised in order to determine a model store volume and markup.

The model food distribution system was designed to be a realistic model with the expenses of operation liberally estimated. The construction of the cost curves for the individual stores has made ample allowance for all economic costs except entrepreneurial profit, which has not yet been taken into account. Therefore an additional markup must be entered here to assure that the actual costs of operating the model system will not be underestimated.

Constructing a smoothed curve based on the plotted cost curves provided an opportunity for bringing into the picture the entrepreneurial profit. This was set arbitrarily at 1 per cent of goods sold.[3] A new cost curve was then drawn at one percentage point above all the highest coordinate points. This gives a cost curve that is satisfactory for estimating the volume and markup of the model stores. This curve is designated the "upper limit cost curve."

It will be noted that Store No. 17's third projection in Figure 1 does not fit the pattern well. This is because the owner estimated that at three times his present volume he would need a refrigerated display cabinet to supplement the ten cubic feet home-type refrigerator which he now uses and which he thinks would be adequate to handle twice his present volume of sales. A number of other individual cost curves show areas of increasing cost caused by the addition of discrete units of one input factor or another. In view of the curves for No. 12 and No. 3, it appears defensible to ignore the final segment of No. 17's curve when constructing the upper limit curve.

The decision as to optimum volume must be modified by a number of factors. In the first place, the model food distribution system will require a considerable number of the isolated rural stores merely to assure that all rural dwellers will be within walking distance of a store. A lower volume for the model isolated rural store should be

[2] Ideally, the cost curves would be plotted against a horizontal axis calibrated in physical units. Because this is nearly impossible with the heterogenous output of retail food stores, dollar values were used. Expressing the sales volume in terms of cost of goods sold rather than in terms of revenues from sales avoids the distortion of the curves which would result from the great variation in gross margins now received by different stores.

[3] Corporate chain stores on the mainland usually show a net profit of less than 2 per cent; from this should be deducted the return on the investment in order to arrive at the "pure" profit of economic theory.

chosen, therefore, than would be the case were geographical distribution of no importance. Secondly, it is obvious that the upper limit curve is determined at the high volumes by Store No. 3 solely, whereas in the $4,000 and $5,000 range it is certainly conceivable that store No. 12 would also be able to operate at a markup less than that indicated by the upper limit curve.[4] In view of these considerations, and where the density of population is sufficient, the volume of the model isolated rural store appears to be about $5,000 cost of goods sold per month with a required markup of 11.6 per cent. In municipalities where the individual stores cannot achieve monthly sales volumes of $5,000, the markup necessary to cover the cost of handling the achievable volume would presumably be determined from the upper limit curve. However, the combined operating statement of the twenty-eight consumers' cooperative stores for the fiscal year ending on June 30, 1951, indicates that, in spite of an average monthly volume (valued at cost of goods sold) of less than $1,700, their operating expenses (which include salaries to the managers and a charge for the bookkeeping services rendered by the Federation) amounted to less than 6 per cent of the cost of goods sold.[5] This 6 per cent markup does not include all the economic costs reflected in the cost curves of Figure 1, but indicates that well run rural stores could cover all their economic costs with the 11.6 per cent model store markup even at monthly cost of goods sold volumes of as little as $1,700. It is evident that Store No. 17 has a high cost of operation because of excess capacity or poor management. It would seem wise, therefore, that it be ignored in determining the volume and markup of the model isolated rural store.

If this is done, the isolated rural stores of the model can be presumed to handle a monthly cost of goods sold volume of $1,700 at a markup of 11.6 per cent if no credit or delivery service is offered.

What markup would be required by the model isolated rural stores were they to sell on credit? Survey data described in Chapter III showed that over half the rural stores make at least 75 per cent of their sales on credit. Stores Nos. 4, 12, and 17 reported their credit cost markups to be, respectively, 1.03, 2.23, and 1.58 per cent over the cost of goods sold on credit.[6] A ratio of credit costs to cost of goods sold on credit of 2.25 per cent is the equivalent of a 1.7 per cent markup over the total cost of goods sold if 75 per cent of the sales are on credit. Such a markup is consistent with the credit loss

---

[4] Store No. 3 was an excellent store for this study. A Cooperative store and a member of the Federation, its books were kept by the central accounting office and hence were quite accurate.

[5] Data provided by Cooperative Education Division, Social Programs Administration, Puerto Rico Department of Agriculture. The twenty-eight stores are rural cash stores.

[6] Store No. 3 is a cash store.

expense reported in the larger field study. Hence the model isolated rural store selling on credit can be presumed to require a total markup of 13.6 per cent over cost of goods sold.

Rural Town Stores

Figure 2 shows the data for rural town stores assuming neither credit nor delivery services to be extended to consumers. The upper limit curve, drawn so as to allow a 1 per cent markup for pure entre-

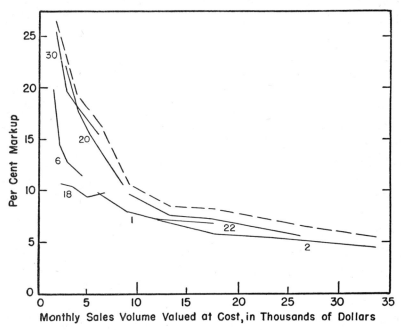

Figure 2   Percentage markup over cost to retailers required by rural town stores, offering counter service, no credit, and no delivery.

preneurial profit, exhibits a definite elbow in the vicinity of $14,000 monthly cost of goods sold. A $14,000 monthly volume, therefore, would appear to be a desirable optimum. An 8.4 per cent markup appears to be sufficient at this volume. It could be argued that $27,000 or $33,000 is more desirable optimum volume because of the lower markup; but these optima would be based on the third projection of only two stores and therefore may not be particularly reliable. The $14,000, 8.4 per cent optimum is obviously within reach of Store No. 2, which is now operating at a volume of more than $11,000 with a markup of less than 7.5 per cent.

When counter service with credit but no delivery is assumed, Figure 3, the slope of the curves changes rather abruptly in the vicinity of $14,000 monthly cost of goods sold. Apparently the model rural town store selling on credit should operate at a $14,000 monthly volume with a markup of not more than 10.9 per cent; but this figure is determined primarily by Store No. 22 which may have atypical credit costs.

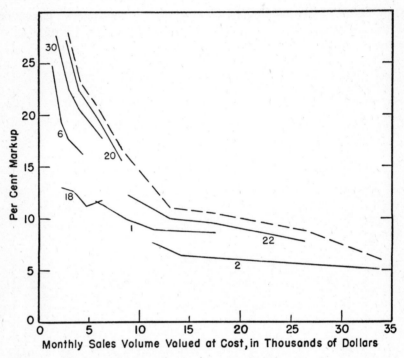

Figure 3   Percentage markup over cost to retailers required by rural town stores, offering counter service, credit, and no delivery.

If this optimum markup is accepted, credit costs for this type of store must be 2.5 per cent of sales (10.9 − 8.4). The seven stores analyzed reported credit cost markups over cost of goods sold on credit of from 1.56 per cent to 7.04 per cent, with 3.69 per cent as the average. The first retail study indicated that the average percentage of sales on credit for all urban stores serving average and low-income areas was about 60 per cent of total sales. A model store credit cost markup of 4 per cent (instead of 3.69, to be liberal) over the cost of goods sold on credit is the equivalent of a 2.4 per cent markup over the total cost of goods sold. So the model rural town store selling on credit will require a markup of 10.8 per cent at a volume of $14,000 per month valued at cost of goods sold.

Credit costs as a per cent of sales will be considerably higher in the model system, then, for rural town stores than for isolated rural stores (2.4 per cent compared with 1.7 per cent) despite the lower proportion of credit sales in the rural towns. This difference may be unrealistic and might have resulted from the small number of stores chosen for analysis. On the other hand it is conceivable that the rural consumers, having fewer alternative stores within reach, are more careful about paying their obligations to the grocer than is the case in the rural towns. Accordingly, the credit costs are presumed to be greater in the rural towns than in the isolated rural areas.

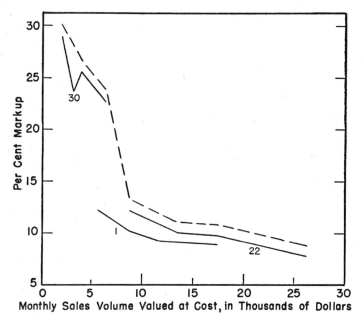

Figure 4   Percentage markup over cost to retailers required by rural town stores, offering counter service, credit, and delivery.

We next consider counter service with credit and delivery. The survey of Chapter III revealed that the average percentage of delivered sales for urban stores serving average and low income areas is about 10 per cent.[7] Only three of the rural town stores analyzed reported any delivered sales, but for these three the delivery costs as a markup over the cost of goods sold of delivered sales were 2.5 per cent, 4.1 per cent, and 5.6 per cent. If 5.0 per cent is taken as achievable, then the model rural town store delivering 10 per cent of

[7] These income areas are defined in a comparatively rough and arbitrary manner and do not correspond with the market areas discussed in this chapter. But the delivery and credit data can be taken as an approximation to the data for the market areas.

its sales will require an additional markup of .5 per cent over its total cost of goods sold to cover the delivery expense. Thus the model rural town store offering counter service, credit, and delivery will require a total markup of 11.3 per cent.

The data for the only three rural town stores which now deliver a portion of their sales are plotted in Figure 4. Again the pattern of curves indicates an elbow in the $14,000 per month range, but not

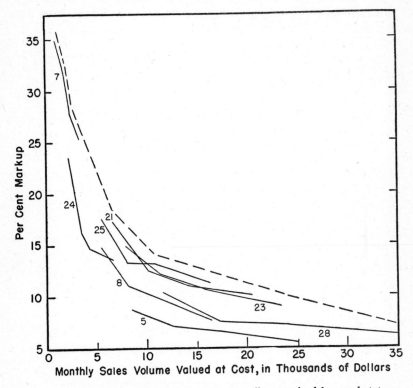

Figure 5   Percentage markup over cost to retailer required by market town stores, offering no credit, no delivery.

as clearly as in Figures 2 and 3 simply because the latter contain more cases. Judging from Figure 4, a model store markup of 11.3 per cent at a volume of $14,000 is ample for these services.

For rural town stores, regardless of the number of services offered, the model store volume of $14,000 monthly (valued at cost of goods sold) seems justified. By way of summary the model markups are as follows: assuming neither credit nor delivery service is offered, 8.4 per cent; assuming credit but no delivery service, 10.8 per cent; and assuming both credit and delivery, 11.3 per cent.

Market Town Stores

None of the isolated rural or rural town stores studied operated on a self-service basis nor have any such stores come to our attention in the rural areas of Puerto Rico. In the market towns, however, self-service stores are occasionally found. Cost analyses were completed for three counter-service and five self-service market town

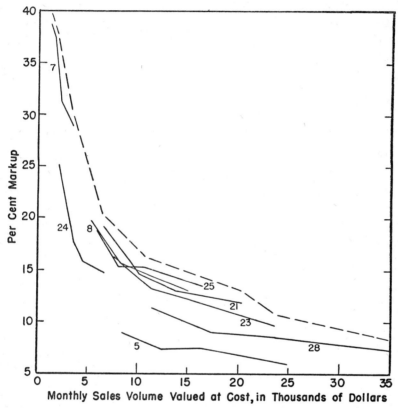

Figure 6 Percentage markup over cost to retailers required by market town stores, offering credit and no delivery.

stores. Because the differences in operating costs for the two stores types were not significantly different, self-service and counter-service stores are considered together in this section. (See the discussion of self-service and counter-service costs in Chapter III.)

Figure 5 shows the required markups for market town stores at various sales volumes (valued at cost of goods sold), assuming neither credit nor delivery. Stores Nos. 5, 7, and 23 are counter service, but their cost curves are neither consistently higher nor lower than those of the self-service stores. The summary cost curve is constructed as on the previous charts and similarly shows no indication of an increasing cost phase.

It might be argued that the "optimum" sales volume and markup which should be used are $35,000 and 7.3 per cent. This estimate would be based, however, only on the third projection of one store's costs. A similar argument could be brought to bear on the $24,000 volume. A volume of about $20,000 at a markup of 11.1 per cent has much to recommend it, however, for use in the construction of the model system. This volume is based on the projections of four stores, two of which (Nos. 5 and 28) could operate at markups of less than 11.1 per cent at their present volumes. This optimum point appears to be sufficiently realistic for use.

Figure 6 presents the information for market town stores assuming credit is offered, but no delivery service. For the same reasons as in the "no credit, no delivery" case, the $20,000 monthly volume appears most realistic. The markup indicated by the summary cost curve is 13.2 per cent, 2.1 per cent greater than when all sales are for cash, but this does not take into account the possibility that the stores analyzed do not sell the same proportion of total volume on credit as do the stores for the island.

The stores studied must have an average markup of 2.7 per cent over the cost of goods sold on credit to cover their credit expenses. The individual percentages range from .4 per cent to 5.29 per cent.[8] The retail field study suggested that credit losses of retailers selling $10,000 per month and over (valued at retail) were well under 1 per cent, but there is no indication of what per cent of the sales of the stores studied in this sales range are on credit. Considering that their credit sales are probably in the vicinity of the island average of about 60 per cent and that credit costs may include some bookkeeping costs as well as credit losses, a markup over cost of goods sold on credit of 2.7 per cent (the equivalent of a 1.6 per cent markup over total cost of goods sold) seems adequate.

Thus the model market town store selling on credit will handle a monthly volume of $20,000 (valued at cost of goods sold) with a markup of 12.7 per cent.

In Figure 7, showing the projections where both credit and delivery are offered, the curve for Store No. 5 has been omitted because this store does not deliver. Nevertheless a model market town store volume of $20,000 per month again seems advisable, this time because

---

[8] These percentages were computed by (1) subtracting, for each store, the total operating costs assuming no credit and no delivery from the total operating costs assuming credit and no delivery, then (2) dividing this difference by the value (in terms of cost of goods sold) of the store's monthly credit sales.

Store No. 28 could operate at less than the optimum indicated markup of 14.7 per cent at its present volume and because two other stores could operate with this markup if their third projections are accurate.

The 14.7 per cent markup to cover delivery and credit costs is 2.0 per cent higher than when credit only is extended, but this percentage is probably unduly influenced by Stores Nos. 21 and 25.

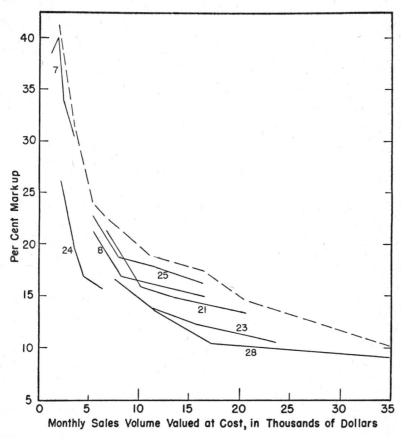

Figure 7   Percentage markup over cost to retailers required by market town stores offering credit and delivery.

The stores studied reported delivery costs to be 2.6 per cent of delivered sales (value of cost of goods sold) with the range being from 1 per cent to 4.2 per cent. Chapter III indicated that about 10 per cent of the sales of all urban stores were delivered and that about 58 per cent of the sales of urban stores located in high income areas were delivered. Since many of the urban stores catering to average and low income areas are located in the rural towns, the average percentage of sales delivered by market town stores must be well above 10 per cent but still below 58 per cent. If on the basis of this we arrive at a crude estimate of 30 per cent for delivered sales, the model market town store will require an additional markup of .9 per cent to cover delivery costs rather than the 2.0 per cent additional markup indicated on Figure 7. Therefore, the model market town store offering credit and delivery service will be assumed to operate at a monthly volume of $20,000 (valued at cost of goods sold) with a markup of 13.6 per cent.

In summary, market town stores in the model system will operate at volumes of $20,000 per month (valued at cost of goods sold). If they are assumed to operate on a cash and carry basis, the markup required will be 11.1 per cent; if credit but no delivery service is assumed, the required markup is 12.7 per cent; if both credit and delivery are offered, the required markup is 13.6 per cent.

Metropolitan Stores

As with the market town stores, self-service and counter-service stores in the metropolitan areas were treated together because of the absence of any significant difference in operating costs of the two types.

Figure 8 presents the metropolitan store data for cash-and-carry operations. Immediately it is clear on Figure 8 that Stores Nos. 26 and 27 must be relatively inefficient stores. Their required markups appear excessive in view of the volumes and required markups of Stores Nos. 9, 10, 13, and 19. For this reason curves Nos. 26 and 27 are ignored in the construction of the upper limit curve. The third projection of No. 13's required markup appears to have been over-estimated by the store's owner. He estimated that his accounting service costs would increase by $300 per month over the costs incurred in the second projection in spite of the fact that he had already esti-mated his new labor requirements in such a way as to increase the markup necessary to cover labor costs from 2.2 per cent in the second projection to 3.8 per cent in the third projection. Since the labor expense can be expected to increase proportionally with sales or nearly so, the third projection of No. 13's costs appears unrealistic and is ignored.

Again the upper limit curve does not show an increasing cost phase, as has been the case with all other curves in the study. A model monthly sales volume of more than $40,000 will require that the markup be based on rather slim evidence, namely, the third cost projection of one store and the second and third cost projections of another. At a monthly volume of $35,000 it is apparent that the markup of 10.1 per cent is based on the projections of four firms and that three firms (Nos. 10, 13, and 19) could now operate at a markup nearly as low as 9.8 per cent or lower.

Therefore, the model metropolitan store offering no credit and no delivery will be assumed to have a volume of $35,000 per month with a markup of 10.1 per cent.

For the same reasons as in the above case, the model volume with credit but without delivery appears to be $35,000 (see Figure 9). The cost curve indicates a markup of 11.3 per cent, implying that the credit costs of metropolitan stores amount to 1.2 per cent over cost of goods sold.

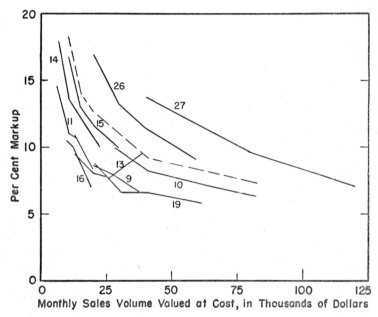

Figure 8   Percentage markup over cost to retailer required by metropolitan stores, offering counter service, no credit, and no delivery.

The stores selling on credit reported credit costs to require, on the average, a 2.7 per cent markup over the cost of goods sold on credit. It appears from the field study data that about 60 per cent of the metropolitan sales are on credit. Expressed as a markup over total cost of goods sold, the credit costs would thus be about 1.6 per cent. This markup seems consistent with the data reported in Chapter III.

Therefore the 1.6 per cent additional markup is adopted for the model metropolitan store; the total markup for the metropolitan store selling on credit will be, then, 11.7 per cent at a volume of $35,000 per month.

Figure 10 gives the data for metropolitan stores offering credit and delivery service. The smoothed cost curve is constructed as in the "credit, no delivery" case, and for the same reasons an optimum volume of $35,000 per month seems desirable. The model markup indicated for this volume is 12.7 per cent, but this percentage may be unduly influenced by Store No. 10 because of the method of constructing the summary curve, and by the fact that the panel stores

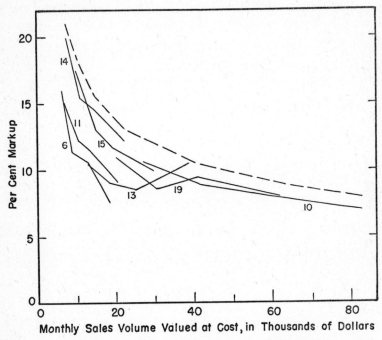

Figure 9 Percentage markup over cost to retailer required by metropolitan stores, offering counter service, credit, and no delivery.

deliver a considerably greater percentage (74 per cent) of their sales, on the average, than do all metropolitan stores. Judging from survey data, the urban stores serving average and high income areas deliver about 40 per cent of their sales, compared with only 14 per cent delivered by all urban stores. Because "urban" in this sense means all town stores regardless of the size of the town, a higher proportion of the urban stores tabulated offer no delivery service than is the case in metropolitan areas. Hence the 40 per cent figure is more realistic for the present purposes.

The stores studied required, on the average, a markup of 4.4 per cent on delivered sales to cover the delivery costs at their present sales volumes. The range was from 1.05 to 10 per cent. Assuming that the stores requiring markups above this average at their present volumes would be able to achieve at least some economies of scale in their delivery equipment and labor, use of the 4.4 per cent markup seems defensible for the model store. Delivery expenses will require a markup over *total* cost of goods sold of slightly less than 1.8 per cent.

The model metropolitan store offering credit and delivery service will therefore operate at a volume of $35,000 per month with a markup of 13.5 per cent.

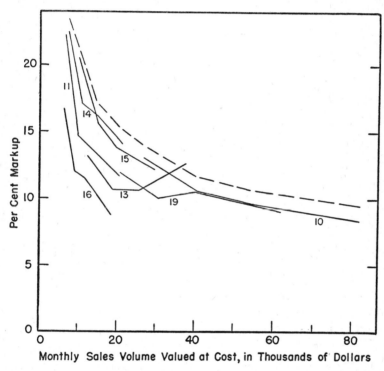

Figure 10   Percentage markup over cost to retailer required by metropolitan stores, offering counter service, delivery, and credit.

In summary, the metropolitan stores in all the model systems will be presumed to operate at a monthly volume of $35,000, valued at cost of goods sold. If neither credit nor delivery service are offered, the markup will be 10.1 per cent; if credit service only is offered, the markup will be 11.7 per cent; and if credit and delivery are both available, the markup will be 13.5 per cent.

Table 32 summarizes the findings. The pattern of markups required in the "limited service" case is unusual. One might expect the

Table 32   Percentage markups over cost of goods sold, required by model stores
offering no services, credit but no delivery, and credit and delivery,
by market area served

Market area type	No services	Credit, no delivery	Credit and delivery
Metropolitan	10.1	11.7	13.5
Market town	11.1	12.7	13.6
Rural town	8.4	10.8	11.3
Isolated rural	11.6	13.3	—

markups to increase from a low for the isolated rural stores to a
high for the metropolitan stores because of higher wages, rent and
equipment costs in the latter instance. On the other hand, it can be
argued that managerial efficiency is lowest in the rural stores and
highest in the metropolitan stores. It is possible, however, that the
stores analyzed in each market area were not of the same average
level of efficiency, relative to the norm for the market area, in each
of the four groups. The methodology has assured, however, that the
markups of Table 32 are, if anything, too high rather than too low,
and they do reflect realistic operating conditions. They can be used
with confidence to compute the cost of operating a model food distribution system. As will be seen presently the maximum conceivable
error in the markups can affect but little the difference between the
cost of the present system and the model.

8

THE OPTIMAL WHOLESALE UNIT

The cost analysis schedules and the principles applied in using them were basically the same for wholesalers as for retailers. The original balance sheet and the original income statement were completed at the time of the first visit to the wholesaler. From these data the original cost analysis was prepared. Three projected cost analyses, assuming sales increases of 50 per cent, 100 per cent and 200 per cent, were completed at the time of the second interview with the wholesaler. The entire cost analysis procedure for wholesalers, as contrasted with that for retailers, was simplified by the more accurate and complete accounting records available and the absence of unpaid employees.

The three projected cost analyses assumed the proportion of credit and delivery sales to remain constant. Delivery and credit costs were identified so that projected cost analyses assuming any combination of these services (or neither of them) could be constructed. Valuation and depreciation were handled as in the case of the retailers. Full insurance coverage was assumed and a 10 per cent return on the investment was recorded as an operating expense.

Considerable difficulty was encountered in determining the wage component of the owners' salaries. The owners were asked what they would pay managers if managers were substituted for themselves. The common answer was that it would be impossible to find a suitable manager, and that the salary could be anywhere in a wide range, depending on how good the man was. Estimated salaries were submitted, however, and on the basis of these it was apparent that the following scale would provide appropriate standardized owners' salaries for the cost analyses: Wholesalers handling less than $50,000 worth of goods per month were presumed to pay an owner's salary of $75 per week; firms with monthly sales of $50,000 up to $100,000 were assigned owners' salaries of $90 per week. All other firms were assumed to pay their owners $100 per week.

The wholesalers' inventories were assumed to increase proportionally as sales — this is based on the assumption that the island's stock of food should remain constant when expressed as a proportion of total sales. In view of the fear of dock strikes which on occasion have prevented food from coming into the island for several weeks at a time, it is doubtful if the food distribution system could operate safely on a smaller stock more frequently replaced.

The Findings

Unlike the retailer analysis, the wholesaler analysis is intended primarily to reveal the markups necessary to support one pattern of services, that is, credit but no delivery, rather than three. The markups required to cover wholesaler credit *and* delivery service are of no concern because in the model system the wholesaler-to-retailer trucking costs are computed independently of retailer and wholesaler operating costs. The assumption of altered wholesaler-retailer credit relationships is investigated later. The present discussion of wholesaler markups will provide the necessary information for the Models LS, C, and CD, assuming the existing wholesaler-retailer credit structure.

The wholesaler cost-analysis data (offering credit, and assuming no delivery) are presented in Figure 11. The pattern of the curves in Figure 11 is noticeably at variance with those formed by the retailer cost curves. The economies of scale in wholesaling appear to be considerably less than in retailing. Increasing cost phases which are reversed at higher volumes are more common in the wholesaler curves.

It was apparent in the course of the cost analyses that the wholesalers as a group were less certain of their input requirements at expanded volumes than were the retailers. This was to be expected. Wholesaling is a more complicated operation than is retailing and more employees and more equipment are involved. This difference in the nature of the two types of firms thus accounts for the lesser clarity of the wholesaler cost curve pattern and for the appearance of nearly constant costs. This more complicated character of wholesale operations may also account for the sporadic increasing cost phases with expanded volume and for the low rate of fall in required markups as well. However, general observation of wholesale and retail firms in Puerto Rico provides evidence that the existing wholesale firms, with the exception of a very few low-volume operators, are utilizing the resources they employ at or near capacity. Because hired cartage is cheap, trucks are not owned by wholesalers unless they are going to be used intensively. Labor appears to be idle a smaller proportion of the time in wholesaling — to cite one reason, because unpaid family labor is less common in wholesaling than in retailing.

Although data for thirteen firms were collected, only ten curves appear in Figure 11. One of the original panel firms, No. 4, proved to be a very high cost firm (requiring a markup at present and at projected sales volumes of at least 10 per cent) and so its cost curve is omitted as being atypical of the group. The two other omitted firms

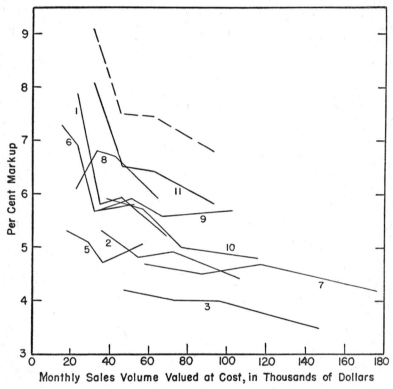

Figure 11 Percentage markup over cost of goods sold required by wholesaler at present and projected sales volumes, assuming no delivery.

showed low markups (not more than 6.7 and 4.7 per cent at present or projected volumes) but their sales were so large (in excess of $300,000 per month) that presentation of their data would risk identification and violation of their confidence.

An upper limit curve is constructed in Figure 11 as in the case of the retailer cost curves, which provides an entrepreneurial profit of 1 per cent of the cost of goods sold. Such an allowance to wholesalers may seem excessive — the same rate of profit as was allowed to retailers on a smaller volume of sales. However, the owners' salaries may well be underestimated in the case of the wholesalers, and also the lack of a more definite pattern in the wholesalers' cost curves may indicate a greater uncertainty on the nature of costs at expanded sales volumes. In view of these uncertainties and of the general policy of overestimating rather than underestimating the operating cost in the model distribution system, the 1 per cent entrepreneurial profit seems justified.

The optimum volume and markup, as in the case of the retailers, must be placed somewhere in the decreasing cost phase of the summary cost curve simply because there is no increasing cost phase. A conservative estimate of the optimum volume and markups appears to be in the vicinity of a monthly volume of business of $75,000, valued at cost of goods sold, with a markup of 7.1 per cent. A volume greater than this amount would be based primarily upon second and third projections of present operating costs, and on fewer cases.

The 7.1 per cent markup is conservative not only because of the conservative cost analysis method but also because the two large volume wholesalers not shown on Figure 11 are now operating at markups of less than 7.1 per cent. In addition, it is apparent that were Nos. 6 and 11 dropped from consideration because of apparent inefficiency, the model markup would be reduced by approximately 1 per cent. But in the interest of a conservative savings estimate, the optimum wholesaler markup shall be left at 7.1 per cent, assuming credit but no delivery. All but one of the thirteen firms sold from 65 to 90 per cent of their volumes on credit, typical for the island.

In order to construct Models LS, C, and CD assuming retailers to buy from wholesalers only on ten-day rather than thirty- to ninety-day terms as at present, it is necessary to identify the savings which such a shift would realize. Identification of credit costs was attempted but the wholesalers were quite uncertain as to the savings which could result from such a shift in retailer buying practices. This stemmed primarily from uncertainty about the probable savings in billing costs, which some wholesalers considered would be significant while others did not.

In view of this difficult estimating problem, an aggregative, rather than model firm makeup, approach was used. Were retailers to buy on ten-day terms from wholesalers rather than on thirty- to ninety-day open account, as is the practice at present, the reduction in billing costs might be insignificant. However, some interest would be saved. The wholesalers' accounts receivable amount to about 7.3 per cent of their annual sales, according to the original field study, or $954 million, slightly less than one month's sales. If wholesalers' invoices to retailers were paid within an average period of ten days instead of thirty, these accounts receivable supposedly would be reduced to about 3.18 million. This would require the retailers to borrow the difference, $6.36 million from the banks instead of from wholesalers. In the model the wholesalers are allowed a 10 per cent return on their investment, hence this $6.36 million reduction in their investment would cut their costs by $.636 million. But the retailers would have to pay perhaps an average of 7 per cent interest on bank loans for this amount, which expense would approximate $.445 million. The net saving to the system, then, would be about $.2 million per year.

No estimates are available as to the proportion of wholesaler purchases from mainland suppliers which do not take advantage of cash discounts. If, for example, retailer payment within ten days were to make it possible for wholesalers to take a 2 per cent discount on one-half of their purchases, $1.11 million could be saved per year. Adding this to the $.2 million interest in saving gives a total saving of $1.3 million but this is, of course, a very crude approximation. It would appear conservative, however, because it assumes no reduction in billing costs and no reduction in bad debt expense.

In summary, the wholesale sector of Models LS, C, and CD assuming the present wholesaler-retailer relationship, will require a markup of 7.1 per cent. In the Models LS, C, and CD assuming less wholesale credit service, the markup required by the wholesale sector will be 7.1 per cent less $1.3 million per year.

9

THE COMPLETED MODEL

A comparison of model food distribution systems with the present system and the analysis of potential economies in food marketing requires that three estimates be kept in mind. These are (1) the island food bill valued at cost to the original wholesaler-importer, hereafter referred to as the island food bill CTW; (2) the island food bill valued at the cost to the retailers, hereafter referred to as the island food bill CTR; (3) the island food bill valued at cost to the consumer, hereafter referred to as the island food bill CTC. These concepts are qualified and clarified below.

The Present Island Food Bill

The island food bill CTW can be defined as the total of whole-salers' direct purchases, both from local producers and from mainland exporters, of food to be resold to other wholesalers or retailers. In other words, the island food bill CTW is the quantity of food which the original wholesalers buy and which they sell within the food distribution system. Table 33 shows the method of calculating a first approximation of this food bill. It is only a first approximation because the final figure in Table 33 includes not only wholesaler imports but a certain amount of imports which bypass wholesalers and go direct to retailers. Added to the value of the edible imports in Table 33, is the value of the local production of processed foods. Fresh produce and meat purchased from local truckers, farmers, and slaughterers are not included in this figure. Also, the data on which estimates are based do not include the output of processed foods by those industries which produced less than $1,000,000 worth of goods in the calendar year 1949.[1] In column three are listed the imports

[1] The source table for the local production of processed foods uses a broad definition of industry so that the omissions are probably minor. For instance, "canned fruits, fruit juices, and vegetables; jam, jellies, preserves, etc." were included in the same industry.

Table 33 Computation of island food bill valued at cost to the wholesalers
July 1, 1949 to July 1, 1950[a] (in dollars)

	Imports	Plus local production of processed foods[b]	Less imports for processing	Less exports to U.S.	Less exports to foreign countries	Total through system
Meat products	16,727,120				21,139	16,705,981
Animal oils and fats	7,211,199					7,211,199
Dairy products	14,254,939				311,245	13,943,694
Fish and fish products	6,895,169				2,662	6,892,507
Other animal products	2,324,642					2,324,642
Grains and preparations	31,496,134	4,028,304	5,646,598		7,612	29,870,228
Vegetables and preparations	13,559,562	2,885,904		3,614,021	207,986	15,608,344
Fruit and preparations	2,984,885					
Nuts and preparations	187,905				1,010	186,895
Vegetable oils and fats	1,964,307					1,964,307
Table beverages materials	2,209,915					2,209,915
Spices	119,704					119,704
Sugar and related products	2,202,617			453,811		1,748,806
Total	102,138,098	6,914,208	5,646,598	4,067,832	551,654	98,786,222
Plus: Refined sugar produced and sold locally[c]						13,460,400
Plus: Local meat and produce bought by wholesalers[d]						700,236
Total intake						112,946,858
Less: Inventory increase of 1.5 per cent of purchases[e]						1,694,203
Final total						111,252,655

[a] Source, unless otherwise noted: *Annual Book of Statistics of Puerto Rico, Fiscal Year 1949–50*, Economic Development Administration, San Juan, Puerto Rico: Tables 128, 129, 130, and 132.
[b] *Statistical Yearbook, Puerto Rico, 1950–51*, Economic Development Administration, San Juan, Puerto Rico: Table 89. Data cover industries producing goods valued at one million dollars or more in calendar 1949.
[c] Source: Sugar Producers Association of Puerto Rico, San Juan, Puerto Rico.
[d] Estimated from wholesaler survey data; see text.
[e] Estimated percentage change based on data provided by General Supplies Administration, San Juan, Puerto Rico.

which went to processors rather than into the wholesale-retail distribution system. More than $5,000,000 of this amount is accounted for by wheat imports — importers estimated that 90 per cent of the imported wheat goes to processors. Exports to the mainland (principally locally canned fruits and fruit juices) and exports to foreign countries are listed in columns four and five. The exports to foreign countries include some reëxported foods which originated on the mainland. Because such foods are exported at a slightly higher value than that at which they are listed in the import column, the figures in column five are slightly higher than they should be. However, the error here is undoubtedly slight. The algebraic totals of the five columns give the totals of the different food items going through the system in Puerto Rico. The local production of sugar, however, was not included in column two. The Sugar Producers Association of Puerto Rico provided data on the refined sugar produced and sold locally during the period in question. The value of locally produced meat and fresh fruits and vegetables bought by wholesalers was estimated from the data obtained in the wholesale study, described in Chapter IV. Totaling these figures gives a final value of purchases by wholesalers of $112,946,858.

Up to this point, no allowance has been made for possible changes in inventories during the fiscal year 1950. Fortunately the General Supplies Administration in Puerto Rico requires all wholesalers to file monthly statements of their inventories of fourteen basic imported items. During the period, 1.5 per cent of the imports of these items, by value, were used to increase inventories. Accepting this as an index of the percentage of purchases used to increase inventories of all items purchased gives an inventory adjustment of —$1,694,203. The final figure for the island food bill valued at cost to the wholesaler is $111,-252,655.

Because the value of the local production of processed food does not include the output of industries producing less than $1,000,000 in calendar 1949, the final $11.3 million figure contains some error. A partially balancing overestimate of the refined sugar sold into the system is probable because the $13.5 million intake of refined sugar includes an unknown proportion of sales to local processors. Judging from 1947 per capita consumption data for sugar, about $2 million worth of the $13.5 million sugar total must represent sales to processors.[2]

The $6.9 million total for the local production of processed foods does not include the output of bakeries. It is generally observed in Puerto Rico that bulk of the baked goods is sold directly to the consumers from the bakery rather than through retail food stores. However, the retail stores do handle a very small proportion.

Two further corrections have not been considered. No deduction has been entered for the food purchases of hotels, institutions, and restaurants; nor has any adjustment been made to correct for an under-valuation of imports. Economic Development Administration personnel charged with collecting import information state that shipper's declarations sometimes express value c.f.i., while other declarations are in terms of value at the point of shipment. Shipping costs from the mainland to Puerto Rico amount to about 5 per cent of landed value in the case of food.[3] If only one-half of the value of

[2] Roberts and Stefani, *Patterns of Living,* Table 200, p. 387. Per capita sugar consumption times 1950 population gives 153.1 million pounds, or about 85.4 per cent of the 179.5 million pounds reported sold locally by the Sugar Producers Association.

[3] See Samuel E. Eastman and Daniel Marx, Jr., *Ships and Sugar,* University of Puerto Rico, Rio Piedras, 1953, p. 185.

imports are expressed in terms of landed costs, import values must be understated by about 2.5 per cent.

Offsetting this error, at least in part, are the institutional purchases. According to the survey of metropolitan San Juan wholesalers (see Chapter IV), 2.7 per cent of the metropolitan wholesalers' sales are to hotels, institutions, and restaurants. Because this type of business is concentrated in San Juan, it seems likely that the average for all wholesalers on the island is not more than 2 per cent, which amount should be deducted from the island food bill valued at cost to the wholesalers if we wish to deal only with that part of the food moved through the wholesale-retail structure to the consumer.

Because so little is known about the magnitudes of these latter adjustments, the final $111,252,655 figure arrived at in Table 33 does not take them into account. It is believed that the correction would cause no significant change in the estimate.

The $111.3 million constitutes only a first approximation to the island's wholesale food bill because it includes retailers' direct imports. The proportion of the $111.3 million figure consisting of retailers' direct imports can be computed only by estimating all the components of the island food bill CTR and CTC in a simple algebraic formulation, as follows:

It is known that wholesalers' purchases (from abroad and from local producers and processors) plus retailers' direct imports equals $111,252,655. Table 29 indicates a gross profit margin of 11.8 per cent of sales for limited-line wholesalers and 15.5 per cent of sales for full-line wholesalers. Weighting these percentages by the sales of the sample firm gives an average margin of 14.14 per cent. However, it seems justifiable to use 15 per cent as an island average because the sample over-weighted the San Juan, and hence the limited line, firms. The effect of using this margin, rather than the much lower one reflected by other wholesale margin studies, is discussed later. The 15 per cent margin is the equivalent of a markup of 17.6 per cent over cost. Therefore, we assume that 1.176 times wholesalers' purchases equals retailers' purchases from wholesalers. The latter is, of course, one of the components of the island food bill CTR. However, retailers also imported some goods directly and they also bought some locally produced goods directly from the producer. The survey of retail outlets, Chapter III, indicates that about 3.5 per cent of retailers' sales consisted of locally produced goods purchased by the retailer direct from the producer. The original survey also revealed that about 7.4 per cent of retailer sales consisted of goods imported directly. In view of the intentional oversampling of large retailers in that survey, it would seem reasonable to presume that for the entire retail structure of the island the direct imports would account for not more than 5 per cent of sales. To these three components of the island food bill CTR, namely retailers' purchases from wholesalers, retailers' direct imports, and retailers' direct purchases from local producers, the retailers add a markup of 30 per cent, on the average. This is the equivalent of the 23.1 per cent average gross profit margin of Chapter III. Therefore, we know that 1.3 times retailers' direct imports equals .05 times the island food bill CTC, and 1.3 times the retailers' direct purchases from local producers equals .035 times the island food bill CTC.[4] Finally, we know that the sum of retailers' purchases, multiplied by 1.3 equals the island food bill CTC.

Therefore, if:

a = wholesalers' purchases
b = retailers' purchases from wholesalers
c = retailers' direct imports
d = retailers' direct local purchases
x = island food bill CTC

the following equations are given:

$$1.176\,a = b$$
$$1.3\,(b + c + d) = x$$
$$a + c = \$111,252,655$$
$$1.3\,c = .05\,x$$
$$1.3\,d = .035\,x$$

Solving these gives the island food bill CTC as \$174,658,079. Wholesalers' purchases are \$104,534,956, retailers' direct imports \$6,717,699, retailers' purchases from wholesalers \$122,933,108, and retailers' direct purchases from local producers are \$4,702,319. Thus the island food bill CTW is \$104,534,956, while the island food bill CTR is \$134,353,126 and the island food bill CTC is \$174,658,079.

This estimate of the island food bill does not take into account the double handling of some food by wholesalers. Wholesalers report that such double handling is significant with rice, lard, beans, codfish, and pork products. Although double handling does not mean that the average wholesaler markup is applied twice (sales by wholesalers to wholesalers typically carry lower margins than sales to retailers), nevertheless, it seems likely that ignoring the double handling of these important items may result in a significant understatement of the actual distribution costs.

The cost of operating that part of the food distribution system with

[4] Assuming the retailers' average markup of 30 per cent is applicable to their direct imports and direct local purchases is a simplification which probably has little effect on the final estimates.

which we are concerned is estimated, therefore, at approximately $58.7 million for 1949–50. This is obtained by subtracting from the island food bill CTC of $174.7 million the sum of the island food bill CTW ($104.5 million) plus the retailers' direct purchases of $11.4 million. The total markup charged by the entire food distribution system, therefore, is just under 50 per cent.

The gross product data for Puerto Rico for 1949–50 show goods and tobacco consumption expenditures (including food produced and consumed at home as well as alcoholic and non-alcoholic beverages) to have been $322.9 million, and this might be considered as a basis for a check on the CTC estimate of $174.7 million. However, this gross product food expenditures figure involved estimated wholesale and retail margins and hence cannot be used to check the present margin estimates. Nor are census data notably more satisfactory. The 1949 Census of Business for Puerto Rico shows the total sales of all food group retail stores (which includes milk dealers, confectionary stores, and bakeries) to amount to only $109,112,100, or less than net imports plus locally processed foods moving through the island's distribution system. It is apparent that the Census retail food sales are grossly understated. The merchant wholesalers of groceries and food specialities, on the other hand, reported sales of $177,691,100 to the 1949 Census. This contains an unknown amount of double handling; if the present estimate of $122.9 million worth of wholesaler sales to retailers is correct, the remaining $55 million in sales by wholesalers must be double handled — surely an exaggeration. It would appear, therefore, that the estimated CTC of $174.7 million is a very conservative estimate.

The Model Wholesale System

If the 1949–50 island food bill CTW of $104.5 million had been handled by the wholesale firms of the model, only 132 firms (selling the model volume, valued at cost to the wholesaler, of $75,000 per month or $900,000 per year) would have been needed.[5] If the model wholesalers had offered credit service but no delivery at the required markup of 7.1 per cent, the cost of supporting the wholesale system would have been only $8,456,878:[6] Thus, instead of paying $122.9

[5] The model volume is in terms of 1952 prices. In terms of 1949 wholesale prices, the model wholesaler volume is approximately $790,000 which, when divided into the island food bill CTW of $104.5 million, gives the number of wholesale firms required.

[6] The 7.1 per cent markup is the markup required at the time the cost analyses of wholesalers was accomplished and so is expressed in terms of 1952 prices. The same *dollar* margin would represent a markup of 8.09 per cent over the model wholesaler volume expressed in terms of 1949 rather than 1952 prices. Thus the procedure assumes that the prices of wholesalers' input factors (labor, utilities, etc.) were no higher in 1952 than in 1949, again giving a conservative estimate of the savings which could be realized through rationalization.

million for the food purchased from wholesalers, the retailers would have paid only $113 million for the same quantity.

The 7.1 per cent markup allowed the wholesalers in the model is net of delivery costs. Because the model retail store markup is based on the cost of goods sold defined to include the trucking costs, it is necessary to insert the island trucking bill before proceeding to the construction of the model retail food distribution system.

Brief questionnaires were mailed to at least three retail grocers in each of the seventy-five *municipios* on the island requesting the rate per hundred-pound bag and per medium-sized box shipped from each of the three port cities. Replies were received from fifty-one of the *municipios;* the data from these replies provided an adequate basis for estimating the trucking rates to the other towns. For each town, only the lowest of the three rates was used in the computation of trucking costs; thus, the model assumes each town will be supplied from the port from which trucking costs are least.

The import information in the *Statistical Yearbook for Puerto Rico, 1949–50,* gives the dollar value and the shipping weight of all food items. The data for locally processed food entering the distribution system are in terms of dollars only. Application of the weight to value ratio for each of the imported food items to the same item produced locally provided a shipping weight for the locally produced and processed food. Adding this weight to the total weight of imports and deducting the weight of exports (estimated by a similar procedure) gave the approximate total weight of the island's food in 1949–50. This total weight (more than 1.1 billion pounds) was distributed among the seventy-five *municipios* in the same proportion as the retail sales reported in the 1949 Census of Business, giving the estimated total weight of food imported into each of the *municipios*. For each town, the trucking cost was computed by applying the box rate from the nearest port city to 32 per cent of the weight imported, and the bag rate was applied to the remainder. Totaling the trucking cost for each town gave a final figure of $1,595,064. The total cost of trucking the island's food in the model distribution system is estimated at the round figure of $1.6 million.

In the model, the retailers buy $113 million worth of goods from wholesalers, $6.7 million from abroad, about $4.7 million from local producers and pay a freight charge of approximately $1.6 million. To determine the cost of supporting the model retail system, the $124.4 million paid to suppliers, that is, total retailer purchases less freight in, was distributed among the seventy-five *municipios* proportionally as were the food retail sales as reported in the Census of Business for Puerto Rico for 1949. The procedure assumes that the understating of retail food sales mentioned above was uniform as between all *municipios*. The Census indicates for each *municipio* the sales accounted for by rural stores and by urban stores, which made possible a rural-urban breakdown of each *municipio* model food bill CTR less freight. The *municipio* trucking cost was distributed between rural and urban stores proportionally as the sales. For each *municipio*, then, the urban trucking cost was added to the urban model food bill CTR less freight to arrive at the urban food bill CTR including trucking cost and the same method was used to compute the total model food bill CTR for the rural area of the *municipio*.

From this listing of the model food bill CTR for each *municipio* (by rural and urban areas within it) the model food bill CTR to be handled by metropolitan stores, by market town stores, by rural town stores, and by isolated rural stores was determined by summation. The model metropolitan stores would handle a total of $47.3 million worth of food CTR, the market town stores $17.2 million worth, the rural town stores $30.1 million worth, and the isolated rural stores $31.5 million worth for a total of $126.0 million.[7] This is the island model food bill CTR, equal to the sum of the retailers' purchases from wholesalers, from local producers, and payments to truckers.

The next step was to apply the model store markups as derived from the cost curves in Chapter VII to the market area food bills CTR. These markups, listed in Table 32, however, must be subjected to two adjustments. First of all, these markups are markups over the actual cost of goods sold rather than the model CTR value of the same goods. Secondly, Table 32 markups are based on 1952 prices rather than 1949–50 prices. Price adjustment is accomplished by multiplying the model markups of Table 32 by the product of two ratios: the ratio of the wholesale price index of May, 1952, to the average wholesale price index, July, 1949 to June, 1950; and the ratio of the actual island food bill CTR to the model island food bill CTR. This product equals 1.214. The adjusted markups for each of the four types of market areas and for each of the combinations of credit and delivery service offering were then applied to the total model food bill CTR for each of the market areas. That is, the adjusted model metropolitan store markup, assuming neither credit nor delivery to be offered, was applied to the total metropolitan model food bill CTR of $47.3 million; and so on for the total market town food bill CTR, rural town food bill CTR and isolated rural food bill CTR. In this manner, the total dollar cost of supporting the model stores of each type market area was determined under each of the three assumptions concerning services offered.

Model LS, assuming existing wholesaler-retailer credit relation-

---

[7] The computed figure is $126,006,916. Market area food bills CTR do not total $126.0 million due to rounding.

ships, would require \$15.6 million to support the retail sector whereas Model C would require \$18.4 million and Model CD would require \$19.8 million. (See Table 34.) The island food bill CTC in this version

Table 34   Total operating margins, in dollars, required by retailers in model systems LS, C, and CD, by market area type

Market area type	Area food bill at CTR	Model LS	Model C	Model CD
Metropolitan	47,308,945	5,800,077	6,717,870	7,753,936
Market town	17,169,340	2,314,427	2,647,512	2,834,658
Rural town	30,057,617	3,065,877	3,940,554	4,123,905
Isolated rural	31,471,014	4,431,119	5,082,569	5,082,569[a]
Total	126,006,916	15,611,500	18,388,505	19,795,068

[a] In none of the models is it assumed that the isolated rural stores offer delivery service.

of Model LS would be \$141.6 million, compared with \$144.4 million for Model C and \$145.8 million for Model CD. Thus Model CD would represent a saving of \$28.9 million under the estimated \$174.7 million cost of food to the consumers at present, a reduction of more than 17 per cent. Model C would save about \$30.3 million and Model LS about \$33.0 million (19 per cent).

Yet another adjustment, however, was considered. Up to this point it has been assumed that each store in the model would operate at the optimum volume of business. Earlier it was stressed that the final model would assure each inhabitant of the island of a store within walking distance. To meet this requirement, the detailed land-use maps of the Puerto Rico Department of Agriculture and Commerce, which show the location of every building in rural Puerto Rico, were consulted and the few uninhabited areas of any size (primarily portions of the two national forests, and some of the coastal caneland) were blocked out. The number of stores necessary to service the remainder of the island was determined by counting the number of paper discs, each the equivalent of two miles in radius, required to blanket the inhabited areas of the island. The resultant number of stores presumably assures every Puerto Rican of having a store located within two miles "as the crow flies," although the rough terrain in the interior may mean that covering the distance requires walking more than two miles in some instances. It is not uncommon, however, for people in the interior now to walk greater distances to their stores. Furthermore, the paper disc procedure actually left relatively few people a full two miles from the nearest store because of the overlapping of the circles.

The minimum number of isolated rural stores required by this procedure was shown to be 278, well under the 1872 optimum volume stores required to handle the isolated rural store sales CTR of $31.4 million. Furthermore, for each *municipio,* the number of optimum volume isolated rural stores exceeds the minimum number required to cover the rural area, so no adjustment in the cost of operating the model retail system is necessary when the distance requirement is taken into account. The entire island has an area of 3,418 square miles, so the model system would have each isolated rural store serving an area of less than two square miles. In view of this large number of isolated rural stores plus the assurance that no consumer should have to walk much more than two miles, it can be said that the model system could be achieved without requiring people to travel unreasonable distances to obtain their groceries.

If the Chapter VIII estimates of probable savings resulting from less wholesaler credit are admissable, Models LS, C, and CD assuming wholesalers to extend only ten-day credit would reduce the island food bill CTC by another $1.3 million, or a little more than .7 per cent. Integration supposedly would involve still greater economies, but as was explained in Chapter VI, the savings are probably impossible to estimate with any desired degree of reliability.

Each model retail food distribution system has a total of 2,311 stores, including 136 metropolitan stores (61 in San Juan and Santurce), 86 market town stores, and 1,872 isolated rural stores. This figure may be compared with the 16,747 food group retailers which were reported in the 1949 Census of Business for Puerto Rico, of which over 14,000 were classified as grocery stores. Thus the model contains less than 20 per cent as many stores as were in existence in 1949. The contrast between the model and the actual retail distribution system is striking. If the model retail system were to offer credit and delivery service, about $19.8 million would be required to support the retailers' operations as contrasted with the present actual total retail margin of $40.3 million. To gain the $20.5 million difference, however, the Puerto Rican consumer would be required to walk somewhat farther for his groceries.[8]

The impact on employment in food retailing would not be nearly as great as on the number of retail stores. The estimate of employment in the model retail system is based on the maximum sales per worker estimated by the panel retailers. For example, if the four isolated rural stores in the panel were operating at the volume at which each would maximize sales per worker, the four would employ a total of twelve persons, including owners, and would be selling $18,030 worth of

---

[8] But those who have their food purchases delivered, of course, would not face this inconvenience. Nor would delivery distances increase to the same extent as the decrease in the number of urban stores (thus increasing delivery costs) because of the overlapping delivery areas in the present system.

merchandise per month or $1,503 per worker. This is the equivalent of $1,238 per worker per month in terms of 1949 model CTR values. The total isolated rural food bill in the model is $31,471,014 per year or $2,622,584 per month. This amount divided by $1,238 gives 2,118 workers required in the retail sector if neither credit nor delivery are offered. (See Model LS in Table 35.)

Table 35   Number of stores and employment in retail sector of model systems LS, C, and CD, by market area type

Market area type	Number of of stores	Number of employees		
		Model LS	Model C	Model CD
Metropolitan	136	1,523	1,543	2,440
Market town	86	697	697	855
Rural town	217	1,097	1,097	1,478
Isolated rural	1,872	2,118	2,118	2,118 [a]
Total	2,311	5,435	5,455	6,891

[a] In none of the models is it assumed that the isolated rural stores offer delivery service.

If the retailers offer credit, very few additional employees are needed; the panel retailers usually considered it possible for the same employees required to handle a strictly cash business to handle also the little extra work involved in credit sales. Monthly statements are not common and each credit sale is simply entered in a notebook, so the additional bookkeeping time is not significant. To estimate the additional work force requirement when credit is granted (Model C, Table 35), the volume of credit sales of the panel metropolitan stores was divided by the estimated number of additional employees required to handle the credit business (this information taken from the cost analysis schedules) to give the volume of metropolitan credit business which would require the services of one more employee. Data in Chapter III indicate that about 60 per cent of the metropolitan sales are credit sales, or $28.3 million of the total metropolitan model food bill CTR of $47.3 million. The panel metropolitan store owners now selling on credit estimated that selling on a cash basis would reduce their work force by only one man; in other words, of the five such stores, four would require the same work force on a cash basis as on a credit basis, and one store could dispense with one employee. The five stores reported total credit sales of $146,995 per month, valued at CTR. Converting this into model CTR terms and dividing it into the total metropolitan credit sales in the model reveals that only twenty additional employees would be required by the metropolitan stores if they were to sell 60 per cent of their volume on credit. None of the market town, rural town, or isolated rural panel store owners estimated that dropping credit would affect the number of employees. In summary, the Model C would require only twenty more employees than Model LS, or 5,455 in all, a negligible difference.

A similar procedure was used to estimate the work force requirements with credit and delivery, Model CD, Table 35. For the panel retailers in each of the four market areas, the number of additional employees required to handle the sales delivered at present was computed and used as a basis for estimating the increase in workers occasioned by the delivery service. An estimated total of 6,891 persons are required to operate the Model CD.

In Model CD credit and delivery service are used to the same extent as in the present existing system. The Model CD retail structure employment figure of approximately 7,000 persons is thus comparable with the approximately 15,000 persons apparently now employed in food retailing.[9] Comparing Table 35 with Table 34, it is clear as might be expected that the additional cost of credit service causes an increase in the labor expense. The number of additional employees necessitated by delivery service appears surprisingly great, by mainland standards. It must be remembered, however, that the method of providing delivery service provides a clear illustration of the substitution of labor for capital in a low-range economy. Several delivery boys on foot or on bicycles are used instead of one boy using a truck. Furthermore, the scarcity of telephones requires that a store messenger make the daily rounds to the store's customers, picking up the grocery lists from the housewives. The purchases are then delivered on a second trip. It is immediately apparent that delivery service, therefore, requires a considerable expansion of the work force in retailing.

Evaluation of the Savings Estimate

For the sake of consistency, the dollar savings achievable by the models have been estimated on the presumption that the present wholesale margin is 15 per cent of sales, in accordance with the statistical findings of Chapter IV. In view of the lower wholesale margins reported by other studies and by some representatives of the trade, it is necessary to examine carefully the possible margin of error in the savings estimate.

If the average wholesale margin were 8 per cent instead of 15 per cent of sales, and if no double handling by wholesalers was presumed, the calculation of the island food bill CTC would render a figure of

---

[9] Data in Chapter III show average sales per worker to be about $12,000 per year. If the present food bill CTC estimate of $175 million is accurate, at least 14,500 persons must be presently employed in this phase of food distribution.

$162,182,005 instead of $174,658,079, a difference of almost $12,500,-000. Because the estimating equations render different values for the island food bills CTW and CTR under the new assumption, the dollar savings are reduced not by $12.5 million but by $12.1 million. The Model CD saving would amount to a little less than 10 per cent instead of 17 per cent of the island food bill CTC, or $15.1 million rather than $28.9 million.[10] But the $15 million annual saving to the people of Puerto Rico is surely a gross understatement of the potential saving, and a strong argument can be put forward to the effect that the $28.9 million annual savings is a more realistic figure.

First of all, the dollar value of the goods going through the distribution system in 1949–50 is probably underestimated. If so, the percentage saving would be applied to a larger base, giving a larger absolute (dollar) amount saved. According to the original food bill estimate, wholesalers' sales to retailers amounted to $122.9 million. If the food bill estimating equations is solved assuming a wholesale margin of 8 rather than 15 per cent, wholesalers' sales to retailers amount to $114.2 million. Both estimates assume no double handling. But the Census reports grocery and food specialty wholesalers' sales of $177 million, indicating that the island food bill estimate has understated wholesaler sales to retailers and wholesaler sales to other wholesalers by a total of from $55 million to $63 million. If these are exclusive agents' sales to other wholesalers, and even if the agents' margin were only 7 per cent, the amount paid for the double-handling services would be between $3.85 and $4.41 million. Presumably much (but not all) of this double-handling margin could be eliminated by vertical integration. If some of this $55 to $63 million represents sales to retailers, then the CTR and the CTC are understated and the dollar savings also.

At least some of this $55 million does represent sales to retailers, for the calculation of the value of the imports plus local production moving through the food distribution system in Puerto Rico, shown in Table 33, makes no allowance for the alcoholic beverages moving through the food stores. Total imports of malt liquors plus local production less exports in 1949–50 amounted to about $9.7 million valued

---

[10] The total annual savings possible in the three models under each of the wholesale margin assumptions are as follows:

	15 per cent wholesale margin assumption		8 per cent wholesale margin assumption	
	Millions of dollars	Percentage of CTC	Millions of dollars	Percentage of CTC
Model NS	33.0	18.9	19.3	11.9
Model C	30.3	17.3	16.5	10.2
Model CD	28.9	16.5	15.1	9.3

at cost to the wholesaler. If only one-half of this amount goes through food stores rather than eating and drinking places, the food bill CTC is understated by $4.8 million plus the wholesale and retail markups. Furthermore, island production of distilled liquors in 1949 amounted to $9.5 million, imports of liquors and wines were about $.6 million the same year, and exports over $3 million. Hence $5,000,000 to $7,000,000 worth of liquors and wines were distributed on the island, and a small portion of this merchandise went through the food stores.

Coffee sales through food stores were also omitted because of an imperfection in the retailer survey data, and because of great uncertainty as to the proportion of the coffee production taken by food stores. Coffee typically moves directly to the retailer from the roaster, so coffee production was not included in the Table 33 calculation. Retailers' direct purchases from local producers amounted to $4.7 million dollars according to the calculations of the present food bill, this representing the 3.5 per cent of sales which retailers reported were goods bought by them directly from the local producer. The original survey of retailers, however, shows this 3.5 per cent to consist solely of produce and meat. The proportion of the $5.1 million worth of coffee roasted in Puerto Rico in 1949 which went through food stores is unknown, but two-thirds is probably a conservative guess. This $3.4 million plus the retail markup would increase the food bill CTC and so would increase the potential savings.

If it were possible to estimate accurately the value of beer and liquor sales through the system, the value of the coffee sales and the distribution of the $55–63 million of unexplained wholesale sales revenues between sales to wholesalers and sales to retailers, the estimated food bill CTC of $173.1 million (or $162.2 if the wholesale margin is assumed to be 8 per cent rather than 15 per cent) would surely be increased by another $10 million or more. Thus the dollar amount of potential savings would likewise be increased significantly above the minimal estimate of $15.1 million per year.

This estimate is low for a number of other reasons. First of all, the cost analyses of both wholesalers and retailers were carried out so as to overestimate rather than underestimate operating costs at present and expanded sales volumes. The upper limit curves were drawn not as averages of the individual cost curves on which they are based but were drawn *above* all the individual cost curves. In the case of the wholesalers, a cost curve based on the markups required at the present sales volumes would reflect considerably greater economies of size than does the upper limit curve, which is tempered by the projections. The possible economies which might result from integration have not been considered; they would surely be significant. Furthermore, the dollar savings are based on 1949–50 volume and prices and given percentage saving on the current food bill would be somewhat greater than that indicated above because of higher prices as well as greater volume.

In conclusion, the minimal savings estimate of $15.1 million does indeed appear to be much too conservative. It is based on an 8 per cent wholesale margin rather than the 15 per cent margin found in the present survey. It does not even recognize any of the aforementioned $55–63 million worth of wholesaler sales as being either double handled or sold to retailers. An unknown proportion of $9.7 million worth of beer, of $5 to $7 million worth of liquor, and $5.1 million in coffee, *plus retail markups,* was marketed through food stores, and the $15.1 million savings estimate does not take into account any potential savings on this volume. The allowed operating costs of the model firm have been ample, no savings due to integration have been recognized, nor does the minimum savings estimate include the additional four million savings which could redound from elimination of credit and delivery. It would seem reasonable, therefore, to estimate the minimum potential annual savings at about $20–25 million, while recognizing that there is a very good chance that the potential savings might exceed $30 million.

10

NON-FOOD MARKETING:

SETTING AND METHOD

We turn now to an examination of the Puerto Rican distribution system for products other than food. For many years students of the island's economy have believed that the marketing system which brings clothing, utensils, consumer's durables, and other consumer requirements to the people of Puerto Rico is, like that which brings them food, unduly expensive and also, perhaps, unreliable in the quality of goods it provides. Here, as in the case of food, it is necessary to describe the system by which important non-food merchandise is marketed and to assess its efficiency. It should be noted that stores carrying non-food products are much less homogeneous — both in volume of business and character of merchandise carried — than food stores; accordingly, it is difficult to classify them. No attempt has been made to establish a model system by which the present efficiency of non-food retailing in Puerto Rico might be tested. Comparisons between different stores in Puerto Rico and between stores on the island and mainland, however, have provided reasonably satisfactory clues to the efficiency of operations.

As with food, the distribution of non-food products is shaped by the low level of incomes of the people of the island, its irregular receipt, and the comparatively limited range of products which Puerto Ricans can afford. However, poverty and irregular income payments lead to a somewhat different scheme of distribution in the non-food lines from that for foods. Although stores that are small by continental United States standards predominate, most of these stores are located in urban *barrios* and the average store in the non-food lines here considered sells about five times as much as the average food store listed in the Census.[1] These estimates do not take into account the peddlers operating in both types of products.

[1] *Census of Business, 1949, Puerto Rico,* Bureau of the Census, Department of Commerce, Washington, D.C., United States Government Printing Office, 1952, pp. 12–13.

For many families clothing, furniture, drugs, and other non-food products have only a residual claim on the family income. According to a study made in Puerto Rico in 1939–40, an average of 45 per cent of the consumption expenditures went for food. Wage earners' families, however, were spending about 60 per cent of their total expenditures on food and in the poorer families even larger proportions went to supply the basic food needs.[2]

The purchases of non-food items by country people and the poorer urban dwellers, therefore, are few and far between. Clothes, medical supplies, and home furnishings are often makeshift; and a purchase is usually made only after long consideration.

A 1949 study reveals the few articles demanded from a store by the average Puerto Rican.[3] The very restricted income dictates a simple and unvarying diet, which in turn requires a minimum of utensils. For the type of cooking common in the majority of Puerto Rican homes, it is estimated that only some fifteen to twenty items are needed, namely:

iron kettle	cooking spoon
other kettle	frying pan
kitchen knife	two large cans or pails for water
large bowl	coffee bag
can or pot for coffee	two dishes or cans to hold food
mortar and pestle	strainer
kitchen fork	dishpan
	grater

But even these minimum requirements are possessed by only 27 per cent of the rural families and 43 per cent of the urban families. Many of the utensils are in fact improvised. Thus gourds are used for bowls and plates, and even for spoons; large cracker or lard tins are used for carrying water; and reclaimed tin cans are used for cooking and eating utensils.

This pattern, existing in kitchen requirements, shows up even more clearly in furniture for the house. Nearly half of the families have less than fifteen pieces of furniture — most commonly beds, cots, hammocks, benches, chests, and chairs. In some rural areas only six articles, some improvised, are found in as many as half of the homes. These were the bed, *baúl* (chest), table, bench, hammock, and mirror. Such common articles as a rocker, arm chair, wardrobe, sewing machine, dresser, buffet, sofa, or bookcase are found in only 6 to 18 per cent of the homes. The articles of furniture which the families have are frequently homemade. Shelves, cupboards, tables, and chairs are

[2] Harvey S. Perloff, *Puerto Rico's Economic Future,* University of Chicago Press, Chicago, Ill., 1950, pp. 168–171.

[3] Roberts and Stefani, *passim.*

made from boxes and barrels which also provide the wood for home construction.

Consumer durable goods play an even smaller role in the life of the average Puerto Rican. Although almost all of the urban areas are wired for electricity, only about 23 per cent of the rural areas have electric service. Therefore, for many in the rural areas, electric appliances are of no interest. Even radios are a luxury, though the most common of all electrical appliances purchased.

Clothing supplies are meager for most families. Much is made from reclaimed materials or yard goods purchased in the country from the ambulant vendors who roam the hills. In many of the poorer urban areas peddlers with a few yards of material over their shoulders and a measuring tape supply the needs of the families for clothing material.

Even some medical supplies are provided by the herbs and roots of the district. Teas, brews, and poultices of various sorts are used by rural families for a variety of ills.

This forced independence of the average Puerto Rican from commercial supplies of clothes, furnishings, and medicines explains the concentration of the non-food stores in the urban communities. (Only *bazares,* in reality expanded dressmaking shops, have located in the rural areas to supply the basic needs of the surrounding population.) If a rural family feels that it can afford a store purchase it can also probably afford the cost of transportation to the larger centers where available choice is greater. It is for these reasons that, as compared with the approximately 15,000 food stores (excluding *cafetines*) on the island, approximately 3,000 stores supply the major non-food requirements of the Puerto Rican people.

Sources of Information

For Puerto Rico the main source of information on retail outlets has been the United States Census of Business, but this is a rather recent development. Moreover, it has as the basis for its classifications divisions suitable for the United States economy which are not really applicable to the simpler scheme of distribution in Puerto Rico. Thus the Census of Business does not enumerate peddlers and hawkers who have no permanently established place of business. Although the actual volume of sales by peddlers cannot be estimated reliably, they are of some significance in Puerto Rico, and their omission from the statistics affects the accuracy of the reports. Peddlers have been of decreasing importance since the advent of better roads, better means of transportation, and the attempts of some municipalities to restrict their activities. However, the mountain areas and the poorer urban *barrios* are still served by peddlers with small stocks of notions and materials.

In addition, much information collected by government agencies in Puerto Rico is in connection with legislation which specifically exempts small firms. Therefore, these reports are also incomplete.

To obtain the necessary information for a description and appraisal of the present system it was necessary to organize a special survey of non-food retailing and wholesaling. Interviews, based on a detailed questionnaire which requested data on store policies, investments and expenses, were conducted with retailers and wholesalers. This information was supplemented by the opinions on business organization expressed by successful businessmen. We now turn to the sampling procedure employed in this survey.

Sampling Procedure

There was no doubt that all non-food stores in Puerto Rico would not be homogeneous — differences would be apparent in markups, expenses, and policies. Further, a sample would have to be large enough and drawn in such a manner as to give every item an equal chance of being chosen. However, to draw such a random sample it is necessary to have a complete listing of the universe from which the sample is drawn. This was unavailable in the present survey; there was no record of the total universe of retail stores nor of any given part of it. Moreover, six different types of stores had to be represented in the sample. Lists which were available as guides to the universe were inaccurate in a great many instances, and definitions of individual store types did not conform to the requirements of the survey. Prior to drawing a sample, therefore, it became necessary to find some means of determining the universe.

Licensing lists were available by *municipios* and, in order to minimize the problems of enumerating the universe, fourteen representative *municipios* were chosen. The licensing lists from these communities were used as the first estimate of the universe.

A large survey was then made of the stores which could conceivably be non-food outlets in the fourteen *municipios*. This provided the necessary information for the stratification of the universe. The final sample was then drawn at random from the firms surveyed.

The most common non-food stores on the island are clothing stores, and this category includes everything from the large specialty stores in the metropolitan areas to the small *bazares* selling only a limited range of goods to rural customers. Because of the diversity of firms represented in this category, it was decided to select a large sample in the hope that adequate representation would be given to each type and that the summary statistics derived would be valid for the universe. For the other types, about forty stores were considered sufficient to represent the areas and volume of sales ranges of the stores. Specialized appliance stores are rather uncommon on the island; thus the sample of these firms is the smallest.

In order to concentrate attention on that part of the distribution system which is most important in the expenditure patterns of the people, six major store types were included. These were chosen to correspond as closely as possible with the census divisions to make practicable, within certain limitations, the comparison of data obtained from the censuses taken in Puerto Rico in 1949 and 1939, and with different areas in the continental United States. These six types cover stores selling clothing and yard goods, shoes, furniture and furnishings, appliances, hardware, and drugs. The retail sales of the lines studied (excluding hardware) amount to about one-quarter of all the retail sales in Puerto Rico. Almost 14 per cent is spent on clothing, 4 per cent on drugs, 3 per cent on furniture and furnishings and on appliances, and 2 per cent on shoes.

Following the Census of Business classifications, all stores having over 50 per cent of their sales in any one category were counted as belonging to that type. For example, a store selling 60 per cent appliances and 40 per cent home furnishings was considered an appliance store. Clothing and dry goods stores included those that had 50 per cent of their sales in either clothing or yard goods or a combination of these two. In accordance with the Census definitions, all firms making over one-half of their sales to final customers were considered retailers. Therefore, in the final sample of retailers there were a few firms who made a small proportion of their sales at wholesale.

The universe was also stratified to insure representation in the sample of four regional sub-divisions of the island. The San Juan area, including Rio Piedras, constituted the first class for this purpose; Ponce and Mayaguez were the second. These two classes comprise the main population centers of the island. The third was composed of those *municipios* with an urban population of over ten thousand — elsewhere referred to as market town areas. The fourth classification, rural town *municipios,* includes those with an urban population of less than ten thousand. The fourteen *municipios* in the final sample represent the full range of population and include areas concentrating on the cultivation of cane, pineapple, coffee, and tobacco; small truck farms; fishing; and industry.[4] They represent 69 per cent of the total urban population and 40 per cent of the total population of the island. In order to obtain a list of stores in each *municipio* suitable for the

[4] The fourteen *municipios* are San Juan, Ponce, Mayaguez, Caguas, Arecibo, Fajardo, Manatí, San Germán, Aibonito, Ciales, Peñuelas, Patillas, Ceiba, and Rincón.

purposes of the study, a large sample was drawn from the licensing lists in each *municipio*. In San Juan, Rio Piedras, Ponce, and Maya-guez, every fifth non-food store on the licensing lists was included in the survey; in the market town *municipios* every second store was covered; and all stores in the rural *municipios* were included. This gave 1,009 stores to be interviewed with a short questionnaire asking for information on volume of sales and percentages of sales in the various lines. This information permitted classification of the stores according to the categories determined. In each of the small towns any stores which were not listed on the licensing lists but which were sell-ing non-food products were added, bringing the total number of firms surveyed to 1,051.

The replies to the survey questions were classified according to the store type and the area in which the stores were located. Of the 239 clothing stores, 45 were located in San Juan, 38 in Ponce and Maya-guez, 83 in the market towns, and 73 in the rural towns. Since a sample of about 120 firms would include about 5 per cent of the total number of such stores on the island, firms replying to the survey questionnaire were selected at random, distributed evenly among the four areas. A similar method was used for all but the appliance stores, where only three of the firms surveyed are not included in the final sample.

The final sample represented 5 per cent of the firms classified as clothing stores by the 1949 Census, 34 per cent of the shoe stores, 14 per cent of the furniture and furnishings stores, 19 per cent of the appliance stores, and 8.5 per cent of the drugstores.

Although the survey was made in April and May and the retail interviews were completed by September, within that period some of the stores had changed their primary line — for example, from fur-nishings to hardware, shoes to clothing, or clothing to furniture and furnishings. Small stocks of various lines are added or dropped peri-odically; in the smallest stores an automatic shift can occur in response to the demands of the customers in the previous period. Thus the composition of the final working sample as given in Table 36 differs slightly from the final sample as tabulated in the following chapter.

Data obtained in the survey of food stores undertaken in Puerto Rico in 1949–50 show important differences from the Census data obtained the previous year. Such discrepancies are less severe for non-food retailing. The food store managers have consistently shown a reluctance to give Census information. The lack of adequate book-keeping facilities in the numerous small stores makes it difficult for them to do so. Government offices collecting data on retailing in Puerto Rico have found the owners of clothing, furnishings, and drug firms

Table 36 Distribution of stores in the final working sample,
by lines handled and by location

	San Juan area	Ponce and Mayaguez	Market towns	Rural towns
Clothing	30	33	30	27
Shoes	9	8	11	10
Furniture and furnishings	11	7	13	10
Appliances	8	6	6	2
Hardware	9	8	12	8
Drugs	9	9	9	11
Total	76	71	81	68

not only more willing to give information, but also more able to give accurate data on their operations.

With appropriate allowances for price changes, data collected in this survey check generally with the Census information on those points where the latter is available. In general, markups in drugs and clothing, available from studies of the Office of Price Stabilization, were also in agreement with the data collected in the sample. Although there are certain qualifications which will be explicitly stated below it is probable that the sample results give a reasonably accurate picture of the operations of the types of non-food stores considered.

11

RETAILING OF NON-FOOD PRODUCTS

As noted only 3,000 retail stores handle the diverse non-food lines compared with the 15,000 stores engaged in the distribution of food in Puerto Rico. However, a comparison with the corresponding store types in the continental United States shows that small stores are also important in the distribution of non-food products in Puerto Rico. For example, according to Census of Business for 1949–50, over 54 per cent of the clothing stores in Puerto Rico did less than $5,000 worth of business a year.[1] Only 7.7 per cent of the mainland firms had such a small volume of sales.[2] Almost 23 per cent of the drugstores in Puerto Rico sold less than $10,000 a year, but only 6.3 per cent of the firms on the mainland fell into that sales class. Average sales in the continental United States of non-food stores of the types here considered were $84,369, varying from an average of $88,250 in the East-North-Central section to $80,511 in the East-South-Central area. This compares with an over-all average of $12,924 for Puerto Rico.

However, it is interesting to note that when Lorenz curves are constructed, showing the per cent of total sales within the various sales classes against the per cent of stores in the various sales classes there is a remarkable correspondence between Puerto Rico and the United States. In other words, although the absolute size of the stores is very different in the continental United States and Puerto Rico the proportion of sales by relatively small and relatively large stores is similar.

According to the Census, over two-thirds, or 2,254, of the non-food retailers in 1949 were clothing and yard goods stores. The average volume of sales reported in the Census was only $20,375; that for the

[1] *Census of Business 1949, Puerto Rico*, Bureau of the Census, Department of Commerce, United States Government Printing Office, Washington, D.C., 1952, pp. 12–13.

[2] *Census of Business 1948, United States*, Bureau of the Census, Department of Commerce, United States Government Printing Office, Washington, D.C., 1950, pp. 202–207.

112 clothing and yard goods firms in the sample was $26,304. Since some purchases of clothing or yard goods are made by nearly all families, a relatively large number of such stores situated throughout the island with a correspondingly low volume of sales is to be expected. It is in the sale of clothing and yard goods that peddlers are most important. The Census does not cover firms without an established place of business, so data on these operations are not included in Census averages. The average volume of sales for all sellers of clothing and yard goods would undoubtedly be smaller than the figures quoted above.

Frequently in the smaller towns the clothing and yard goods stores are located in the front room of the storekeeper's house, fitted with a few shelves, possibly a sewing machine, and a table or counter. In the rural areas the returns from these small *bazares* may constitute a supplementary income for the family which raises a part of its own food and hires out during the busy season as farm laborers.

Drugstores were second in number to clothing stores, again reflecting the need of the people to have some access to drug supplies. Here the average volume of sales per year of the sample firms was $31,068. Other types of stores are less numerous and do a larger volume. They sell articles which constitute larger unit purchases than do apparel or drugs, and it is customary for purchasers to make a trip to the nearest town to have the advantage of choice from several stores. It should be noted, also, that the small *bazares* as well as some food stores carry work shoes, machetes, and other common requirements.

Table 37 gives the distribution by sales class size of the six types of stores studied.

When store volume is related to location there is a general tendency for the average volume of sales to be larger in the San Juan area and in Ponce and Mayaguez than elsewhere on the island. This difference is somewhat disguised by the fact that the *municipios* of the San Juan area, Ponce, and Mayaguez encompass rural districts with small stores. In the rural towns, there were only seven stores from the whole sample that had a volume of sales exceeding $50,000 a year, and only one with annual sales in excess of $100,000. On the other hand in the San Juan area twenty-two stores, or one-third of those considered, had sales of over $50,000 per year.

As previously noted, the large number of small stores actually accounts for only a very small proportion of the sales made in any one line. Thus the 13 per cent of the hardware stores which sold less than $5,000 a year accounted for less than 1 per cent of the total hardware sales. The 8 per cent of the stores which sold more than $100,000 per year accounted for almost 50 per cent of all hardware sales. In clothing

Table 37   Number of stores and total sales in non-food stores,
by sales class and by store type

			Yearly sales (dollars)			
	Less than 5,000	5,000 to 9,999	10,000 to 24,999	25,000 to 49,999	50,000 to 99,999	Over 100,000	Total
Clothing							
Number	39	25	15	14	14	5	112
Total sales	99,936	195,912	235,500	517,056	949,272	947,700	2,945,376
Shoes							
Number	3	3	4	9	10	7	36
Total sales	8,400	21,024	69,996	322,704	783,828	1,036,416	2,242,368
Furniture and furnishings							
Number	4	3	9	9	8	6	39
Total sales	12,288	21,996	156,324	344,028	569,784	1,252,836	2,357,256
Appliances							
Number	3	2	3	5	2	4	19
Total sales	7,500	16,200	59,796	172,663	122,004	1,197,000	1,575,163
Hardware							
Number	5	6	7	11	6	3	38
Total sales	14,880	49,200	110,400	386,964	442,728	947,892	1,952,064
Drugs							
Number	2	5	13	13	4	—	37
Total sales	3,840	34,560	272,004	498,084	341,184[a]	—	1,149,672

[a] Includes one firm selling over $100,000.

and yard goods, the firms selling less than $5,000 annually represented 54 per cent of the stores, but made only 3.4 per cent of the sales. At the other end of the scale the top 5 per cent of the stores sold about 35 per cent of the goods.

An outstanding characteristic of the retail firms studied was the great variety of goods which many of them handled. Drugstores alone seem to concentrate on specified lines — only one such store in the sample sold clothing and yard goods in addition to drugs and sundries. In the other store types over 50 per cent handled at least two lines, and 17 per cent handled as many as three to five lines. Table 38 shows this characteristic in more detail, where the sample stores are classified according to volume of sales in the various lines handled.

A comparison of the number of years in business with information on volume of sales gives no clear indication of the relative ability of large and small stores to survive. The median age in each case was between five and ten years. Clothing stores and drugstores — the two types with the smallest average volume of sales — did show that a

Table 38   Number and percentages of stores, by lines handled and by sales class

	Yearly sales (dollars)						
	Less than 5,000	5,000 to 9,999	10,000 to 24,999	25,000 to 49,999	50,000 to 99,999	Over 100,000	Total
Clothing							
Number	70	25	15	11	8	3	132
Per cent	53.0	18.9	11.4	8.3	6.1	2.3	
Shoes							
Number	23	8	10	9	12	4	66
Per cent	34.8	12.1	15.2	13.6	18.2	6.1	
Yard goods							
Number	31	17	8	5	2	3	66
Per cent	47.0	25.8	12.1	7.6	3.0	4.6	
Furniture and furnishings							
Number	23	12	11	11	6	6	69
Per cent	33.3	17.4	15.9	15.9	8.7	8.7	
Appliances							
Number	10	10	10	7	2	4	43
Per cent	23.3	23.3	23.3	16.3	4.7	9.3	
Hardware							
Number	14	13	6	11	3	3	50
Per cent	28.0	26.0	12.0	22.0	6.0	6.0	
Drugs							
Number	14	5	13	13	4	—	49
Per cent	28.6	10.2	26.5	26.5	8.1 [a]	—	

[a] Includes one firm with sales of over $100,000.

critical time in relation to survival is reached after two or three years in business. The capital needed to open such stores is modest. Hence it is possible that a number of potentially submarginal stores are opened, exist for a short period, and then are closed or sold. This was substantiated by interviews with owners of recently established retail stores.

Employment and Employment Functions

With increasing volume, sales per worker increased though at a decreasing rate, for clothing, shoes, furniture and furnishings, and appliance stores. (See Table 39.) In hardware a slight decline in sales per worker occurred in the largest sales class. A consistent decline in sales per worker was found in drugstores with sales of over $50,000 per year. This may in part be due to the concentration in the largest

Table 39   Average number of employees and sales per employee,
by class and by store type

	Yearly sales (dollars)						
	Less than 5,000	5,000 to 9,999	10,000 to 24,999	25,000 to 24,999	50,000 to 99,999	Over 100,000	Average
Clothing							
Average number of employees	1.4	1.7	2.4	4.7	5.6	11.8	3.0
Sales per employee	1,817	4,556	6,542	7,834	12,170	16,063	8,743
Shoes							
Average number of employees	1.3	2.0	2.5	3.4	7.3	11.3	5.6
Sales per employee	2,100	3,504	7,000	10,410	10,737	13,119	11,046
Furnishings and furniture							
Average number of employees	1.2	1.3	2.1	4.0	3.6	10.5	4.0
Sales per employee	2,458	5,499	8,228	9,556	19,648	19,886	15,110
Appliances							
Average number of employees	1.7	2.0	2.3	2.8	7.0	17.3	6.0
Sales per employee	1,500	4,050	8,542	12,333	8,715	17,348	13,939
Hardware							
Average number of employees	1.0	1.7	2.0	3.5	4.7	20.3	4.1
Sales per employee	2,976	4,920	7,886	10,183	15,812	15,539	12,512
Drugs							
Average number of employees	1.0	1.6	3.5	4.2	11.0	—	4.2
Sales per employee	1,920	4,320	6,045	9,056	7,754[a]	—	7,465

[a] Includes one firm with sales of over $100,000.

drugstores on the prescription business and its attendant requirements
for prescription druggists rather than clerks.

The average sales per worker in the various stores in Puerto Rico
fall far short of the figures on the mainland. For example, the average
sales per worker (paid and unpaid) in continental United States
apparel stores were $15,840 — a figure achieved in Puerto Rico only
in the highest sales class. Among mainland shoe retailers the average
sales per employee were $18,549, and in drugstores $13,303, levels not
achieved in any sales class in Puerto Rico. For furniture and furnishings and appliance stores in the United States, the averages were
$16,735 and $17,338.

Unpaid workers in the United States constituted between 5 and 10 per cent of the employees in the various types of stores, a much lower percentage than is common in Puerto Rico, where, for example, over one-half of the clothing stores paid no wages, and over one-third of the hardware stores had no regularly paid employees.

It is not surprising that sales per worker are lower in Puerto Rico than on the mainland, in view of the wage differential. Nevertheless, these comparisons are striking. Thus one store selling less than $1,000 a year and over one-third of the stores selling less than $5,000 a year had at least two employees. It is apparent that employment policy is often dictated not by economic considerations, but by the number of relatives who need work.

Prices and Merchandising Policies

Although it is fairly common for Puerto Rican food retailers to enter wholesaling operations by beginning to sell some goods to nearby smaller stores, this practice of combining wholesaling and retailing services is rare in non-food distribution. Over 90 per cent of the sales of each of the types of non-food stores were made directly to the ultimate consumer. A few of the hardware stores sold a small percentage of their products to contractors, but the only significant deviation from the standard pattern is in the stores selling yard goods which act as the suppliers for the peddlers. About 10 per cent of the stores selling yard goods sold to peddlers, and most of these were located in the market towns. However, these stores sold an average of only 10 per cent of their total sales to peddlers, and no firm sold over 30 per cent.

There are several reasons for the smaller use of intermediate wholesalers in non-food lines. In the first place, there are very few non-food stores in remote areas. Therefore, most stores have access to a wholesaler or his representative and do not have to rely on nearby retailers to supply them. This is in contrast to the great number of small food stores in remote places which are not serviced by the regular wholesalers.

Secondly, with improved transportation facilities and rising incomes on the island, the importance of the peddler has declined, reducing the amount of sales to this group. Thirdly, most market or rural town retailers are not large enough to maintain the variety of stocks necessary to supply the needs of other stores, and the problems of style and obsolescence discourage part-time entrance into wholesaling. Finally, many of the arrangements with mainland firms encourage direct purchase through company salesmen, thus minimizing the place of the wholesaler in the whole scheme of distribution.

From the interviews with store managers it was evident that price cutting was frowned upon as a means of increasing the volume of business although small sales to get rid of dead items in the inventory were not considered unfair competition. It was widely believed that the market for most goods was strictly limited and that sales would not really bring new customers to the store. The pattern of clearance sales of the sample stores verified this attitude. Less than 4 per cent of the retailers had more than two general sales a year, and over 75 per cent never had a general sale. Clearance sales were most rare in drugstores, including those selling sundries and cosmetics. Sales were most common in shoe stores; almost 60 per cent of these firms had at least one clearance sale a year. As would be expected, clearance sales were more common in the larger stores where, with the exception of drug firms, over half the stores had at least one clearance sale a year.

On the other hand some sort of individually offered discount was granted by at least half of the stores of each type. Discounts were most often given in haggling or for quantity purchases. Since no general agreement as to what constituted a quantity purchase existed, this type of discount undoubtedly reflects the bargaining ability of those customers who convince clerks that their purchases warrant some price concession. In addition some price concessions were made to regular customers. It was not unusual for a firm to mark up each item 60 to 70 per cent, expecting to sell it finally at a markup of about 50 per cent.

Nearly all stores did some form of advertising, using sound truck, newspaper, radio, hand bills, calendars, or fans. Radio advertising was the most popular, and only furniture and appliance stores made any substantial use of newspaper advertising as an alternative. Sound truck and newspaper advertising were for obvious reasons confined to the larger urban areas, but radio advertising was popular even with the rural town stores where approximately one-third of the stores made some use of it.

Asked about attitudes toward increased scale of operations, over half the respondents stated that they would like to expand their businesses. Expansion would provide access to more capital and with larger unit purchases suppliers might be induced to offer quantity discounts. As a larger volume does not necessarily imply reduced prices in Puerto Rico, an increase in sales would usually be expected to lead to an increase in profits.

Most retailers, in considering expansion, anticipated difficulty with employees and seemed unwilling to turn over responsibility to them. Additional problems which were mentioned were inadequate resources for financing an expansion, and bad location. The latter included such barriers as absence of room for expansion in the present place of business and unavailability of adjacent facilities. This barrier ranked first in importance in the larger urban areas but was relatively less important in the rural areas.

As with food retailers attitudes toward expanded operations and the attendant difficulties are deeply colored by an impression of a limited market, by the desire to avoid unfair competition, and by a live-and-let-live philosophy. There were a few retailers who felt that they could, through advertising or pricing policies, obtain a larger share of the market. More frequent were such comments as:

I do not believe that lowering prices in this business will bring a substantial increase in sales volume that will compensate for the difference in price.

As I said before, we count on a limited number of customers; a lower price will increase the volume of business for a limited time, but from then on the market will be saturated, and customers will not buy any more, even if prices are lowered further.

I am not interested either in expanding this business or in opening branches, because the customers are limited and there would be the same volume of business whether I have branches or not.

We do not deem it necessary to lower prices to increase the volume of sales. As long as you can satisfy the wishes of your customers by having a varied supply of items they will come to your store.

Furthermore, there was a general feeling that it is unethical to expand sales at the risk of forcing someone else out of business.

In this business there is a share for everyone engaged in it. I do not like to see any of my competitors driven out of business because of a price war or unfair competition. It is not necessary for you to keep up in business by hampering other businesses with practices which you wouldn't like any other person to use against you.

To prevent price competition explicit as well as implicit price agreements were quite general.

I have price agreements with most of the business men that carry my same lines. With the ones with whom there is no possible agreement, I try to do as they do or else use certain tricks to attract the public's attention.

Investment

Information on investment, both working and fixed capital, is probably the least reliable of data collected for this study. Few firms, if any, had a consistent inventory policy, and few stock records were maintained. As the types of stores and lines of goods handled were diverse, the interviewers were unable to make more than a very general estimate of the value of the inventories. Therefore, the managers' estimates of inventory, cash, and accounts receivable were accepted.

Similar difficulties were encountered in valuing the fixed capital involved in the business. Much of the property was rented and estimates of value by the retailer were thus of doubtful value. In cases where the store had been purchased, the original equipment and inventory were frequently paid for in one lump sum and store managers were unaware of the separate asset values. Some storekeepers had built their own equipment or repaired secondhand equipment thus enhancing its value. Even when some accounting records were maintained, depreciation accounts were rare, and a consistent depreciation policy between different firms would have been unlikely.

For these reasons estimates of equipment and property valuation were not requested from those interviewed and alternative valuation standards were devised. The equipment valuation represents depreciated replacement cost. The interviewers made a complete listing of all the equipment and its age, estimating shelf space, type of construction, values of materials used, and other relevant information. The value of the equipment was then estimated from the figures compiled giving present costs of equivalent equipment. Rates of depreciation of equipment were taken from dealers' estimates of the life of the equipment and Bulletin F of the Federal Bureau of Internal Revenue.

For property and building valuation the records of the Office of Scientific Assessment were used. The only parcels for which such a valuation was unobtainable were those owned by the various municipal governments and for which no valuation have been set. Hence those stores which rent building and land from the government, including those maintaining stalls in the *mercado* (market), are not tabulated in the tables on total capital and total capital turnover ratio.

Adjustments were made in each case for the proportion of the building used for business purposes. The total capital figure represents, therefore, not the investment of the storekeeper himself, but an estimate of the total amount of capital which is being used by the business. Table 40 presents the data on inventory and capital turnover.

There was a large variation in all the figures on investment and particularly in those on inventory. The inventory estimates for clothing stores ranged from less than $150 to over $200,000. There was a consistently higher inventory in shoes and appliances than other merchandise, and as expected there was a high correlation between inventory and sales.

But even within the various size classes there were large variations in inventory. Thus in clothing stores selling less than $5,000 a year, inventories ranged from $125 to $9,000. With sales of $5,000 to $10,-000 the range was from $550 to $10,000. In the smallest furniture and furnishing stores inventories varied from $100 to $1,500. Above the

Table 40   Average inventory, total capital, inventory turnover rates,
and capital turnover rates, by sales class and by store type

	Yearly sales (dollars)					
	Less than 5,000	5,000 to 9,999	10,000 to 24,999	25,000 to 49,999	50,000 to 99,999	Over 100,000
Clothing						
Average inventory (dollars)	981	3,164	7,249	14,720	20,165	96,998
Total capital (dollars)	3,451	6,617	12,901	25,143	34,866	126,261
Inventory ratio	5.5	3.8	3.7	2.9	3.8	2.3
Total capital ratio	1.1	1.4	1.7	1.6	2.1	1.7
Shoes						
Average inventory (dollars)	1,483	3,000	5,675	18,219	43,400	65,267
Total capital (dollars)	2,871	6,087	14,063	25,499	63,929	86,474
Inventory ratio	3.5	3.9	4.0	2.2	2.5	3.3
Total capital ratio	1.2	1.7	1.7	1.6	1.5	2.3
Furniture and furnishings						
Average inventory (dollars)	582	1,667	6,327	14,363	14,349	70,167
Total capital (dollars)	3,201	7,789	19,072	39,121	44,117	191,994
Inventory ratio	13.6	7.0	3.6	5.9	8.6	7.3
Total capital ratio	1.1	1.5	1.0	1.2	2.1	1.3
Appliances						
Average inventory (dollars)	1,833	2,500	5,153	18,000	20,000	80,206
Total capital (dollars)	3,361	5,772	22,181	38,858	37,506	106,111
Inventory ratio	1.6	3.3	7.2	3.7	3.1	11.4
Total capital ratio	0.5	1.5	1.4	1.1	1.8	2.5
Hardware						
Average inventory (dollars)	710	4,940	6,286	21,000	16,963	125,000
Total capital (dollars)	3,171	7,603	13,538	31,917	29,709	249,109
Inventory ratio	4.0	2.6	2.9	1.9	4.7	2.9
Total capital ratio	1.2	1.3	1.3	1.3	2.8	1.4
Drugs						
Average inventory (dollars)	375	3,600	6,469	14,046	24,750	
Total capital (dollars)	2,853	6,775	12,765	21,224	38,117	
Inventory ratio	1.7	2.7	3.8	3.1	4.2	
Total capital ratio	0.5	1.2	1.7	1.9	2.5[a]	

[a] Includes one firm selling over $100,000.

smaller sales classes a more consistent relationship between sales and inventory was found.

Inventory requirements were usually lower in the rural towns though there were some exceptions. The particularly low inventory figures for appliance stores in the market and rural towns reflects the fact that these stores sell appliances primarily on consignment for a store in a nearby larger town, and their stocks consist mainly of radio repair parts. The high inventory figures in hardware for the market and rural towns are explained by the fact that these stores frequently handle some lumber and building supplies.

There was only slight correlation between accounts receivable and the volume of sales. Some firms reported a volume of accounts receivable in excess of yearly sales. The owners of these stores admitted that bad debts were never written off but were held in the hope that good fortune would smile on the debtor and enable him to settle his account. (In such cases the figures were adjusted to include only those accounts receivable which could conceivably be current.) With the exception of appliance and furniture stores, less than 10 per cent of the stores had accounts receivable of more than $10,000. The accounts receivable were consistently lower in the rural areas, reflecting both the smaller volume of sales of rural stores and perhaps a better knowledge of the customers to whom credit is offered.

The amount of total capital is the sum of the working capital (inventory, accounts receivable, and cash), and fixed capital (equipment, building, and land). Over 35 per cent of the clothing and yard goods stores had a total investment in their business of less than $5,000. This reflects the meager equipment and inventory sufficient for the small *bazares*. In some of the urban *barrios* as well as the rural areas these stocks can be replaced easily by purchases from traveling venders.

There was no consistent pattern of inventory turnover ratios, either by sales class, area, or types of products sold. The figures on the whole compare favorably with the information available from the mainland. For example, the *Hardware Retailer,* summarizing data collected from 1,198 firms for 1951, gave stock turnover ratios as varying between 1.8 and 2.7. These depended on the volume of sales with higher turnover rates at larger volume of sales.[3] The values obtained for Puerto Rico ranged from 1.9 to 4.7. The high turnover may result from the smaller variety stocked by the stores in Puerto Rico. In shoes, a study by Dun and Bradstreet of 258 firms gave inventory turnover ratios of from 1.6 to 2.5 depending on volume of sales.[4] Figures for Puerto Rico ranged from 2.2 to 4.0.

The ratio of sales to total capital gives a more consistent pattern, with higher ratios for firms with the larger volume of sales. There were, however, some instances of a downturn at the largest sales class, indicating that perhaps there is more effective utilization of capital at the slightly lower volume of sales between $50,000 and $100,000. This is

[3] *The Hardware Retailer* published by the National Retail Hardware Association, Indianapolis, Indiana, 82, (June 1952), 13.
[4] *National Footwear News,* published by National Shoe Retailers Association, New York, 18 (November 1952), 23.

particularly true for the hardware firms in this category which maintain essentially efficient operations.

The use of store earnings gave additional information about the position of the firms with respect to investment. Almost 10 per cent of the firms replying stated that they were using their profits to pay off existing debt, presumably ahead of the required payments since these latter were considered part of the expenses of the firm. An additional 10 per cent were investing in store building and equipment with their profits, and slightly over 20 per cent were increasing their inventories as a preliminary to an attempt to increase their volume of sales.

Retail Costs and Margins

Tables 41 through 46 give the volume of sales and major expenses expressed as percentages of sales for the various types of stores within the six sales classes.

Table 41   Average sales, expense ratios, and profit ratios for clothing stores, by sales class

Yearly sales (dollars)	Number of stores	Average sales (dollars)	Cost of goods sold (dollars)	Per cent of sales					
				Gross profit	Total expenses	Wages	Rents	Other expenses	Net profit
Less than 5,000	39	2,562	1,817	29.7	13.6	1.8	4.8	7.0	16.1
5,000– 9,999	25	7,836	5,814	25.9	10.3	3.0	3.2	4.1	15.6
10,000–24,999	15	15,696	11,784	25.1	11.7	4.1	2.7	4.9	13.4
25,000–49,999	14	36,936	25,676	29.0	17.0	8.7	3.2	6.1	12.0
50,000–99,999	14	67,800	48,940	28.5	11.6	5.7	1.6	4.3	16.9
Over 100,000	5	189,540	131,227	30.0	14.7	7.6	1.5	5.6	15.3
Average for 112 stores		26,304	18,780	28.0	12.8	4.0	3.4	5.4	15.2

Table 42   Average sales, expense ratios, and profit ratios for shoe stores, by sales class

Yearly sales (dollars)	Number of stores	Average sales (dollars)	Cost of goods sold (dollars)	Per cent of sales					
				Gross profit	Total expenses	Wages	Rents	Other expenses	Net profit
Less than 5,000	3	2,800	2,119	24.0	14.7	2.3	6.0	6.4	9.3
5,000– 9,999	3	7,008	5,336	23.6	18.4	8.4	1.8	8.2	5.2
10,000–24,999	4	17,496	13,611	21.5	15.7	8.2	4.0	3.5	5.8
25,000–49,999	9	35,856	25,740	33.5	10.9	4.2	2.9	3.8	22.6
50,000–99,999	10	78,384	55,910	28.6	15.4	8.8	2.3	4.3	13.2
Over 100,000	7	148,058	101,472	30.5	14.3	9.1	1.5	3.7	16.2
Average for 36 stores		62,292	43,830	28.6	14.3	7.1	2.7	4.5	14.3

Table 43   Average sales, expense ratios, and profit ratios for furniture and furnishings stores, by sales class

Yearly sales (dollars)	Number of stores	Average sales (dollars)	Cost of goods sold (dollars)	Per cent of sales					
				Gross profit	Total expenses	Wages	Rents	Other expenses	Net profit
Less than 5,000	4	3,072	2,250	28.0	9.0	1.9	0.5	6.6	19.0
5,000– 9,999	3	7,332	5,804	21.5	11.9	—	2.8	9.1	9.6
10,000–24,999	9	17,364	11,027	36.4	21.3	5.9	2.3	13.1	15.1
25,000–49,999	9	38,220	24,861	34.9	18.8	6.0	2.8	10.0	16.1
50,000–99,999	8	71,220	45,809	35.7	13.6	4.1	0.9	8.6	22.1
Over 100,000	6	208,806	175,808	43.7	13.8	5.9	2.9	5.0	29.9
Average for 39 stores		60,444	36,388	34.8	15.8	4.7	2.0	9.1	19.0

Table 44   Average sales, expense ratios, and profit ratios for appliance stores, by sales class

Yearly sales (dollars)	Number of stores	Average sales (dollars)	Cost of goods sold (dollars)	Per cent of sales					
				Gross profit	Total expenses	Wages	Rents	Other expenses	Net profit
Less than 5,000	3	2,500	1,252	45.4	43.7	12.2	11.8	19.7	1.7
5,000– 9,999	2	8,100	5,172	34.9	8.3	1.7	1.8	4.8	26.6
10,000–24,999	3	19,932	14,716	25.9	13.0	2.5	3.6	6.9	12.9
25,000–49,999	5	34,536	22,730	34.2	17.6	5.7	2.6	9.3	16.6
50,000–99,999	2	61,008	42,000	30.7	24.2	6.0	1.7	16.5	6.5
Over 100,000	4	299,250	199,626	32.3	22.0	12.3	1.5	8.2	10.3
Average for 19 stores		82,908	55,500	33.9	21.6	7.2	3.8	10.6	12.3

Table 45   Average sales, expense ratios, and profit ratios, for hardware stores, by sales class

Yearly sales (dollars)	Number of stores	Average sales (dollars)	Cost of goods sold (dollars)	Per cent of sales					
				Gross profit	Total expenses	Wages	Rents	Other expenses	Net profit
Less than 5,000	5	2,976	1,998	31.6	7.8	—	2.6	5.2	23.8
5,000– 9,999	6	8,196	5,508	34.6	11.3	1.8	4.0	5.5	23.3
10,000–24,999	7	15,768	11,511	27.5	12.3	3.8	4.2	4.3	15.2
25,000–49,999	11	35,184	26,084	25.7	13.4	5.7	2.3	5.4	12.3
50,000–99,999	6	73,788	56,808	23.1	10.4	4.6	1.2	4.6	12.7
Over 100,000	3	315,964	239,596	25.2	15.0	8.0	1.1	5.9	10.2
Average for 38 stores		51,372	38,682	27.8	11.8	4.0	2.7	5.1	16.0

Table 46   Average sales, expense ratios, and profit ratios for drugstores
by sales class

Yearly sales (dollars)	Number of stores	Average sales (dollars)	Cost of goods sold (dollars)	Per cent of sales					
				Gross profit	Total expenses	Wages	Rents	Other expenses	Net profit
Less than 5,000	2	1,920	1,296	26.7	22.7	—	—	22.7	4.0
5,000– 9,999	5	6,912	4,606	32.6	19.9	0.8	5.9	13.2	12.7
10,000–24,999	13	20,926	14,928	29.1	18.1	9.7	1.8	6.6	11.0
25,000–49,999	13	38,316	26,650	30.8	15.1	7.8	1.6	5.7	15.7
Over 50,000	4	85,296	57,492	32.1	19.6	9.3	1.8	8.5	12.5
Average for 37 stores		31,068	21,492	30.8	18.1	7.3	2.2	8.6	12.7

Information regarding expenses from all firms interviewed was requested for the calendar year 1951 under the assumption that if records were kept the average figures for the previous year would be the most accurate available. However, if figures for a fiscal year could be obtained, these were also acceptable. Many of the firms interviewed kept no books, and, therefore, lacked accurate records from which to draw the required data. Since it was believed that there would be a downward bias to the figures given when no books were available, the questions were asked for the previous month or months in an attempt to get figures relating to the general conditions of the business for a short, not exceptionally good or bad period. The information was requested for a short period to reduce the magnitude of the figures given since more accurate figures could be expected if the manager were not dealing with large numbers. When stores were located in the owner's home, an attempt was made to prorate such expenses as utilities, rent, and taxes.

Cost of goods sold figures were obtained in some instances from the records of invoices of the firm and in some instances estimated by the owner. There were independent checks on this information from the markups given and from the records of purchases of goods in each line requested in a later portion of the interview. The cost of goods sold was often overstated in an attempt to make the profit margin seem smaller. Correction was made if there was disagreement between the individual purchases per month, the figure for cost of goods sold, and the gross markup.

Wages were included only for employees, the owner's compensation being included in the net earnings of the firm. This policy is also followed in the Census reports and facilitates comparisons. Actual payments to owners varied greatly within each sales class. Frequently no attempt was made by the owners to withdraw a given salary each month; they took out funds as needed or when money was available in the till.

Minimum wage laws obtain for all retail employees with rates varying according to three zones set up for the island. Zone I, including urban San Juan and Rio Piedras, requires payment of the highest wages—$12 a week or 30 cents an hour. Zone II includes urban Aguadilla, Arecibo, Bayamon, Caguas, Fajardo, Guayama, Humacao, Mayaguez, and Ponce. Here minimum wages are $10 a week or 25 cents an hour. The remainder of Puerto Rico constitutes Zone III, and minimum wages there are set at $8 a week or 20 cents an hour. Other regulations hold for apprentices and other special categories. No wages are set, of course, for the self-employed. Retail employees are on the whole poorly paid, even in the large stores, and low wages seem to be both a cause and an effect. Only relatively inefficient workers are attracted into the field by the low salaries, and the employers feel justified in continuing low salaries since the workers are inefficient. Since the smaller stores employ more unpaid workers, wages as a per cent of sales do not fall with a larger volume of sales. In addition there is some small presumption that wages do increase slightly with the larger-volume stores.

Stores in the rural areas consistently paid a smaller amount for rent. In general also a larger percentage of the store buildings in the rural areas were owned by their managers. This substantiates the general assumption that the smaller rural town stores are more frequently located in a part of the house of the storekeeper. In general a higher percentage of the small retailers owned their own buildings, as well as a slightly increased percentage of firms in the highest sales class.

As detailed breakdowns of expenses were not maintained by most of the storekeepers, the replies to the questions referring to minor expenses were frequently incomplete. Some payments, being irregular and relatively small, were classed together as miscellaneous expense by the store owners. For example, utilities expense was in some cases computed as a part of rent, in some instances included in miscellaneous expense, and in other instances listed separately. Furthermore, there was a great variation among firms and many of the averages conceal relatively wide ranges in values.

Depreciation was charged as an expense regardless of the accounting practice of the store owner. The depreciation was computed from the tables set up as described in the section on investment. (See pages 139–143.) The depreciation for buildings was charged only when the building was owned by the storekeeper and the depreciation was computed according to the tables of life expectancy and per cent good set up by the Scientific Assessment Office, depending on type of construction, adjustment in value made for improvements, and so forth.

The Scientific Assessment records also gave a check on taxes paid by the property owners for those cases in which the property was owned by the shopkeeper. These values in almost every instance agreed closely with the figures as given by the individual storekeepers.

There were very few stores which did not make some sales on credit, and the figures for credit losses were consistently high. However, no standard method of writing off bad debts was employed, and allowance must be made for this. The data collected, however, did not reveal a higher percentage of credit losses at either low or high volumes of sales, or in any particular type of market area.

In the larger populations centers, higher sales volume does not entirely offset higher rents, higher wage costs, higher utility expense, greater advertising, and so on. Therefore, expense ratios for the rural and market town stores are lower than for stores in the San Juan area, and in Ponce and Mayaguez, though in some instances the variation is not significant. The most important factors in almost every instance are the wage and rent differentials.

There is no general indication that the larger firms count on a smaller margin for their larger sales. The reverse was apparent in stores handling clothing, shoes, and furniture and furnishings. This may be one further indication of the lack of price competition and the lack of incentive on the part of the larger firms to increase sales further by means of lower prices. The markups of some of the large stores cover both the wholesale and retail functions. Such firms purchasing direct from the states obtain goods at a low price. With no incentive to pass on the saving to the consumer they receive a proportionately high percentage markup.

In general the profit margins obtained in the various lines are consistent with data available from the continental United States. For example, the average profit margin in 1951 for a selected group of hardware stores in the states was about 28 per cent, and precisely the same percentage gross profit was obtained from the sample of hardware stores in Puerto Rico. Expense ratios were not substantially higher on the mainland, averaging in hardware about 24 per cent, leaving a net profit of under 5 per cent. This net figure, however, does not include the owner's salary which as a percentage of sales ranged from 4 to 10 per cent. In Puerto Rico the expense ratios totaled about 16.5 per cent leaving a net profit of about 12 per cent, which did include the owner's salary.[5]

---

[5] *The Hardware Retailer,* p. 13.

Gross Markups

Tables 47 and 48 show gross markups over cost by lines carried, by areas, and by volume of sales. With the exceptions of appliances and furniture and furnishings, the median markup fell in the range from 30 to 39 per cent. This represents the average markup at which the goods are finally sold. It is a general practice as on the mainland to price many items high enough in the first instance to allow for subsequent markdowns.

In general, stores in the San Juan, Ponce, and Mayaguez areas had slightly higher markups on their goods. This presumably reflects the higher costs of doing business in these areas. However, the differences are not very significant in many instances and it seems probable that traditional policies control markups throughout the island. Retailers most frequently explained their markup by stating that they added "what they always had"; very few claimed that they computed the cost of handling any item or considered the effect on the market of the prices which they would charge. However about half of the storekeepers did do some comparison shopping.

The prices and markups set by the Office of Price Stabilization and other regulatory bodies have also been considered nearly sacrosanct and are closely followed. Fair trade agreements are operative in some lines and one retailer stated that if a competitor were selling a branded article below the manufacturer's suggested price he would call the supplier to have the matter remedied. In most lines the rulings of the Office of Price Stabilization on markups constituted less of a restraint than a guide to markup policy.

Credit Policies

As in the case of food, extensive use is made of credit. (See Table 49.) Even in drugs, hardware, and the dry goods lines, between 20 and 30 per cent of the sales were made on credit. As would be expected with the larger unit purchases in furniture and furnishings and appliances a much greater proportion of these lines was sold on credit. In the rural towns less than 13 per cent of the appliance sales were for cash, and the average for all appliance sales for cash was less than 30 per cent.

In the case of drugs, hardware, and dry goods the usual credit device is the regular charge account to be paid off at the end of the month. In agricultural areas, however, this may mean a delay of several months. For appliances the usual means of payment involves a regular installment plan. From about one-half to three-quarters of the

Table 47 Average percentage markups over cost of goods sold for lines handled, by area and volume of sales

	Yearly sales (dollars)						
	Less than 5,000	5,000 to 9,999	10,000 to 24,999	25,000 to 49,999	50,000 to 99,999	Over 100,000	Average
Clothing							
San Juan	50.5	26.3	52.3	46.0	47.0	55.0	47.6
Ponce	36.1	29.9	39.8	49.3	41.5	—	36.9
Market	58.3	33.7	35.6	34.0	32.3	42.0	46.1
Rural	39.8	42.6	26.5	30.0	—	—	39.5
Total	45.6	34.9	39.1	43.3	40.1	51.0	42.4
Shoes							
San Juan	26.5	35.0	—	56.3	45.0	52.5	39.4
Ponce	35.2	25.0	35.0	50.0	50.0	59.0	40.8
Market	27.7	45.0	46.0	29.7	32.0	—	34.8
Rural	35.4	16.0	45.7	46.0	30.0	—	34.7
Total	32.0	29.1	41.5	44.4	38.3	55.8	37.4
Yard Goods							
San Juan	27.5	35.0	—	68.5	—	100.0	46.7
Ponce	30.3	37.8	29.0	—	—	33.0	32.6
Market	34.5	29.3	32.8	30.0	30.0	26.0	32.2
Rural	27.0	37.6	24.0	40.0	—	—	30.0
Total	29.6	35.4	29.6	49.4	30.0	53.0	33.7
Furniture and furnishings							
San Juan	37.7	41.0	37.0	33.0	45.0	75.0	46.6
Ponce	55.0	18.0	63.0	89.0	82.0	75.0	62.6
Market	34.0	44.5	60.0	60.0	49.7	78.0	47.9
Rural	36.3	26.5	49.5	63.0	—	—	44.7
Total	37.9	39.0	50.7	61.5	53.5	75.5	48.5
Appliances							
San Juan	58.3	—	28.5	50.0	22.0	57.0	45.1
Ponce	89.0	88.0	—	68.4	50.0	44.7	63.9
Market	40.5	51.8	27.3	78.0	—	—	43.4
Rural	22.5	50.5	57.5	—	—	—	47.7
Total	47.1	54.9	39.6	67.1	36.0	47.8	50.0
Hardware							
San Juan	41.3	39.5	29.5	35.8	—	—	38.9
Ponce	39.0	74.7	—	—	24.0	42.0	51.3
Market	87.7	40.0	40.8	29.0	—	30.0	51.4
Rural	31.0	41.0	—	31.0	31.5	—	34.2
Total	48.7	48.2	40.3	33.5	29.0	38.0	42.4
Drugs							
San Juan	22.0	60.0	36.3	41.5	50.0	80.0	40.7
Ponce	32.5	50.0	45.0	41.5	33.0	—	41.5
Market	50.0	35.0	61.0	38.5	38.0	—	44.9
Rural	35.7	50.0	30.3	55.4	—	—	42.2
Total	34.4	49.0	42.1	45.9	40.3	80.0	42.3

Table 48 Distribution of stores according to markups and lines carried

Markups over cost (per cent)	Clothing		Shoes		Yard Goods		Furniture and Furnishings		Appliances		Hardware		Drugs	
	Number	Per cent	Number	Per cent	Number	Per cent	Number	Per cent	Number	Per cent	Number	Per cent	Number	Per cent
0–19	2	1.5	4	6.1	3	4.6	2	2.9	4	9.3	2	4.0	1	2.0
20–29	43	32.6	19	28.8	24	36.4	10	14.5	4	9.3	11	22.0	5	10.2
30–39	32	24.2	16	24.2	25	37.9	17	24.6	10	23.3	15	30.0	18	36.7
40–49	11	8.3	11	16.7	7	11.6	7	10.1	2	4.7	9	18.0	8	16.3
50–59	22	16.7	11	16.7	4	6.1	12	17.4	9	20.9	8	16.0	11	22.5
60–79	13	9.9	3	4.6	1	1.5	13	18.8	7	16.3	2	4.0	4	8.2
80–99	—	—	1	1.5	—	—	7	10.1	6	14.0	—	—	1	2.0
100	9	6.8	1	1.5	2	3.0	1	1.5	1	2.3	3	6.0	1	2.0

Table 49   Percentage of sales for cash or on credit to consumers,
by lines handled and by area

	Cloth-ing	Shoes	Yard goods	Furni-ture and furnish-ings	Appli-ances	Hard-ware	Drugs
Immediate cash payment							
San Juan area	83.1	89.0	76.8	58.2	35.6	86.6	86.2
Ponce, Mayaguez	74.0	72.6	75.8	43.9	39.5	66.6	72.5
Market towns	84.3	79.1	82.9	50.2	25.1	83.9	71.2
Rural towns	69.2	80.6	73.0	51.0	12.5	71.0	68.5
Average	77.4	80.1	77.0	51.7	27.8	78.7	73.9
Installment							
San Juan area	—	1.0	—	13.6	51.9	0.3	—
Ponce, Mayaguez	1.9	5.6	3.6	43.3	46.4	10.6	—
Market towns	3.8	2.6	4.5	36.4	63.2	2.7	4.8
Rural towns	6.5	3.5	2.5	32.5	77.5	—	6.2
Average	3.2	3.3	3.0	30.2	60.1	2.4	4.4
Other charge accounts							
San Juan area	16.9	10.0	23.2	28.2	12.5	13.2	13.8
Ponce, Mayaguez	24.0	21.8	20.4	12.3	14.1	22.7	21.6
Market towns	11.9	18.2	12.6	13.4	11.6	13.4	24.0
Rural towns	24.4	15.9	24.5	16.5	10.0	29.0	25.3
Average	19.4	16.7	20.0	18.1	12.0	18.9	21.6

sales are made in this way. Installment purchases of furniture are also more general than regular charge accounts. These provide a means of budgeting payments, and facilitate the reclaiming of the item if payments are not made.

In general cash payments are more customary in the San Juan area; in the rural towns there is a stronger reliance on credit. This, in turn, is related to the lower per capita income in the rural areas, and the dependence on irregular, seasonal wages.

With only a few exceptions all stores sold some of their goods for cash. In clothing, hardware, shoes, yard goods, and drugs, 60 per cent or more of the stores sold between 76 and 100 per cent of their goods for cash. Less than 15 per cent of the stores selling clothing and yard goods sold over 50 per cent of their goods on credit, and less than 10 per cent of the stores selling shoes, hardware, or drugs sold over 50 per cent of their goods on credit. By contrast, over half of the stores handling appliances made 76 to 100 per cent of their appliance sales on an installment basis, and an additional 10 per cent made between 76 and 100 per cent of their sales on charge account basis.

There was no definite relationship between volume of sales and credit, except in appliances and furniture and furnishings. Here the greater proportion was sold for cash in the stores with the lower volume of sales. In the case of furniture and furnishings, sales in such stores are mainly of small household supplies that would normally be purchased for cash. In appliances, the stores with the lower volume of sales are also selling the smaller appliances and also supply some radio parts and service. This again, as might be expected, is predominately a cash business.

Many firms recognize the higher costs of credit sales and place a premium on cash purchases by offering a 10 to 15 per cent discount to a customer paying cash. This is a device employed frequently by firms wishing to expand their sales without incurring the increased cost of operations resulting from credit sales.

Source of Supply

In contrast with food marketing in Puerto Rico, much of the merchandise in the non-food lines is supplied directly by the manufacturer to the retail firm. Only in yard goods was less than 25 per cent of the goods purchased from the manufacturer. In clothing, over 40 per cent was supplied direct. Many of the purchases from the manufacturer were from continental United States concerns. This was particularly the case for drugs, appliances, and shoes. (See Table 50.)

In clothing and furniture, the firms in the San Juan area, Ponce, and Mayaguez purchased a smaller percentage of their goods direct from the manufacturer than did the firms in the market towns. This is because many of the suppliers of the former firms are continental United States manufacturers. The suppliers of the market towns, however, are more commonly the small manufacturers located in or near the market towns. For example, Aguadilla is a center of furniture manufacturing and Mayaguez and Bayamón centers for clothing manufacturing.

Non-food products are commonly handled on the island by manufacturers' representatives who travel around the island and send in the orders obtained to the sales office in the States. The merchandise is then shipped direct to the purchaser. The products of the local clothing and furniture manufacturers are frequently distributed in the same way. The wholesaling functions are thus being assumed by the manufacturer and fewer wholesalers are needed on the island.

For firms selling less than $5,000 per year, direct purchases from the manufacturers were of minor importance except in the case of clothing stores and drugstores. In clothing the small store can purchase from local manufacturers of work and children's clothing. Drugstores

Table 50 Percentage of sales by source of supply, lines carried, and sales class

	Yearly sales (dollars)						
	Less than 5,000	5,000 to 9,999	10,000 to 24,999	25,000 to 49,999	50,000 to 99,999	Over 100,000	Average
Clothing							
Manufacturers salesmen	26.0	53.8	65.5	48.0	75.0	23.3	40.7
Own buyer[a]	8.9	2.2	3.5	13.6	—	1.7	6.7[b]
Wholesaler	65.0	44.0	26.3	30.0	13.8	75.0	50.6
Broker	—	—	4.7	8.4	11.3	—	1.9
Shoes							
Manufacturers salesmen	—	41.9	39.8	28.3	35.8	16.7	22.8
Own buyer[a]	4.5	—	—	5.6	15.0	58.3	8.7
Wholesaler	95.5	57.5	59.2	66.1	49.2	25.0	68.3
Broker	—	0.6	1.0	—	—	—	0.2
Yard goods							
Manufacturers salesmen	—	10.3	27.5	—	42.5	—	7.3
Own buyer[a]	—	11.8	6.3	20.0	17.5	33.3	7.3
Wholesaler	100.0	77.9	53.8	76.0	40.0	—	80.5
Broker	—	—	12.5	4.0	—	66.7	4.8
Furniture and furnishings							
Manufacturers salesmen	4.1	36.5	58.4	71.8	66.7	29.2	36.8
Own buyer[a]	3.5	8.1	9.1	18.1	6.7	51.7	12.0[c]
Wholesaler	88.0	55.4	32.5	10.1	26.7	19.2	49.8
Broker	4.3	—	—	—	—	—	1.4
Appliances							
Manufacturers salesmen	1.0	26.0	21.7	35.7	50.0	43.5	23.5
Own buyer[a]	9.5	—	15.0	—	2.5	—	5.8[d]
Wholesaler	89.5	74.0	63.3	64.3	47.5	56.5	70.7
Broker	—	—	—	—	—	—	—
Hardware							
Manufacturers salesmen	7.1	9.2	33.7	23.5	49.7	89.3	21.9
Own buyer[a]	—	4.6	18.3	7.3	16.3	8.3	6.5
Wholesaler	92.9	86.2	31.3	66.5	34.0	2.3	69.0
Broker	—	—	16.7	2.7	—	—	2.6
Drugs							
Manufacturers salesmen	48.4	36.0	24.1	22.0	30.0	—	32.2
Own buyer[a]	—	—	1.5	—	25.0	—	2.5
Wholesaler	51.6	64.0	74.4	78.0	45.0[e]	—	65.4
Broker	—	—	—	—	—	—	—

[a] Applies to firms sending own buyer to negotiate directly with manufacturer.
[b] Includes 3.4 per cent purchased direct from firm's own factory.
[c] Includes 1.6 per cent purchased direct from firm's own factory.
[d] Includes 2.3 per cent purchased through retailers' purchasing association.
[e] Includes firm selling over $100,000.

similarly purchase through the local outlets which are subsidiaries of the continental firms.

The services of brokers are rarely used. This requires normally a large volume of sales to be profitable for the two parties. Brokers achieved importance only in the sample firms selling over $10,000 annually. They were used most commonly in yard goods where mill ends and out-of-season stocks are handled. Even in yard goods, however, purchases from brokers accounted for less than 5 per cent of total purchases.

Because of the practice of the manufacturers of awarding exclusive agencies in various products, it becomes necessary for the individual store to deal with several manufacturers or several wholesalers to supply the various needs of the store for different brands of appliances, different styles of clothes, or patterns of material. This breaks up the already small purchases required by the smaller-volume stores, and it is most unusual for a store to be in a position to take advantage of quantity discounts. Quantity discounts appeared most frequently in drug lines, where slightly over 25 per cent of the firms were offered quantity discounts. These firms commonly stock the pharmaceutical products of only one or a few major drug concerns. Quantity discounts were offered most rarely in yard goods, where only 3 per cent of the stores selling yard goods reported that they were offered quantity discounts on their purchases. In the other lines between 10 and 18 per cent of the stores reported that they were offered quantity discounts.

While the number of stores offering quantity discounts is small, the number of stores that took advantage of these discounts is even smaller. Less than 15 per cent of the stores handling drugs took advantage of the discounts, and less than 10 per cent took advantage of the discounts in the other lines. The most common discounts offered were 2 and 5 per cent.

Terms of Purchase

The substantial use of credit offered by the wholesalers explains in part the low investment necessary for many of the firms engaged in retailing on the island. This policy of financing purchases through the supplier reduces the amount of working capital which it is necessary for the retailer to maintain since he is to some extent operating on the capital of the wholesaler. He can count on selling a certain proportion of the goods purchased before the bill falls due and paying for the invoiced goods with the actual returns from their sale.

Over 50 per cent of the firms handling each line paid for none of their purchases with cash, and in no instance did more than 20 per cent of the firms pay for 76 to 100 per cent of their purchases within ten days. The most common terms extended by the suppliers were thirty days or sixty days. Goods received on consignment played an important role only in the sales of appliances, where almost 40 per cent of the firms made some purchases on consignment, and almost 30 per cent made between 76 and 100 per cent of their purchases on consignment.

A general charge account with the supplier is quite common among the stores with lower sales volumes. Many of the storekeepers said that they ordered as they needed goods, and paid at the end of a month or two months or whenever they had the funds for payment. There seemed to be no set limit to the amount ordered in this manner, and between 25 and 30 per cent of the small firms selling clothing, yard goods, shoes, and furniture and furnishings made common use of this method of purchase. It was particularly important in purchases of yard goods where almost one-third of the total sales were made on open charge account.

The pattern of substantial cash purchases in the smallest sales class and recurring large cash purchases in the largest sales categories would seem to indicate a dual consideration in cash purchases. It is likely that cash payment is required of the smallest firms, whose credit position might be considered dubious by the supplier. In the largest sales classes cash purchases regain their importance as the firms with sufficient capital are able to take advantage of cash discounts and maintain a strong credit position by early settlement of bills.

Cash discounts were offered more generally than were quantity discounts, but the practice of using the suppliers as a source of credit meant that little advantage was taken of such savings. Cash discounts were offered most frequently in drugs, where almost 70 per cent of the firms were offered cash discounts on some of their purchases, and almost 60 per cent were offered a discount on 90 to 100 per cent of their purchases. Less than 50 per cent of the firms took advantage of the discounts, and of the twenty-three firms who did take some cash discounts almost one-third did so on less than 10 per cent of their purchases.

About 60 per cent of the clothing stores were offered discounts, and between 30 and 50 per cent of the other firms were offered cash discounts. Between 25 and 35 per cent of these firms were offered cash discounts on 90 to 100 per cent of their purchases. However, as in the case of drugs, no more than 30 per cent of the firms took advantage of the cash discount.

The most common cash discount offered was 2 per cent, but, in clothing particularly, discounts of from 3 to 5 per cent and over were not uncommon.

Transportation of goods follows a fairly uniform pattern reflecting the source of supply. A large proportion of the goods comes in by ocean steamer and then is delivered either by hired truck or by the supplier's truck. Only in the case of furniture and furnishings and appliances was a significant proportion of the merchandise picked up by a truck belonging to the purchaser. In these lines the possession of a truck is essential for delivery of sales, and it is thus available for handling supplies.

Rural areas rely more heavily on hired transportation, as normally the store is too small to own a truck or car, and distributors may not service the area. The common practice is to have the goods delivered by *público* or express or, if the items are large enough, to rent a truck for the one occasion.

12

THE WHOLESALING OF

NON-FOOD PRODUCTS

The wholesaler of non-food products plays a markedly different role from that of the food wholesaler. Only a small proportion of food products are purchased direct from the continental supplier by food retailers, and a substantial proportion of the goods pass through the hands of more than one local wholesaler. As noted in preceding chapters a large proportion of the non-food products are ordered direct by retailers from the continental United States through salesmen or catalogues. This, of course, reduces the importance of the local wholesaler. According to the Census for 1949, the retail sales of the lines considered in this study was $112.5 million. The wholesalers of the same types of goods sold only $31.7 million worth of goods in that same year.[1]

The Sample Studied

In 1949, approximately 116 wholesalers were listed by the Census of Business as handling apparel and dry goods, furniture and furnishings, electrical goods, hardware, and drugs. This does not include agents and brokers which comprise a separate Census category. Choosing a sample of wholesalers for detailed study presented many of the same problems encountered in the study of retailers. Here again for establishing categories the Bureau of the Census definitions were used. These definitions presented certain difficulties for present purposes. Thus wholesalers of electrical goods as defined by the Census include firms selling larger commercial equipment, wiring supplies, and elec-

---

[1] A firm is considered a wholesaler if more than half its sales are to retailers or other wholesalers. It is classified according to the line in which the largest volume of its sales are made.

trical construction materials as well as appliances in which we are here interested. Hardware wholesalers as defined by the Census include firms handling exclusively such commercial equipment as plumbing and heating supplies, or air conditioning units. These were excluded from the present study. Finally, wholesalers of furniture and furnishings are not listed separately in the Census.

Several types of wholesalers operate on the island. There are small firms scattered around the island who purchase from importers and supply nearby retailers. In San Juan are the manufacturers' agents and salesmen, brokers, and large importing wholesalers. Differences in the functions which these distributors perform naturally affect the policies and operating costs of the firms. To avoid having replies reflect the variety of services offered rather than the controlled variables of volume of sales and lines handled, the present study is confined to firms offering substantially the same services of assembling goods, storage, financing, and distribution to retailers. Those selling apparel and dry goods and hardware received everything in their own warehouses; those selling drugs and electrical goods had about 5 per cent of their sales sent direct from the manufacturer to the customer. In furniture and furnishings about one-third of the orders were delivered direct to the customers from the factory, probably because of the large unit purchases and the practice of ordering from samples shown by the wholesalers.

To establish the universe from which the sample was drawn municipal licensing lists for wholesalers and manufacturing wholesalers were available. However, as in the case of the retailers, these could not be considered complete or accurate. Nevertheless, lists for the whole island were studied, and all firms which could be wholesalers of non-food products were entered in a master file.

From the replies on the retail questionnaires regarding the source of supply of their merchandise, additional names were obtained and these were added to the master file. The names were then divided according to the *municipios*. All *municipios* with any listing of wholesalers were visited. The firms were visited, asked what products they sold and what per cent they sold to retailers or consumers. They were also asked to supply the names of other wholesalers who might be operating in the area.

Many of the firms on the original list were dropped, either because they were selling primarily food products, had gone out of business because of death, illness, or retirement, or were primarily retail outlets. Out of approximately seven hundred firms interviewed only two hundred were actually non-food wholesalers or manufacturing wholesalers.

The list of wholesalers obtained from this survey was then compared with shipping lists of importers and with available government records. A few additional names were found. The compilation is therefore substantially complete, and any significant omissions are probably in the category of agents and manufacturers' representatives in the San Juan area.

Table 51 gives a comparison of the survey results with the findings

Table 51   Distribution of wholesalers, by lines handled and by area in census, survey, and sample

Type of wholesaler	San Juan area			Ponce and Mayaguez			Market and rural towns		
	Census[a]	Survey	Sample	Census[a]	Survey	Sample	Census[a]	Survey	Sample
Dry goods and apparel	31	67	2	16	20	7	16	6	4
Furniture and furnishings	—	10	2	—	1	—	—	3	3
Electrical goods	9	18	3	3	—	—	2	—	—
Hardware	3	11	—	—	3	2	5	1	1
Drugs	26	33	5	3	9	3	2	6	4

[a] Does not include agents and brokers.
Census figures are for 1949. Survey and sample figures for 1951–52.

of the United States Census of Business for Puerto Rico. The discrepancies in numbers do not necessarily indicate a substantial error of enumeration of wholesalers. They may be attributed in large measure to the inexactness of the categories of agents and brokers in the Census where no distinction is made between food and non-food firms, as well as to the changes which have occurred since 1949 when the Census was taken.

The sample of wholesalers selected for study was chosen specifically to include the various sized firms and the different areas of the island. Since the majority of firms are concentrated in San Juan, a proportionately higher per cent of the firms in smaller towns are included in order to provide regional representation.

Thirteen firms selling dry goods and apparel were selected, five firms selling furniture and furnishings, four selling electrical appliances, three selling hardware, and thirteen selling drugs. In each line there is a range of sales volumes. Of the thirty-eight firms originally chosen for the wholesalers' sample, only one appliances wholesaler did not cooperate fully and is not tabulated. In addition, one clothing wholesaler interviewed was now found to sell over 50 per cent of his merchandise at retail and therefore was considered a retailer and dropped from the sample. One wholesale druggist was unable to give information concerning expenses.

Although the number of firms in the sample for each of the lines considered is small and therefore averages may be misleading in some respects, there is enough consistency in the replies to show the general outlines of wholesaling operations. Strict comparisons with the Census are misleading, for the sample was not chosen as a random sample which would reflect the characteristics of the universe precisely, but rather was chosen to illustrate the various sizes, types, and locations of firms. Beyond these criteria, however, there was no attempt to choose firms which were unusually successful, well known, or in any way exceptional. In other words, there was no control over variables other than size, type, and location.[2]

As with retailers, some wholesalers carried more than one line of goods, for example, both hardware and electrical goods. Therefore, the sales of a hardware wholesaler (which might include a small proportion of electrical goods) are not the same thing as the sales of hardware for that firm. Similarly in the averages, sales for hardware firms represent sales of all products they handle, not just the sales of hardware. Firms are classified according to the predominate line.

Size of Firms

Sales by the individual firms ranged from a low of $30,000 to a high of $3,000,000. The average sales of all the firms considered was $392,944, ranging from a low average of $199,600 in furniture and furnishings to $660,000 in electrical goods. Of the thirty-six firms in the sample, three (8 per cent) sold less than $50,000 per year, and nine firms (25 per cent) sold more than $500,000. The Census in 1949–50 reported fourteen firms (14.1 per cent) selling less than $50,000 and seventeen (17.2 per cent) selling more than $500,000. (See Table 52.)

The average sales figures for the wholesalers in the sample and for Puerto Rican and continental United States firms as reported in the Census are given in Table 53. In almost every instance the sample averages were larger than those given in the Census for Puerto Rico. With the exception of wholesale druggists all averages for United States firms exceeded those in Puerto Rico.

As with retailers, firms supplying drugs at wholesale usually concentrated on that one line. In shoes also there was a tendency for the firms to carry only one line. About half of all the firms considered

---

[2] Statistics are offered in many instances for all wholesale firms taken together, for the tabulation of the small sample would otherwise reveal information concerning individual firms.

Table 52   Percentages of firms and yearly volume of sales for wholesalers, by sales class, in Sample, in 1949 Census of Business of Puerto Rico, and in 1948 United States Census of Business

Yearly sales (dollars)	Sample		Puerto Rico		United States	
	Per cent of firms	Per cent of sales	Per cent of firms	Per cent of sales	Per cent of firms	Per cent of sales
Under 50,000	8.3	0.7	14	1.6	20.6	0.9
50,000– 99,999	16.7	3.2	12	2.9	15.5	2.0
100,000–499,999	50.0	31.6	57	39.7	41.1	18.5
Over 500,000	25.0	64.4	17	55.7	22.8	78.5

Table 53   Number of firms and average volume of sales, by type of wholesaler in Sample, in 1949 Census of Business of Puerto Rico, and in 1948 United States Census of Business

Type of wholesaler	Sample		Puerto Rico		United States	
	Number	Average sales (dollars)	Number	Average sales (dollars)	Number	Average sales (dollars)
Apparel and dry goods	12	210,333	63	176,695	11,090	372,996
Furniture and furnishings[a]	5	199,600	—	—	3,471	348,916
Electrical goods	3	660,000	14	666,886	4,720	826,638
Hardware	3	525,667	8	158,438	5,793	651,507
Drugs	13	543,615	31	450,936	1,883	269,722

[a] Not classified separately in 1949 Census of Business of Puerto Rico.

carried some clothing or yard goods, and almost half of the firms also carried furniture and furnishings.

Much greater stability than in the case of retail firms was evidenced by the number of years which the wholesale firms have been in business. None of the firms chosen had been in business for less than three years. Over 75 per cent of the firms had been in business over fifteen years. There was no evident correlation between volume of sales and the number of years in business.

Employment and Selling Policies

As might be assumed, the average number of workers employed in the various wholesale firms increased with increasing volume of sales.

There was a consistent increase through all five sales classes for the three types of workers—sales, office, and warehouse employees—listed in the questionnaire. In the lowest sales class an average of between two and three employees was necessary to discharge the wholesaling functions. In the largest firms, those selling over $500,000 a year, an average of about thirty employees was used with about fourteen on the office staff, nine in the warehouse, and about seven working directly on sales.

There was a great variation in employment according to the lines handled. Warehouse workers were used most extensively in appliance firms which also had the largest average number of employees. This does not reflect inefficient use of labor, however, since the average volume of sales was greatest in appliance firms. The average number of salesmen employed was about three to five for all the lines handled, the greatest differences coming in the requirements of office and warehouse help. Furniture and furnishings firms which had the largest proportion of their sales shipped direct to the customer, had, not surprisingly, the smallest average number of warehouse personnel. Between five and seven employees were used in furniture and furnishings and apparel, about twelve for hardware, and twenty employees were used in the appliance and drug firms. (See Table 54.)

Table 54   Average number of employees and average sales per worker, by type of wholesaler

Type of wholesaler	Number of firms	Average number sales employees	Average number office employees	Average number warehouse employees	Average total employees	Average yearly sales per worker
Apparel and dry goods	12	3.2	1.9	1.8	6.9	$29,549
Furniture and furnishings	5	2.6	1.8	0.6	5.0	39,920
Electrical goods	3	4.0	7.7	9.0	20.7	31,884
Hardware	3	4.3	3.3	4.3	12.5	42,053
Drugs	13	5.5	9.4	4.2	19.1	37,000

The average volume of sales per worker increased throughout the sales classes except for a slight decrease in the highest sales class. The average volume of sales per worker in the firms selling less than $50,000 per year was $14,879, and was $33,767 for firms with sales of over $500,000.

The volume of sales per worker varied from $29,549 in apparel to

$42,053 in hardware. In appliances the sales were $31,884, and the higher sales per worker of $37,000 and $39,920 were obtained in drugs and furniture and furnishings respectively. These figures are at least two and three times greater than the average sales per worker in the retail stores.

Just over half of the firms interviewed offered discounts to their customers. In almost every instance this was a cash discount. Only three firms, selling between $100,000 and $250,000 per year, offered quantity discounts. By contrast, sixteen firms offered some cash discount to their customers. The terms varied greatly, though the most common terms offered were 2 per cent cash, 2 per cent ten days or 2 per cent thirty days. A 3 per cent discount was offered in some instances.

A larger proportion of the firms in the higher sales classes offered discounts to their customers. Only about 20 per cent of the firms selling less than $100,000 per year offered discounts, but of those firms selling over $100,000, more than 60 per cent offered a discount.

Discounts were offered by less than half of the apparel and dry goods, hardware, or electrical goods wholesalers. Three-quarters of the wholesale druggists offered cash or quantity discounts. Drug firms also offered the most generous terms, usually 2 per cent ten days or 2 per cent thirty days, while furniture and apparel firms usually offered discounts for immediate cash payment only.

Advertising was commonly done by about half of the firms studied. As with retailers the most popular advertising media were first the radio and then the newspaper. Sound trucks were used occasionally by some firms. Most of this advertising is brand advertising directed to the ultimate consumer. Promotion with retailers is confined to the sales force.

Although almost all firms financed their operations primarily through their own resources, many of the firms interviewed have at some time had occasion to borrow money. Local banks were used for this almost exclusively. Occasionally collateral was offered, but this was exceptional. The usual rate which applied to loans, whether for working capital or for new construction or expansion, was 6 to 8 per cent, though for firms considered a good risk by the banks the rates were sometimes as low as 3 to 5 per cent.

In discussing the problems of expansion with the wholesalers, about 60 per cent of them stated that they would like to increase the size of their businesses. The most frequently cited obstacles were a lack of capital for expansion, difficulties encountered in obtaining additional workers and supervising the larger staff, and limited space for expansion in the present quarters combined with existing high building costs.

Twelve firms mentioned insufficient purchasing power and too much competition among the present firms to permit expanded sales for any of them.

One of the wholesale firms stated that the major obstacle to expansion was in selling to small retailers on credit. Since the costs of handling credit sales are high it was not to their advantage to expand further into credit sales. Moreover, this ties up the wholesaler's capital and leaves him without the flexibility which would make for more efficient operations.

Many of the wholesalers felt that their present space was adequate for at least half again the present volume of sales and that an increase in sales would increase profits because of the spreading of overhead costs. Although few of the firms ever took advantage of the quantity discounts offered to them, several mentioned that this would be a source of advantage if they could expand their present volume of sales. More efficient operations were anticipated at a larger volume of sales, and one firm also hoped to obtain exclusive representation of additional lines.

Present business earnings, however, were being channeled into expansion of either inventory or building and equipment by less than one-third of the firms interviewed. Other firms were purchasing real estate, paying dividends, or paying off debts.

Investment

The information on investment, as in the case of the retailers, was the least reliable of the information obtained from the wholesalers. The data were subject to wide variation and the variations were not always directly correlated with either line or volume of sales. Many of the firms did not, for example, have an established policy for inventory control. Though some records were available, it is probable that their accuracy is questionable. Also inflated inventory values may come from not writing off obsolete stock.

Inventories ranged from an average of $5,000 in one of the smaller firms to over $400,000 in the largest firms. Taken broadly there was an increase in the average size of inventory with an increased volume of sales. But there were exceptions to this in every line.

There was, however, a definite pattern by lines, with lower inventories maintained in furniture and furnishings (at least in part because of the policy of direct shipment of sales to the customer from the manufacturers), apparel and dry goods, and drugs. Average inventories of about $150,000 and over were held in hardware and electrical goods.

The volume of accounts receivable was more directly correlated with the volume of sales than were inventories, though exhibiting a great range of values. The lowest volumes of accounts receivable were in furniture and furnishings and in dry goods. Six firms reported no accounts receivable, and these were found in almost every sales class. The average of accounts receivable for dry goods was $30,500 and for furniture and furnishings $10,015. In hardware and drugs the average volume of accounts receivable was $33,000 and $50,000 respectively. The highest volume of accounts receivable was reported by the firms handling electrical goods where the average was over $250,000.

To compute total capital, both equipment and building and land values were obtained from the Office of Scientific Assessment. Approximately one-third of these values could not be obtained because action on appeals was pending, the buildings were new and had not yet been assessed, or records were missing from the office.

For the remaining twenty-five firms total capital figures have been computed. The most consistent patterns were in wholesale firms selling furniture and furnishings and drugs. In apparel, average investment by sales classes varied from less than $50,000 to over $400,000, and in electrical goods from less than $100,000 to over $1,200,000.

A more relevant picture was given by the various turnover rates. When all the firms were taken together, the inventory turnover ratio increased through the first four sales classes, from 2.0 to 7.7, and in the highest sales class fell to 4.6.

The turnover ratios showed a more common pattern throughout the lines than did the absolute figures. Table 55 gives the averages for the types of wholesalers, and Table 56 the averages by sales classes, when all the firms are taken together, for inventory ratios, working capital ratios, and total capital ratios.

Expenses

The great number of retail stores to be supplied is an important factor in the operating costs of the various wholesale firms. This particularly affects such costs as delivery, advertising, and credit losses. Tables 57 and 58 give the breakdown of expenditures according to volume of sales and types of wholesalers.

The average gross profits were lowest for apparel wholesalers and highest for wholesale druggists. Wholesalers of electrical goods had the highest expense ratios, due in most part to the higher labor, rent, and advertising costs. The average gross profits had a range of a little over 4½ per cent of sales, and the average total expenses fell within a range of about 5½ per cent. However, high gross profits were not related in these instances to high expenses, and the net profits exhibited a range of almost 6½ per cent.

Table 55   Average yearly inventory, working capital, and
total capital turnover ratios, by type of wholesaler

Type of wholesaler	Inventory turnover	Working capital turnover	Total capital turnover
Apparel and dry goods	3.87	2.90	1.94
Furniture and furnishings	10.16	4.57	2.97
Electrical goods	3.85	3.26	1.34
Hardware	3.90	3.50	1.35
Drugs	5.23	3.45	2.12

Table 56   Average yearly inventory, working capital, and total capital
turnover ratios for wholesalers, by sales class

Yearly sales (dollars)	Inventory turnover	Working capital turnover	Total capital turnover
Less than 50,000	1.99	1.98	1.47
50,000– 99,999	4.51	3.89	2.17
100,000–249,999	5.73	4.32	2.53
250,000–499,999	7.66	3.45	2.13
Over 500,000	4.64	2.94	1.44

The expenses were computed in the same way as for the retailers. Wages do not include the compensation of the owner, which is included as a part of the net profit. Wage expense was highest for hardware, drugs, and electrical goods wholesalers, those who had the greatest number of employees.

Rents were highest for drugs and electrical goods wholesalers, where there was a larger proportion of San Juan firms. Also some of these firms had joint retail-wholesale outlets, and rents in these instances were also higher. Only six firms owned all their own warehouse and store facilities; four were apparel wholesalers, and two sold furniture and furnishings. (Some firms, however, owned one warehouse and rented another.) Building depreciation is calculated only where the building is owned by the owner of the business and an account for building depreciation occurred in every line except hardware, where no firm owns its own building.[3]

Delivery expenses were highest for wholesalers of furniture and furnishings and apparel. In the former case, this was because of the need for more extensive equipment for each firm, and in the latter case it represents the higher costs of servicing the greater number of

---

[3] Equipment depreciation has not been computed since only a general figure for equipment could be obtained from the Office of Scientific Assessment.

Table 57 Average expenses and profit ratios for wholesalers, by sales class (percentage of total sales)

	Yearly sales (dollars)						
	Less than 50,000	50,000 to 99,999	100,000 to 249,999	250,000 to 599,999	Over 500,000	Total	Average
Number of firms	3	6	10	8	8	35	
Average sales (dollars)	34,667	75,500	183,200	330,000	1,019,500		318,458
Cost of goods sold	71.93	76.77	81.37	82.29	81.44		80.00
Gross profit	28.07	23.23	18.63	17.71	18.56		20.00
Wages	4.30	4.45	5.18	5.14	5.43		5.09
Rents	1.33	0.94	0.73	0.75	0.97		0.88
Utilities	0.19	.17	.25	.17	.23		.21
Delivery	3.77	1.64	.34	.26	.55		.89
Repairs and maintenance	0.32	0.37	.10	.08	.03		.14
Credit losses	.17	.66	.24	.11	.47		.33
Advertising	—	.18	.33	.55	.74		.42
Interest	0.26	.34	.54	.54	.65		.51
Insurance	.36	.28	.56	.32	.57		.44
Dept. Bldg.	.02	.01	.06	.01	.09		.05
Charity	.22	.04	.08	.08	.03		.07
S.S.W.C.[a]	—	.04	.05	.01	.07		.04
Property tax	0.02	.28	.67	.66	.39		.48
Licenses	.43	.16	.19	.10	.06		.15
Acct. fees	—	.21	.25	.17	.19		.19
Supplies	0.18	.23	.06	.04	.16		.12
Other	.33	.93	1.59	1.63	.98		1.24
Net profit	16.30	12.30	7.42	6.79	6.96		8.77

[a] Social Security and Workmen's Compensation.

retail stores selling clothing and dry goods. Credit losses seemed not to be directly correlated with the volume of sales on credit. Relative advertising outlays were highest in those firms which served the larger number of retail stores, and in the lines where brand names are particularly important.

The residual category of expenses represented primarily travel and per diem for salesmen, supplies, general administrative expense, and commissions.

In viewing the breakdown of expenses according to volume of sales, certain patterns emerge. There was a variation of less than 1 per cent in the expenses in the various sales classes. In general, gross profits were highest for the small firms and net profits were also higher. The average net profit of 13.6 per cent in the smallest two categories represented approximately $5,000 per year, and in the highest category the average net profit of 7 per cent represented $53,000 per year.

Table 58   Average expenses and profit ratios for wholesalers, by types of wholesaler (percentage of sales)

	Type of wholesaler				
	Apparel and dry goods	Furniture and furnishings	Electrical goods	Hardware	Drugs
Number of firms	12	5	3	3	12
Average sales (dollars)	210,333	199,600	660,000	525,667	338,917
Cost of goods sold	82.24	79.00	80.72	81.27	77.68
Gross profit	17.76	21.00	19.28	18.73	22.32
Wages	3.73	4.12	6.89	5.83	6.23
Rents	0.73	0.27	1.42	0.94	1.13
Utilities	.15	.24	0.32	.13	0.24
Delivery	1.36	1.42	.33	.63	.40
Repairs and maintenance	0.14	0.34	.04	.07	.10
Credit losses	.32	.14	.31	1.08	.23
Advertising	.14	.08	1.69	0.16	.59
Interest	.71	.62	1.04	.20	.20
Insurance	.48	.26	0.78	.31	.42
Dep. Bldg.	.02	.03	.04	—	.09
Charity	.09	.07	.19	0.08	.03
S.S.W.C.[a]	.03	.03	.04	.04	.05
Property tax	.60	.12	.56	.60	.47
Licenses	.09	.16	.07	.12	.24
Acct. fees	.23	.15	.35	.45	.06
Supplies	.15	.22	.09	.11	.05
Other	1.93	.85	.71	.79	.96
Net profit	6.91	11.88	4.41	7.19	10.82

[a] Social Security and Workmen's Compensation.

Operating expenses expressed as a percentage of total sales for continental United States service wholesalers range from 15 to 22 per cent. The lowest operating expenses were in electrical goods and the highest in drugs. These percentages are universally higher than the percentages for Puerto Rico, but the continental figures include a return to officers of the various corporations and regular salaried managers, although not including the return to owner proprietors. The operating expenses for Puerto Rico do not include any return to owner-managers.

Information by Lines Handled

Between 65 and 97 per cent of the wholesalers' sales in every line were sold to retailers.[4] This averaged 76 per cent for all lines taken together. The wholesalers interviewed sold an average of 13 per cent to other wholesalers. Sales to other wholesalers were most important in drugs, furniture and furnishings, and hardware. No sales were made by the wholesalers of electrical goods to other wholesalers.

Markups varied among the lines and also according to the purchaser of the goods. Table 59 gives the breakdown of this information

Table 59   Percentage markups over cost of goods sold by wholesalers to various customers, by lines handled

Line handled	Retailers	Whole-salers	Con-sumers	Manu-facturers	Peddlers
Clothing	23.6	18.0	51.7	—	25.2
Shoes	18.0	15.0	—	—	—
Yard goods	21.3	17.0	58.3	19.3	30.0
Furniture and furnishings	24.9	20.5	60.0	—	31.5
Electrical goods	22.0	—	70.0	—	—
Hardware	20.0	12.5	48.0	—	—
Drugs	28.7	22.6	45.0	23.5	22.7
Average	24.1	20.0	54.9	21.0	27.1

by the lines handled. Some of the wholesalers interviewed sold everything on a cost-plus-commission basis. Others had a fixed markup and allowed a commission to be added as an extra return to the salesmen. This practice was most common in furniture and furnishings and hardware.

Wholesaler markups on goods sold to other wholesalers averaged about 20 per cent. Sales to retailers carried a markup of approximately 24 per cent. The markups to consumers represented a joint wholesaler-retailer markup, including the approximately 24 per cent average wholesaler markup and the customary 30 per cent retail markup, as noted in the retail study. No definite pattern of markup policy by area was evident, and the average markup to retailers for the firms in each area taken together all fell at about 24 per cent.

Tradition plays the same role in the determination of markups for wholesalers as for retailers. In practically every instance a traditional pricing policy was mentioned as the basis for the determination of selling price. In addition there was some attention paid to the market

[4] It must be remembered that only firms making at least 50 per cent of their sales to retailers were considered to be "wholesalers."

conditions, or "judging the best price" for that particular time. Others estimated a reasonable retail selling price for the article and then figured out the price to the retailer by working backwards from this.

Credit was offered fairly extensively to the various purchasers. Cash payment was most customary in clothing, furniture and furnishings, and hardware; between 45 and 56 per cent of the sales in these lines were for cash within ten days. In shoes sixty-day terms were most common, and thirty days in electrical goods. Over half of the sales of yard goods were made on open charge account, the remainder being cash sales. Ninety-day terms were used by only one firm. On the whole, cash payment was used most often, and the thirty-day, sixty-day, and open charge accounts terms were used approximately equally.

The most common means of delivery for wholesalers was by their own trucks, and this was used by about half of the firms interviewed. Hired trucks were used almost as frequently, and there was some use of the railroad and express services for delivery.

Most of the supplies purchased by the wholesalers came from continental United States manufacturers and wholesalers. The larger firms more often sent representatives to the mainland to do the purchasing, and smaller firms were served by representatives of the continental wholesalers and manufacturers. In general the wholesaler supplier was less important to the larger firms, and no firm selling over $250,000 per month purchased as much as 50 per cent of their goods through wholesalers, continental or local. Only nine wholesalers bought any supplies from local wholesalers or manufacturers, and only about 50 per cent of the purchases of these nine firms were made locally. Purchase by catalogue or sample was used extensively in electrical goods and was also used by firms selling drugs, hardware, furniture and furnishings, and yard goods. (See Table 60.)

Table 60 Percentages of purchases by wholesalers from various sources of supply, by lines carried

| | Direct from manufacturer through | | | |
Lines carried	Manufacturer's Salesman	Own Buyer	Mail Order	Wholesaler
Clothing	61.0	16.0	—	23.0
Shoes	32.5	66.8	—	.8
Yard goods	7.0	28.8	8.3	55.8
Furniture and furnishings	49.1	18.2	4.5	28.2
Electrical goods	20.0	16.7	63.3	—
Hardware	35.0	31.7	16.7	16.7
Drugs	42.8	35.6	8.4	13.1

The credit terms received by the wholesale firms were more generous than the ones they offered. On the average less than one-third of their purchases were made for cash, and over 40 per cent of their purchases were made on thirty-day terms. Sixty-day terms were used for over 20 per cent of the purchases, and only insignificant amounts were purchased on open charge account, consignment, or on ninety-day terms. As indicated in Table 61, there was great variation among the lines in the credit terms received.

Table 61   Percentages of purchases on various credit terms by lines carried

Lines carried	Cash 10 days		30 days		60 days		90 days		Con- signment		Charge account	
Clothing	7	34.5	7	44.2	6	21.3	—		—		—	
Shoes	2	2.8	4	56.3	4	41.0	—		—		—	
Yard goods	4	17.7	6	72.3	2	10.0	—		—		—	
Furniture and furnishings	5	29.1	9	47.0	6	23.9	—		—		—	
Electrical goods	3	63.3	2	33.3	—	—	—		—		1	3.3
Hardware	3	50.0	3	25.0	3	25.0	—		—		—	
Drugs	12	29.3	13	32.3	10	23.9	3	3.8	2	6.9	3	3.9
Total	36		44		31		3		2		4	
Average of 36 stores		31.1		42.6		22.0		1.1		2.0		1.3

Cash discounts were offered to well over half of the wholesale firms and on almost half of the total purchases of the firms. However, even though about one-third of the purchases were made for cash, the cash discount was taken on only about 15 per cent of the purchases of the wholesalers. The percentage terms offered varied greatly, from 1 per cent to 5 per cent, and some of the discounts were offered for payment in ten days or thirty days as well as for immediate cash payment.

About one-fourth of the firms were offered quantity discounts on their purchases, but less than 20 per cent took advantage of the discount offered. Wholesalers in many of the lines were plagued with the same difficulties which prevented the retailers from taking advantage of quantity discounts. To obtain a varied line of merchandise to distribute on the island, they were forced to purchase from a great variety of manufacturers, jobbers, or wholesalers, and could not purchase enough from any one of them to make a quantity discount possible. Ultimately the wholesalers received the quantity discounts on only about 6 per cent of the purchases. This quantity discount ranged from 2 per cent to 20 per cent, with the most generous terms being offered in drugs.

Manufacturing Wholesalers

Local manufacturers often take on the function of a wholesaler in distributing their own goods. Other wholesalers manufacture a few lines — primarily men's work clothes, children's clothes, and furniture — to add to their other merchandise range and to take advantage of government tax exemption policies. Such firms are required to have a wholesaler's license and thus are a recognized part of the distribution system of the island. However, they are frequently small firms and do not keep accurate breakdowns of expenses of manufacturing and wholesaling and could not, therefore, be tabulated with the general wholesalers.

In the survey that was made of the general wholesalers the manufacturing wholesalers were interviewed and listed separately. Approximately sixty firms were surveyed and seventeen of these were chosen for the sample. There is no comparable category in the Census for these firms, which are probably classified as manufacturers according to their primary occupation.

The manufacturing wholesaler represents in part an attempt, commonly encountered on the mainland, to simplify the distribution system and to lower costs by eliminating middlemen. But some of these firms are remnants of an underdeveloped distribution system in which functions have not as yet been differentiated. The twelve clothing manufacturers and five furniture manufacturers who were interviewed in this study gave some indication of both characteristics.

The average annual volume of sales for the firms interviewed was $210,624 for clothing manufacturers and $148,000 for the furniture manufacturers (sales and expense information from one furniture firm is lacking, and the averages there represent only four firms). The firms were in general well established — the average age of the furniture manufacturing firms being almost eight years, and that of the clothing manufacturers over fifteen.

Few employees were used for sales, office, and warehouse jobs, and most of the employment was concentrated in strictly factory occupations. In clothing this included a good many domestic workers for finishing and hand work. The average number of home and factory workers in clothing firms was over sixty and about forty-four in the furniture manufacturing firms. About one-sixth of the clothing workers are domestic employees.

The clothing manufacturers' average gross profit was 40.5 per cent, the net being 19.1 per cent. Of the 21.4 per cent expense ratio, 15.4 per cent represented wages. The furniture manufacturers reported an average gross profit of 58.5 per cent and a net profit of 21.7 per cent. As in the case of the clothing manufacturers, over three-fourths of the expenses were wages.

13

THE CONTEXT OF POLICY

In a sense, Puerto Rico can be thought of as exporting sugar and a very few processed goods in exchange for its food and most of its consumer goods. The distribution system is relied upon, therefore, for a far greater proportion of consumer goods than in more primitive and more nearly self-sufficient underdeveloped areas. Because of the comparative poverty of the island, at least by mainland standards, a costly distribution system is also a luxury which the people of Puerto Rico can ill afford. This is especially true for an inefficient food market-ing system. About 40 per cent of all consumer expenditures go for food — compared with about 20 per cent on the mainland; this per-centage is, of course, considerably greater for the lower-income families of the island. Under these circumstances, improvement of the market-ing system, particularly the food marketing system, has a high priority in the island's development program. Before suggesting the lines along which such improvement might proceed, let us review the salient features of the situation with which we are dealing.

The wholesalers and retailers who distribute the consumer goods are typically far smaller firms than are common on the mainland. The food retailers' annual sales average less than $12,000, compared with about $62,000 on the mainland. The usual food store is extremely small, with less than 250 square feet of floor space. The meager equip-ment and furnishings afford questionable sanitation. The bulk of the stores are owner-operated with some unpaid help from family members, although paid clerks are found, of course, in the larger stores. The majority of sales in both rural and urban areas are on credit, and personal relationships based largely on this credit are relied upon by the retailer to assure him customers. The wholesalers' practice of attracting retail customers by extending credit, plus the lack of price competition at retail assures easy entry into food retailing. As a result, there is a steady and large influx of untrained personnel into the grocery business. Modern management methods are unknown to the great majority of these newcomers. They compete not on the basis of price but rather on credit and, to a considerable degree, location. The one chain organization does not engage in price competition in the manner of chain stores on the mainland.

Wholesaler firms are less significantly small, reporting about two-thirds the annual volume of sales of their mainland counterparts in 1949. Price competition is considerably keener between wholesalers than between retailers, but credit from his supplier is as important to the retailer as it is to the consumer. Exclusive agent agreements are relied upon by many wholesalers to assure a minimum volume of sales, and personal relationships between wholesaler and retailer, growing out of the credit service, are again important.

Entry into wholesaling is not especially difficult. It is common for the successful and ambitious retailer to expand into wholesaling rather than into multiple retail outlet operations. This involves fewer personnel and other management problems and is motivated also by the greater prestige of wholesaling.

The conditions of entry, the attitude toward price competition, and the reluctance to expand are the outstanding causes of a high-cost food distribution system. The mass of very small and inefficient operators, although they account for a relatively small proportion of total sales, nevertheless set a price level which rewards the more efficient retailers with handsome margins. The 23 per cent average gross margin at retail is in sharp contrast with the 16 per cent and 13 per cent averages for mainland independents and chains, respectively. The average wholesale gross profit of 15 per cent compares with a gross of about 9 per cent for mainland wholesalers, but the island wholesale margin may be overstated.

The existing market structure both at wholesale and at retail persists because of restraints on the ability of the typical firm to expand its sales volume. The lack of familiarity with modern management methods makes it difficult for the owner to increase his business with a minimum increase in his own contribution of time and effort. Retailers readily suggest that a doubling of sales would require twice as much work, which is an unappealing prospect.

Management attitudes and behavior in Puerto Rico are profoundly affected by tradition and by cultural values which are slow to change. Imagination and initiative are not commonly stimulated in agricultural economies, and Puerto Rico appears to be no exception. Among the food retailers, the great majority of merchants are using a traditional system of establishing markups, regardless of the competition. A live-and-let-live attitude marks their relationships with other retailers. They are reluctant to introduce new products as well as new techniques of merchandising. Knowledge of bookkeeping methods is extremely limited, so the retailer has little idea of how he might handle, for example, a branch store. His attitude toward his employees frequently resembles the paternalism which characterized the coffee *haciendas* and the cane plantations of a generation ago. At the same time he is conscious of his prestige as a businessman as contrasted with his customers. This is sometimes paired with a distrust of untried employees which excuses the low wage which in turn excuses pilferage by the clerk which justifies the low wage.

The above generalizations are directed to food retailing. They can also be extended to the retailer of non-food consumer goods, except that in these enterprises the attitude toward price competition is of a somewhat different sort. The druggist considers himself in a position similar to that of the grocer, and he considers price advertising to be relatively ineffective as well as predatory. The other non-food retailers, however, condone price advertising and special "sales" as long as the purpose of the sale is to move the dead stock. Constant price competition even in non-food distribution is considered unfair.

Here and there a more aggressive type of entrepreneur has appeared. Perhaps fifteen or twenty Puerto Rican retail firms, in food and non-food lines, can be described as seriously engaged in price competition as a regular practice. A very few branch stores also exist. But it is apparent, nevertheless, that with these few exceptions, the men engaged in food and non-food marketing in Puerto Rico think in terms of single-unit firms competing on the basis of service rather than price and operating at a small volume with a comparatively high gross-profit margin.

Many characteristics of the Puerto Rican distribution system are controlled by the buying methods of the public. One of the most troublesome problems stems from the use of credit. Because of the seasonality of the cane industry many families have little or no income for the last six months of the year. Accordingly they look to the grocer as a source of credit. The retailer in turn must buy on credit from his suppliers. Credit from suppliers is used all along the distribution channel so that it is not uncommon for importers to forego cash discount terms from the mainland exporters. The cost of extending credit is, of course, hidden in the final price of food and the consumer does not know how much the credit is actually costing him.

Some additional credit buying, particularly by urban consumers, is a matter of habit rather than of necessity. Urban food retailers long ago made this a regular service and by now their clientele is thoroughly accustomed to it. This, in turn, is related to another relatively costly service, that of delivery. Ordering by telephone, giving the order to the store's messenger (as well as sending the maid to do the shopping) encourage credit buying. The demand for delivery service in the larger towns and cities is partially attributable to *la dignidad* (dignity or position in life); for the Puerto Rican housewife of the middle- and upper-income classes, shopping and parcel-carrying are somewhat unfashionable. An observable fondness for "conspicuous consumption" of services may also contribute to the demand for delivery of goods. Other factors are also of importance. Automobile ownership is still limited by mainland standards. Furthermore, an insular "closing law" forbids food stores to operate after six in the evening on any date, so if the family breadwinner uses the car during working hours it is not available for a trip to the store. Finally, comparatively cramped living quarters even among the middle-income families means limited storage space. Delivery mitigates the burden of frequent buying.

The demand for locational convenience is of special significance not only in low-income rural areas but in high-income areas as well. This, inevitably, increases the number of outlets. Low-income consumers unable to afford telephones or transportation must be serviced by retail outlets within easy walking distance. Moreover, daily food purchases are the rule for such consumers both because of their lack of refrigeration space and because of their meager incomes. Since the daily purchases are very small, they require more selling time and more packaging expense on items sold from bulk and wrapped at the counter than if larger and less frequent purchases were customary. Some (although by no means all) of the cost of retailing in Puerto Rico is thus traceable to the low and seasonal income of the Puerto Rican consumer.

Proposals for improving the marketing of consumer goods in Puerto Rico must be designed with the foregoing economic and cultural factors well in mind. All communities exhibit opposition to social change. Practices and attitudes which have grown out of an economic and social *milieu* of long standing can be so firmly imbedded as to preclude alteration by what seem to be simple and direct measures. History offers many examples of legislated reforms which have failed because this simple fact has been ignored.

Because of the restraints imposed by the environment, reorganization of the distribution system to be successful may have to be gradual. In any case policy must be designed not to force sudden change on an unwilling and resisting system, but rather to establish a context within which movement toward improved efficiency is assured. The object must be to forestall change inimical to greater efficiency and to encourage movement toward lower-cost distribution methods. There is no doubt that steps *can* be taken which will gain some or all of the economies which our analysis in preceding chapters has shown to be intrinsically possible. Change may have to be gradual but it can be definite.

14

MEASURES TO IMPROVE THE EFFICIENCY OF

THE MARKETING SYSTEM: CONSUMER AND

RETAIL EDUCATION

We come now to a consideration of the practical steps that can be taken to improve the marketing system in Puerto Rico — and also to a consideration of some measures which, although they have attractive features, are not recommended. Attention is concentrated first on food marketing for several reasons. Food accounts for a far greater proportion of the consumption expenditures in Puerto Rico than does any non-food product.[1] Moreover, we have not found markups on non-food items to be significantly higher than on the mainland, and certain recent developments in non-food merchandising are clearly in the right direction. Some chain department and clothing stores are beginning to appear; with their development price advertising will become more common. In addition there is the simple fact of the comparative number of retail outlets involved. In contrast with more than 14,000 grocery stores reported in the 1949 Census, only 3,000 retailers were handling *all* of the non-food consumer goods selected for examination in this study.[2]

The policy proposals which follow attempt, directly or indirectly, to diminish the number of food stores in order to increase the average sales volume. This is with a view to reducing excess capacity and making possible the lower, yet profitable, markups that our model

[1] According to the 1949 Census of Business, food sales were more than twice as great as the sales of the apparel and accessories group. Due to the gross under-reporting of sales by grocers, food sales actually must be at least three times as great as apparel and accessory sales.

[2] Chapter XI above.

analysis has shown are possible. With any such development must come a reduction in the number of workers in the distributive trades and this, of course, would appear to portend an increase in unemployment. At the present time employment opportunities on the island are improving, and with continued and accelerating advances of the industrialization program, it would not seem unduly optimistic to hope that many persons moving out of the distributive trades can find more useful employment elsewhere. However, it is important both on humanitarian and practical economic grounds that improvement in the distribution system be paced by an expansion of employment opportunities elsewhere. By providing employment and by increasing incomes, industrialization will also increase the average volume of sales so as to make lower markups profitable. Higher incomes should also ease the credit problem and alter some of the costly buying practices caused by the present low incomes.

Consumer Education

Consumer and retailer education can do much to alter the environment of marketing in Puerto Rico and is an important part of any program to improve the marketing system. At present, four agencies are engaged in consumer education on the island: the Division of Community Education in the Department of Education, the Home Economics Division of the same department, the Agricultural Extension Service of the Department of Agriculture, and the Home Economics department of the University of Puerto Rico.

The Home Economics Division of the Department of Education is in charge of the home economics courses in the junior and senior high schools of the island. One year of home economics is required of all junior high school female students in Puerto Rico; the senior high school home economics offerings are elective and are offered in about fifty of the seventy high schools on the island. One course entitled "Consumers' Problems," offered in five high schools, emphasizes particularly the improvement of buying methods to give the consumer maximum value for price paid. Apparently the emphasis on buying methods in the general home economics courses varies considerably among schools and teachers. In view of the still relatively small proportion of Puerto Rican children in high school, it appears that consumer education reaches only a small segment of the population through the high schools. A still smaller group is enrolled in home economics at the University. In 1952–53, about 190 students were taking this subject, many of whom expected to become teachers of home economics.

Consumer education for those persons not in the schools is handled by the Division of Community Education in the Department of Education and by the Agricultural Extension Service of the Department of Agriculture. The Agricultural Extension Service engages in several types of educational activities. In the summer of 1952 it was operating three information centers in public markets (in Santurce, Ponce, and San Germán) at which centers the use of local produce in season was advertised and demonstrated. The Extension Service also reaches several thousand persons through short courses, meetings, and conferences held for consumers. In these programs the Extension Service has been emphasizing the advantages of local fruits and vegetables in an attempt to improve local diets and to create a better market for such products.

The Division of Community Education in the Department of Education has been in existence for about four years. By means of movies, discussion groups, and the distribution of educational pamphlets in the towns and villages of the island, this division is attempting to teach the Puerto Rican more about his island and to encourage him to improve his lot through his own efforts. Considerable emphasis is placed on voluntary community cooperation as a means of solving community problems rather than appeals to the Commonwealth government for aid.

These consumer education programs reach a very sizable proportion of the population. Any consumer education aimed at improving the efficiency of the distribution of consumer goods should be developed within the framework of present efforts and with a view to making these efforts more effective and comprehensive in their coverage. The most important need is to so adjust the content of the existing programs as to insure that consumer buying practices will exert pressure for improvement in the marketing system.

What sort of education would help improve distributive efficiency in Puerto Rico? Consumers will serve both themselves and the marketing system to the extent that they are (1) conscious of quality and (2) conscious of prices in their purchases of consumer goods. As long as credit plays an important part in determining the buying habits of the Puerto Ricans, there is certain to be considerable indifference as to sources of supply, and the benefits of greater price and quality consciousness will not be fully realized. Some improvement is possible, however, even while a large volume of credit buying continues.

Accordingly, consumer education programs now operating should be redesigned so as to emphasize, wherever possible, price and quality information and their effective use. The Division of Community Education appears to be especially adaptable to this kind of education because it reaches a very large proportion of the population outside the major cities and thus concentrates on the adult population which is in the greatest need of help. All the consumer education work, and the Community Education program in particular, should stress wherever possible the following topics:

(1) The desirability of occasional experimenting among different brands of a food article. Grocers complain that their customers are intensely brand conscious and that as a result new brands are extremely difficult to introduce, even at lower prices. Were experimentation among brands and a knowledge of comparative qualities more common with consumers, the monopolistic position held by some brands would be far more difficult to maintain than it now is.

(2) The advantages of buying food, whenever possible, in the larger packages and cans should be stressed. Worthwhile economies can be achieved by this method, although in some items the economies are more limited than on the mainland because of the practice of some grocers of pricing the larger packages so that the price per ounce is the same regardless of the size of the package.

(3) The high cost of buying on credit should be emphasized. Most Puerto Rican consumers do not now have the alternative of buying their food for less at a cash-and-carry store. However, an increasing number of consumer cooperative stores do provide this alternative and the consumers should be brought to recognize its advantages. The high cost of credit is particularly apparent in Puerto Rico in the market for consumer durable goods, primarily furniture and appliances. Consumers need to be apprised of the very high cost of installment buying.

(4) Price and quality consciousness needs especially to be developed in purchases of cloth and clothing. It is common for the Puerto Rican consumer to favor certain fashionable or otherwise attractive fabrics which do not withstand washing as well as, for example, more durable cottons. The requirements for careful purchasing of both yard goods and ready-made clothing could be stressed to good advantage.

If, by means of such educational programs, the Puerto Rican consumer becomes a better buyer, competition among retailers would grow sharper. If consumers react to good quality at lower prices, retailers will be encouraged to increase their sales volume by meeting such consumer preference—consumer education can increase the elasticity of the demand curve of the individual firm. Price competition will thus become more profitable for the efficient retailer and this will encourage larger-scale operations and a more efficient distribution system.

Retailer Education

In contrast with consumer education, retailer education in Puerto Rico is now conducted on a very limited scale. In 1938, the George-

Deen Act was passed by the United States Congress providing for the appropriation of funds for financing education on distribution in the public schools. In recent years these funds have been reduced, and in fiscal 1953 the Federal appropriation for such education in Puerto Rico amounted only to about $8,600. This money has in the past been used by the Insular Board for Vocational Education, a division of the Department of Education, to help finance cooperative part-time classes for high school students and part-time evening classes for adults. The high school classes have been conducted in San Juan, Ponce, Mayaguez, and Caguas and reached about 270 students during the fiscal year of 1953. These students worked in stores half-time and attended the classes on distribution methods half-time. The classes for adults were held in seventeen communities and reached about 3,900 persons, all of whom were either actively engaged in distribution or were planning to go into the distributive trades.[3] Such subjects as occupational English and Spanish, salesmanship, retail arithmetic, advertising, and human relations were covered. According to the persons in charge of the program, the supply of students always falls short of filling merchants' demands for trained clerks.

In December 1952, the Chamber of Commerce of Puerto Rico was planning a short course in advertising and salesmanship for merchants and their employees. Presumably very few merchants outside the metropolitan San Juan area were able to avail themselves of this program. The Chamber was also taking steps toward a school-work program for the students of business administration at the University of Puerto Rico whereby the interested student would work one or two afternoons each week for a local merchant so that by the time of graduation he would have some experience.

The problem of retailer education is twofold. A vigorous retailer education program might improve rather quickly the typical retailer's knowledge of accounting methods, buying practices, advertising techniques, and similar matters. But the needed changes in retailer practices are not to be gained solely by instilling in the merchants some basic managerial "know how." Some *attitudes* must be altered, including attitudes toward competitors, employees, and potential partners, and also perhaps the attitude toward making money itself.

Retailer education designed to alter attitudes raises a question not involved in a program to improve managerial techniques. One problem concerns the justification for changing the attitudes at all. A live-and-let-live attitude toward one's competitors can be considered as stemming from Christian ethics. To say that the Puerto Rican merchant's system of personal values is improperly constructed involves a value judgment which cannot readily be defended. Nonetheless it does block

[3] Information provided by the Insular Board for Vocational Education.

movement toward more efficient behavior. On this ground, if not on any other, merchants can properly be urged to seek increased volume, to price accordingly, and to view increased earnings as both a measure of and a reward for the service they render.

Retailer education in managerial practices will also remove some of the barriers to expansion of the average firm. It means that branch stores or larger enterprises can be handled, by management methods required in such larger-scale operations.

To increase the retailers' familiarity with modern management methods, it will be necessary to do a much more effective job than at present. The two Chamber of Commerce programs should be encouraged, but it is doubtful whether their influence can be felt much beyond the metropolitan area. Judging from the merchants' demand for students trained in this field, it would appear worthwhile for the Commonwealth government to provide necessary funds, and emphasis on education of the owner of the business as well as on training his employees is required.

It would appear that the problem of retailer education could be attacked most profitably through the distributive education program of the Insular Board of Vocational Education. In the seventeen centers for adult education that now exist in this field, it should not be difficult to alter the courses so as to emphasize bookkeeping, buying methods, personnel policy, advertising techniques, and other managerial techniques. These centers should be shifted every year or two, if possible, so that all the towns on the island would eventually be covered by the program. It has been our observation in the course of this study that most of the small town and rural storekeepers readily welcome and adopt suggested improvements in their accounting systems.[4] If this is a true indication of the retailers' desire for knowledge, a more ambitious retailer education program should be readily accepted by the merchants.

Other means for extending retailer education should be considered. Thus the Insular Board of Vocational Education, the Agricultural Extension Service, the Community Education Division of the Department of Education, and perhaps the College of Business Administration at the University of Puerto Rico could furnish the personnel for three- or four-session extension courses in the towns of the island,

[4] One of the retailers in the cost analysis panel, who had his accounts in at least seven or eight different notebooks and ledgers, immediately adopted the simplified system drawn up for him by Maximino Velez Nieves, a research assistant on this project. The left-hand page of the double-page spread in the journal book carried the revenues, broken down into cash sales, credit sales, and other. On the right-hand page the expenses, including inventory purchases, were listed in three or four categories. When visited six weeks after starting to use the new system, the retailer reported that he was really delighted to learn, for the first time in at least ten years of business, just how much he was making.

each course on a different phase of retailing operations. The total expense of such a program would not have to be large in order to be effective. The more accurate bookkeeping might conceivably increase income tax revenues by enough to pay for the educational program.[5]

The trade journals warrant brief mention as an educational medium. Only a few of the merchants interviewed indicated that they ever saw a trade journal of any sort, but those few were the more progressive businessmen among those studied. If the retailer does not read English well, he obviously will not be interested in the journals from the mainland. A very few journals in Spanish, circulating throughout most of Latin America, are available in Puerto Rico, but few retailers follow them closely.

The retailers' trade associations might conceivably undertake retailer education programs, but except for the Chamber of Commerce, the associations do not now appear to enjoy as much support as would be required for such work. Many of the mainland retailer and wholesaler trade organizations maintain statistical services and information facilities, offering assistance in advertising, pricing policy, store arrangements, and inventory policies. Membership in these organizations and access to their services is available to Puerto Rican firms, if they wish to take advantage of them. If existing Puerto Rican trade associations could translate and edit such material to fit the needs of the local merchants, it would be of undoubted benefit; and, were the members of the associations provided with such a service by the organization, interest and support might well be increased to the point where further retail education programs could be initiated through these groups.[6]

If by a combination of the above programs, retailers were to become familiar with modern management methods — were enabled to run larger firms, engage in more active competition to attract customers, and make larger incomes, they would be equipped to do so. In other words, retailers would be able to capitalize on the elasticity of the demand curve they face. Retailer education could as a result be a very powerful factor for rationalization of the distribution system.

In summary, then, retailer and consumer education must be intensified if the environment within which distribution takes place is to be

[5] One grocer encountered in the course of the study said that he computes his income tax by estimating his sales, subtracting 90 per cent of this amount as his cost of goods sold (since he keeps no record of purchases), subtracts his operating expenses from the remaining gross margin and pays his tax on the balance.

[6] It is conceivable that more effective retail trade associations might lead to restrictive practices and an extension of the live-and-let-live attitude, rather than an improved competitive atmosphere. Since the difficulties of enforcement of restrictive practices would be very great in an organization of many small firms, however, this might not be a serious threat.

improved. A survey of the current work in the two fields indicates that it is unnecessary to establish new programs to meet the educational need; rather the existing Community Education and Distributive Education programs, which appear to be best suited for the work, should be redesigned and strengthened to attack the marketing efficiency problem more directly and more intensively than they do at present.

15

MEASURES TO IMPROVE THE EFFICIENCY OF

THE MARKETING SYSTEM: DIRECT STEPS

Intensive retailer and consumer education can, over a period of time, alter buying and retailing methods so as to establish an environment within which distributive efficiency might be improved. More direct and positive methods of accomplishing the same objective, however, should be instituted at the same time in order to hasten improvement.

Chain Store Operations

At present, only one chain distributor (defined as an organization consisting of more than four retail outlets) operates in food retailing in Puerto Rico. It originated as a chain of company stores owned by one of the *centrales,* but it is now owned and operated independently of the sugar mill. Its operations have been extended until now about thirty retail outlets (an infinitesimal proportion of the 14,000 grocery stores on the island) are operated in the cane workers' rural settlements, at the mills, and also in some of the nearby towns. Although the chain engages in considerably more price advertising than is common on the island, competitive pressure exerted by the firm apparently does not approach that of chains on the mainland. The chain's policy on this matter apparently stems in part from a reluctance to be charged with predatory competition, especially in view of its former close association with the sugar company.

In the past, Puerto Rican retailers have attempted to organize into cooperative buying groups, but with a marked lack of success and all plans failed before operations began. The seemingly unsurmountable problems included the difficulty of raising capital among the retailers, the absence of a mutually acceptable manager of established ability to oversee the operation, and the fear on the part of the smaller retailers that the larger retailers, in their role as large stock-holders in the cooperative, would bend the new organization to their own advantage. At least one plan had the apparent weakness of in-cluding a very high proportion of the retailers in one of the major towns, thus minimizing the competitive advantage accruing to mem-bership. Although complete details of these proposed organizations were impossible to obtain, interviews indicated that the management responsibility and controls required in such an endeavor were not adequately established. For example, control of policy by the members was not assured in one attempt, independent auditing of the organiza-tion's accounts was not provided for in another, and bonus incentive schemes for the manager of the cooperative were not established. Examination of these abortive plans provided additional evidence that a lack of familiarity with business management methods is a serious deterrent to cooperative wholesaling in Puerto Rico.

On a priori grounds it would seem that development of an inte-grated chain store operation on a large scale in Puerto Rico is the most promising single project for improving distributive efficiency. This, of course, has been the experience on the mainland where, with the advent of chain retailing and related developments, there has been a marked reduction in average gross margins in food distribu-tion.

The Economic Development Administration has been interested for some time in attracting mainland chain store organizations to the island. It has carefully studied the possibilities of developing shop-ping centers in the metropolitan San Juan area. Several alternative sites for a shopping center, the core of which is conceived of as a food supermarket of the modern big-city mainland variety, have been chosen and shown to representatives of the interested continental firms.

Entry of mainland chains has been blocked, however, by a number of problems, the most important of which, apparently, is the uncer-tainty of a sales volume sufficient to support a chain organization. Even in San Juan, the most prosperous market area on the island, there has been doubt whether family incomes and the number of family automobiles are great enough to support a modern super-market like those built since the war in the larger metropolitan areas on the continental United States.

The habit of buying groceries on credit is disturbing to mainland chains considering expansion into the Puerto Rican market. In view of the experience of a handful of successful grocers who sell exclu-sively for cash, however, it would seem that a larger proportion of the public would be willing to forego the credit service in exchange for slightly lower prices than is generally granted. How far this willingness to buy for cash extends into the rural areas is a moot point, but the experience of the rural consumer cooperatives, discussed below, is encouraging.

Besides the income and automobile problem, mainland chain operators evidence concern over the availability of personnel and also over the question of warehouse space. The present warehouse problem in San Juan is acute. Solution waits on the completion of the new central market and dock facility now under construction.

However, in view of the experience of the potential savings which chain distribution could bring to the island, clear and positive action to encourage such outlets seems nonetheless worthwhile. This action should be directed both toward bringing mainland chain firms onto the island and toward encouraging the growth of locally owned integrated operations.

The program to encourage entry of mainland firms must emphasize, of course, the many real factors which would seem to promise success in the Puerto Rican market if the chain operations were adapted to local conditions. Continental operators should not be led to believe that the island can be serviced by the same type of organization as the mainland. Income levels and distribution are different. The attitude toward credit buying is different. There are fewer automobiles, and so on.

The modifications of the mainland type of chain operation that would appear desirable for Puerto Rico are reasonably clear. Because of the comparative scarcity of automobiles and the apparent importance to the consumer of convenient location, it would be wise in a market like San Juan to locate several small (say 10,000 square feet of selling space) self-service cash-and-carry outlets with parking space for perhaps fifty cars. These would promise considerably more efficient operations than one or two giant stores. This same formula could be applied to Ponce and Mayaguez and perhaps to a few other large towns. Such a structure might be augmented with smaller counter service cash-and-carry stores in the smaller towns. Such a cash-and-carry chain organization was common on the mainland before the automobile became important.

The competitive advantages of such an organization would be numerous. There would be savings in advertising, in warehousing, and possibly also in trucking costs. However, one of the greatest advantages would result from direct, large quantity purchasing from the mainland. The present markup for the entire system (value of sales at retail over value at landed cost) is apparently about 50 per cent. An efficient chain organization could almost certainly anticipate costs well under this figure. A mainland chain would presumably bypass the exclusive agents for food products in Puerto Rico, who now receive commissions even on sales which are not handled or placed through them.

Because location close to the plaza is important in many small towns, the scarcity of avaliable storerooms might force a chain into incorporating existing firms. This method of development might also assure the chain of higher initial sales than would otherwise be possible. In exchange for centralized accounting and advertising, promising grocers might be induced to surrender their sovereignty over their price policy. The retailer education which could result from this type of organization would appear to be of great significance.

A vigorous program to attract the mainland chains should include not only persuasion of mainland firms, but direct encouragement as well. Thus the Economic Development Administration might offer to build warehouse space in return for sufficient rent to amortize the cost. The building might be designed for conversion to industrial use after the new central market facility is opened at which time chains would presumably move their warehousing operations to the new location. The Economic Development Administration now trains personnel for industrial plants coming onto the island. If the retailer education program does not provide the type of employee needed by new distributive organizations, the Economic Development Administration should consider training persons to fit specific needs. Finally, the Development Bank policy of lending only to industrial concerns should be reëxamined. The shortage of funds led to the present policy. In view of the benefits which could be expected from a strong and aggressive chain organization, the welfare of the population might be improved by a greater margin if some long-term investment funds were allocated to such firms.

Direct encouragement of locally owned chain enterprises is equally important. Were the Economic Development Administration to make warehouse facilities available to a mainland chain at cost it would probably be expected to do the same for similar organizations initiated by merchants now operating on the island. Any other type of assistance should be similarly available to local firms. There is a chance that any mainland enterprise at the outset is likely to reach primarily those consumers least in need of lower-cost food distribution — that is, the well-to-do automobile-owning public. Local chains, operated by men experienced in dealing with the low-income segments of the population, might well do a better job of reaching the smaller towns and rural areas.

In some quarters the fear has been expressed that a chain store organization, once established, might drive out all competition and then abuse its monopoly position by raising prices. Such fears are groundless. Entry into food retailing in Puerto Rico (as elsewhere) is too easy to allow a chain to raise its prices without bringing onto the scene a flood of competitors.

The development of enterprising chain stores in Puerto Rico would undoubtedly be effective in lowering food costs and, as noted, would appear to be the most important single step toward rationalization which can be anticipated in the near future. The core of the problem is the small average volume of Puerto Rican food stores. A firm thoroughly aware of the economies of maximum sales per outlet and of how to achieve the sales volume large enough to realize those economies could take great strides toward rationalization of food distribution. Aggressive price advertising would serve to educate the consumer in the virtues of cash purchasing, thus minimizing what are now very costly buying practices. Direct buying and efficient servicing of retail outlets from central warehouses would bring still further economies of operation. Thus a chain organization modified to fit Puerto Rico's needs could be a very powerful force for improvement of efficiency in food distribution on the island. Every effort should be bent to encourage the development of such organization.

Consumer Cooperatives

The modern consumer cooperative movement in Puerto Rico is only about seven years old. On June 30, 1952, seventy consumer cooperative stores were active and registered with the Inspector of Cooperatives of which more than one-half were in rural areas. Consumer cooperation on the island has been successful and especially in the rural areas.[1] (Members commonly take a more active interest in rural than in urban cooperatives and loyalty to the cooperative runs deeper among the members of the rural organizations.) At present the encouragement of cooperatives is handled by two government agencies. The Department of Cooperatives of the Agricultural Extension Service (part of the University of Puerto Rico) concentrates on cooperative education in the urban areas, and the Cooperative Education Division of the Social Programs Administration in the Department of Agriculture and Commerce handles the rural problem. In the last two or three years the Agricultural Extension Service has shifted the emphasis in their cooperative education program away from the creation of consumer cooperative stores toward the organization of credit unions. This follows the discovery — affirmed by the present study — that the credit problem constitutes the greatest obstacle to the cooperative movement.

[1] The following discussion is based in part on Margaret Bright, *The Cooperative Movement in Puerto Rico,* unpublished manuscript at the Social Science Research Center, University of Puerto Rico.

One reason for the success of the rural cooperatives is the insistence of the Cooperative Education Division of the Social Programs Administration that the rural group interested in launching a cooperative understand the importance of the Rochdale principle that the cooperative shall sell only for cash. After some initial policy errors which were corrected, the number of rural cooperatives has increased slowly but on a sound and firm basis. Of the forty-one consumer cooperatives functioning during 1951–52 as part of the Division's program, thirty-eight distributed surpluses.[2] The average gross margin received by these stores was 12.53 per cent while the operating expenses amounted to 5.39 per cent of sales, leaving a net profit of 7.14 per cent. The average patronage refund was 9.81 per cent of sales.

It is clear that the cooperatives are low-cost, efficient outlets. In part this is due to low depreciation expense on the building, which is typically built in part with free labor time donated by the members. The cooperatives are not subsidized by the government except for the exemption of $50,000 worth of property from the property tax and complete exemption from the income tax. Because these stores are small (the sales of the forty-one stores totaled only $1,181,397 in fiscal '52, or an average of less than $29,000 per store) and located in the rural areas, it is unlikely that typical competitors have any important income tax liability and that the exemption, accordingly, is a significant competitive advantage.

A further indication of the success of the rural cooperatives is provided by the use of the earnings. Fifty-nine per cent of the surpluses earned by the organizations was voted by the members to be used for reserve and share capital. Cash and deposits amounted to 38 per cent of the total surpluses. The retention of surplus in the cooperative, some of which can be drawn on for purchases during the dead season, suggests that the rural consumer can be persuaded to forego credit in return for lower prices. However, the credit problem is not absent from cooperative operations.

In view of the success to date of the consumer cooperative movement in the rural areas, continued and vigorous encouragement is plainly in order. So far the promotion policy has been largely passive. The Cooperative Education Division attempts to establish cooperatives only on the proportional profit farms and in communities which have requested assistance in launching such an enterprise. This restraint was well advised in the initial stages of development. Cooperatives so sponsored are now firmly established and the Division has learned what mistakes to avoid and what methods can hasten and assure sound growth of the cooperative. However, it would appear that

[2] One of the three remaining consumers cooperatives operated with a loss, while the other two did not close their books during the year.

a larger and more aggressive Cooperative Education program could now be instituted. It is now known that rural consumer cooperatives can succeed in Puerto Rico and can distribute food at such low markups. If the Division wishes to continue the policy of establishing cooperatives only in communities requesting assistance, educational work could readily assure that such requests will come out of the villages. (The Community Education Division of the Department of Education could very well develop, as a part of its audio-visual program, a film showing how a community has established its own cooperative and has thereby saved money on food purchases.) The success of the existing consumer cooperatives is the best proof that expansion of the movement in the rural areas would now be well conceived.

Central Warehouse and Dock Facilities

In late 1952, various agencies of the Commonwealth government were cooperating in the planning of a central dock, market, and warehouse facility to be built just south of the point where Martin Pena channel empties into the San Juan Bay. The completed project will provide wharf space for several ships; government-owned warehouses for lease to private wholesale concerns; facilities for a modern wholesale produce market; ample parking space and means of access; and space for a retail development and for wharfside industries. It is believed that the facility will be sufficiently completed for partial use by 1956 or 1957.

Such a facility is undoubtedly a much needed step toward improving the marketing system both of the metropolitan San Juan area and the island as a whole. At present, warehouse space in the warehouse districts of San Juan is extremely scarce. Existing buildings in these areas are inadequate, old, and ill-designed for their present function. Because of the narrow one-way streets, which allow only parallel truck parking and require difficult and uneconomical loading methods, traffic congestion is severe in the warehouse districts. Trucking and handling costs will undoubtedly be reduced with the introduction of modern, well-planned buildings. The rodent, fire, and theft hazards should be minimized. Entry of new, and expansion of existing, wholesale firms will not be blocked by the lack of warehouse and office space as at present. Government ownership of the new buildings should also alleviate the capital barrier to entry of new types of firms. Indeed, availability of modern warehouse space should constitute an important attraction to the mainland chain operators who contemplate expansion into the island market and might also encourage the development of retailer cooperative wholesaling. Finally, the central produce market would stimulate the demand for local produce. These and further advantages need not be examined in detail here as they have been thoroughly explored elsewhere.[3] The central market facility has a high priority among the programs leading to a rationalization of the island's food distribution system.

Promotion of Price Advertising

The advertising of branded foods in Puerto Rico is handled primarily by the exclusive agents. The individual grocers engage in very little radio or newspaper advertising for a number of reasons. Price advertising, as noted, is generally considered unremunerative as well as somewhat unethical. The average store, even in the metropolitan areas, draws customers from such a small area that newspaper or radio advertising coverage would normally be far in excess of the firm's market area and therefore too expensive. Individual grocers are also unfamiliar with effective advertising methods and especially of the importance of a continued advertising program. In at least one somewhat special case, however, continued price advertising by newspaper and radio has been very effective in increasing sales volume.

However, there are forms of advertising that are accessible to the small retailer. Point-of-sale advertising consisting usually of a blackboard in front of the store with prices posted is now used. In several cases grocers have found this to be successful and, of course, inexpensive.

The phenomenon of the weekend special in food stores is also becoming more common in the metropolitan areas. However, the rural consumer is apparently as yet unaccustomed to this innovation. One operator of branch stores reported that although he posted special sale prices in his branch store, he found that the managers whenever possible tried to sell the item to the customer at the regular price. Also the customers, returning the next week, could not understand why the prices on the sale items were back up at their old levels. They argued that if the lard was worth eighteen cents a pound on Saturday, the same boxes of lard could not be worth twenty-one cents on Tuesday.

Retailer education programs should emphasize strongly advertising techniques and the potential gains in volume from active price advertising. It will not be easy to alter the prevailing *attitude* toward the desirability and feasibility of price advertising in foods. No oppor-

[3] *Marketing Facilities for Farm and Related Products at San Juan, Puerto Rico,* United States Department of Agriculture, Production and Marketing Administration, Marketing and Facilities Research Branch in cooperation with Department of Agriculture and Commerce, Government of Puerto Rico, Washington, D.C., June 1951.

tunity should be overlooked for encouraging it. Nothing is more likely to alter the "tone" of competitive behavior than aggressive publicizing of low prices.

Price advertising is becoming increasingly more common among non-food retailers, partly because of the relatively recent establishment of chain department and clothing stores. The radio, newspapers, handbills, and sound trucks are all commonly used by non-food retailers as advertising media. Not only has this advertising sharpened price competition in the non-food lines, but it has also helped give consumers a much better knowledge of the market.

Recapitalization of Progressive Firms

The Development Bank is authorized by law to make loans which will encourage the economic development of the island economy. However, because of the relatively limited funds available (now $27 million), the Bank has followed a policy of lending for industrial purposes only. In view of the potential savings of rationalized food distribution, it would appear highly desirable to modify this policy, to allow lending to firms engaged in distribution. Such aid, whether to local or mainland firms, should be contingent on the establishment of an integrated operation with a minimum number of retail outlets.

Price and Margin Control

Price or margin controls are a possible method of reducing prices and margins and thereby, presumably, eliminating the more inefficient, high-margin firms. But margin controls, whether based on net or gross margins, would require that each firm maintain an accurate set of books. A vast educational program would have to be initiated before such a program could hope to be effective.

Nor is the efficacy of either margin or price controls especially clear. In a retail system in which the consumer is dependent on the grocer because of credit, the consumer cannot be the reliable reporting and enforcement officer that he is in a system where cash sales predominate and where the grocer-customer relationship is more impersonal. In addition, such efforts are relatively expensive to administer, would be unpopular during peacetime, and to some extent treat a symptom rather than the disease. The basic problem is the large number of small stores, which situation has resulted in high margins and prices. A more desirable and effective approach is by methods that reduce the number of stores and increase average volume, methods that are more certain in their effect than price or margin controls.

Outlawing Exclusive Agents

Branded food products produced on the mainland are usually marketed in Puerto Rico through an exclusive agent who has the distributor rights for the product for the whole island or, on occasion, for some part of it. In return for a commission on all shipments of the product into his territory, the agent handles advertising, collections, and claims as well as sales. The agent commonly is also a wholesaler in his own right, that is, he not only acts as an agent in his principal's sales to island firms but also buys on his own account from the principal and resells to wholesalers and retailers. The exclusive agent is also an important source of credit to his customers.

The exclusive agency arrangement is advantageous to the agent and to his principal for many reasons. The principal is relieved of the details of doing business on the island. The mainland producer's sales in Puerto Rico are usually a very small percentage of his total sales and naming the agent is a convenient way to enjoy a small amount of extra business without incurring undue expense. The agent, in return, is given what amounts to a brand monopoly over the distribution of the particular branded product. On the mainland if a buyer does not like dealing with the agent in his territory he can frequently buy from the agent in the next district; this obviously is not possible in Puerto Rico. As a result of this quasi-monopolistic nature of the franchise, the exclusive distributorships have been the basis for a number of the very large incomes on the island.

Certain practices of the exclusive agents and their principals are conceivably, though not certainly, illegal under the Robinson-Patman amendment to the Clayton Act. Section 2(c) of the Clayton Act, as amended, forbids the payment of any commission or brokerage fee except for services rendered in connection with the sale of the goods. Firms in Puerto Rico can and occasionally do order goods direct from the mainland producer, bypassing the agent. In such cases the agent collects a commission on such sales as if he had handled the order himself. This practice would not be in violation of Section 2(c) of the Clayton Act if the agent is viewed as providing certain services, such as advertising, for his principal even on sales not handled through the agent.

Yet another aspect of the exclusive agent operations might violate the Clayton Act. Section 2(a) of the Act, as amended, prohibits price discrimination, direct or indirect, between different purchasers of a commodity where the effect of such discrimination may be substantially to lessen competition "with any person who either grants or knowingly receives the benefit of such discrimination . . ." When the exclusive agent is a wholesaler in his own right, selling to retailers, he is competing with wholesalers who buy from his principal, using him as agent. Thus the agent perhaps might be thought of as enjoying a kind of rebate on his principal's sales to his competitors. If the agent receives a commission on his own purchases from his principal, a practice which would seem illegal in itself,[4] the agent's advantage would be even greater because of his commission on his own purchases plus the commission on those of his competitors.

Objection has been raised in several quarters that the exclusive agents operate a toll gate through which the island's imported food must pass and that they are expensive middlemen for the system to support. The exclusive agents could be abolished or at least restricted by either of two methods. The Federal Trade Commission, charged with enforcement of the Clayton Act, might be requested to investigate and determine whether cease and desist orders should be issued. On the other hand, the Commonwealth might enact legislation minimizing the agents' monopolistic power and income. But the crucial question is, what will be the effect of either of these two steps? Will the resulting change in distribution methods really effect a reduction in costs or will the income now enjoyed by the agents simply be shunted into other hands? Unless a proposal really promises to reduce the expenses of distribution, it is not worth implementing.

Were the Federal Trade Commission to intervene and issue a cease and desist order prohibiting the payment of brokerage fees except on orders handled through the exclusive agent, the mainland supplier would surely refuse to accept direct orders thereafter, in order to protect the agent on the island. If the Federal Trade Commission were to decide that the agent's position as agent and wholesaler constitutes price discrimination damaging to competitors, the agents could readily split the organization into two companies, the second to handle the wholesaling function as a separate entity. These dodges would presumably legalize the existing practices without lowering distributive costs.

The Commonwealth government could pass legislation requiring that all branded consumer goods coming onto the island be handled by not less than a given number of agents, or mainland producers could be required to sell direct to anyone on the island thus prohibiting completely the use of an exclusive agent. Such legislation should have careful study. There would be a specified number of agents without effective competition between them. There is a chance that such

[4] See *Southgate Brokerage Co. v. Federal Trade Commission,* Circuit Court of Appeals of the United States, Fourth Circuit, 1945; 150 F. 2d 607, certiorari denied 326 U.S. 774, 66 Sup. Ct. 230, in which the court upheld the FTC's cease and desist order directing the company to stop accepting brokerage or any commission or compensation on purchases made for its own account.

measures might reduce the dollar volume of each agent so as to necessitate an actual increase in the agents' operating margin. Provisions for direct buying undoubtedly would be thought to infringe on and to overlook important services rendered by the agent.

It is possible that the best means of minimizing the role of the exclusive agent in Puerto Rico's marketing system is an indirect one, namely, the development of a retail chain organization of sufficient size, hence bargaining strength, to deal directly with the mainland supplier. The strength and competitive position of the retail chains on the mainland was derived in large degree from the savings stemming from direct buying. There seems to be no reason why the same cannot happen in Puerto Rico. If a mainland chain were to enter the island market, the exclusive agents would be bypassed since the chain outlets would be serviced from the firm's mainland stocks. The solution of the exclusive agent problem may well have to wait on this sort of development.

Control of Entry

Taxation, licensing, and zoning are alternative methods for controlling the entry of firms into retailing. Thus a lump-sum annual tax, perhaps in the form of a license fee, could be imposed to increase the fixed costs of doing business. The tax could be graduated by market area, being larger for the metropolitan areas and larger towns than for the smaller towns and rural areas. Its effect would be to encourage large-scale operations. Being in effect an increase in overhead costs, the tax would be lower per unit of sales for the larger-volume store than for the small-volume store. It would have the joint effect of encouraging price competition and the demise of marginal small-volume operators.

The effectiveness of this measure, however, appears questionable. The present large-volume operators already enjoy low overhead per physical unit of goods sold, yet the lack of price competition means that these firms realize their advantage in terms of relatively high net profit margins on a relatively small volume of sales rather than in the form of a low net profit margin on a larger volume. Until price competition becomes more common, the lump-sum tax would probably result only in larger government revenues (through a regressive tax) and higher prices to consumers.

An alternative tax measure could be based on gross or net margins, rewarding the firm reporting a low gross with a low tax or perhaps even a rebate while penalizing the high gross operator with a high tax. As with the margin-control proposal, however, this method is burdened with the problem of accurate bookkeeping and reporting by the thousands of retailers on the island.

Restricting the number of store licenses is a possible remedial measure. With the approximate number of food stores necessary to serve each *municipio* determined, the equivalent number of licenses could be made available to the grocers in the area. If only a nominal license fee were charged, the problem of allocation of the few licenses among the many applicants would of course present a very troublesome problem. One solution would be to auction off the licenses to the highest bidders, but this involves the same objection as the lump-sum tax since it is merely a variation on the lump-sum tax methods. If the degree of price competition remains limited, the additional fixed cost may merely afford an excuse for maintaining prices in spite of the larger volume per store, or even an excuse for increasing prices.

Zoning regulations in Puerto Rico are now in force only for the San Juan area, and it will apparently be many years before all the significant towns are zoned. Once zoned, these towns and cities will no longer see *colmados* or *bazares* establishing themselves in residential areas, supposedly, although the existing stores will not be affected by the new regulations and new stores will be allowed to open in the areas open to commercial firms.

In summary we see little hope for effective improvement through the various devices for control of entry. As with price and margin control, the disadvantages would seem generally to outweigh the advantages.

Direct Government Intervention

A complete discussion of possible programs for rationalization of Puerto Rico's marketing system must include consideration of direct government intervention in the form of government-owned retail outlets. This approach to the food distribution problem in Puerto Rico has already been attempted by the Puerto Rico Agriculture Development Company.

The Puerto Rico Agriculture Development Company was established in 1945 for the purpose of developing, on a pilot-plant scale, the findings of the agricultural experiment stations; developing improved fishing and cattle-raising operations; and improving the efficiency of food distribution.

A total of sixteen "Praco" retail food stores were eventually established. In 1951 it was decided that the Praco operation was not realizing expectations and should be discontinued. After unsuccessful efforts to interest various mainland chains in buying the stores as a unit, they were sold as separate units to local individuals.

Various reasons for Praco's lack of real success have been advanced. Political considerations appear to have prohibited some managerial efforts to improve the organization, not only with respect to personnel changes but other managerial problems as well. For example, closing unprofitable Praco outlets was opposed on the grounds that such a move would be a retreat from the plan for a system of government-owned stores. Nor were the Praco operations in the field of distribution clearly separated from the experimental development work; thus it was difficult to identify the operating profits and losses of the distribution phase alone. Praco sales were never sufficient to warrant central warehousing; nor was price advertising emphasized, perhaps because successful advertising campaigns would have drawn such volume as to alienate small grocers.

Although the Praco stores were not continued, they did benefit the island in at least two respects. They introduced self-service operations on a large scale, and they demonstrated that a cash market does exist in the larger towns. Resumption of the Praco operation cannot now be considered feasible, but in view of the rather obvious managerial mistakes that marked the history of the organization, discontinuance of the stores is no evidence that cash-and-carry chain operations are likely to be unsuccessful in Puerto Rico.

INDEX

INDEX

Advertising, 175, 177, 187, 189; non-food retail, 138, 139; non-food wholesale, 163, 165, 167; increased, 192–193

Agents: in food retailing, 23, 27; in food wholesaling, 36, 41, 44, 48; in non-food wholesaling, 157; outlawing exclusive, 194–196

Agriculture, contribution of to total income, 6–8

Agricultural Extension Service (Dept. of Agriculture), 178, 179, 182, 189; Department of Cooperatives, 189

Aguadilla, 77, 146, 152

Alcoholic beverages, and food bill, 115, 122, 123, 124

Apparel. *See* Clothing

Appliances, electric, 13, 180; retail distribution, 129, 134, 135, 136, 141, 144, 147, 149–150, 151, 152, 153, 154; wholesale distribution, 157–158, 159, 160, 161, 162, 163, 164–167, 170–171

Arecibo, 77, 146

Asset and liability accounts, 89

Automobiles, 13, 187

Bakeries, 14, 122, 115

Bayamon, 146, 152

Bazares, 127, 129, 133, 197

Beans, 10, 11, 32, 40, 114

Bookkeeping, 174, 183

Bread, 10

Brokers: in food retailing, 23, 27; in food wholesaling, 36, 41, 49; in non-food retailing, 154; in non-food wholesaling, 157

Buyer. *See* Consumer

Cafetines, 15, 41, 74

Caguas, 77, 146, 181

Cane industry, 8, 129, 175

Canned goods, 19, 23, 24, 29, 39, 44, 76

Cash-and-carry stores, 21, 90, 100; possibility of increasing, 187, 198

Cereals, 19, 23, 24, 29, 40, 44

Chain stores, 177; possibility of increasing, 185–189, 191

Chamber of Commerce, 183; course in advertising and salesmanship, 181, 182

Charge accounts, retail-supplier, 155. *See also* Credit

Chicken, 10, 40

Clayton Act, Robinson-Patman Amendment, 194–195

Clothing, 10, 13, 180; retail distribution, 126, 127, 129, 130, 131, 132–133, 134–135, 136, 137, 141, 143–147, 148, 149–150, 151, 152, 153, 154, 155; wholesale distribution, 157, 158, 159, 161, 163, 164–165, 166, 170–171, 172

Codfish, 10, 11, 40, 114

Coffee, 10, 40, 123, 124, 129

College of Business Administration (University of Puerto Rico), 182

Colmado, 69, 197. *See also* Food distribution

Confectionary stores, 115

Consumer, 17, 19, 28; cost of marketing to, 2–3, 13; buying practices, 23–27, 76, 77, 79, 175–176; dependence of on local store, 69–70, 71; possibilities for educating, 178–180, 183–184; and cooperative stores, 185–186, 189–191; and measures for marketing improvement, 189, 193, 195

Consumers' Price Index, Commonwealth Bureau of Labor Statistics, 11, 12

Consumption expenditures, 9–10

Cooperative Education Division, Social Programs Administration, 189, 190–191

Cooperatives, consumer, 185–186, 189–191

Cooperatives, Department of, 189

Cooperatives, Inspector of, 189

Cost: food retailing, 2–3, 9–10, 31, 32, 74, 87–90, 92–104; and management, 62–63; distribution in model, 78; model food bills, 116–117; non-food retailing, 144–147; and credit, 173–174, 175, 180; and delivery, 175–176

Cost analyses: food retailing, 82–83, 87–104, 106, 107, 123; food wholesaling, 83, 104, 105–109, 123

Credit: in food retailing, 20–21, 62, 76–77; in model, 80, 81, 82–83, 85; loss from, 88–89, 120–121; in cost analyses, 92–104 *passim;* in food wholesaling, 43–44, 105–109, 115; extensive use and cost of, 70–71, 72, 80, 173–174, 175, 180; in non-food retailing, 147, 148, 151–152, 154, 155; in non-food wholesaling, 164, 165, 167, 170–171; and chain stores, 186–187; and cooperatives, 189, 190

Credit unions, 189
Culebra, 38
Customer. *See* Consumer

Dairy products, 40, 76
Delivery service: in food retailing, 17, 21,
    28, 32, 34–35, 77; and model, 80, 81,
    82–83, 85, 95, 98–100, 102–103, 103–
    104, 120–121; in food wholesaling, 105;
    in non-food wholesaling, 165, 166, 170–
    171; cost, 175–176
Development Bank policy, 188, 193
Discounts: food wholesaling, 43–44; non-
    food retailing, 138, 154, 155; non-food
    wholesaling, 163, 171. *See also* Credit
Division of Community Education, Depart-
    ment of Education, 178, 179, 182, 191
Double handling, of products, 114, 122
Drugs, 13, 70, 127; retail distribution, 129,
    130, 131, 132, 133, 134–136, 138, 141,
    145, 148, 149–150, 151, 152, 153, 154,
    156; wholesale distribution, 157, 158,
    159, 160–161, 162, 163, 164–165, 166,
    167, 169–171
Dun and Bradstreet, 142

Economic   Development   Administration,
    112; and chain stores, 186, 188
Economic Stabilization Administration, sur-
    vey on food wholesale markups, 59–
    60
Education: of consumer, 178–180, 183–184;
    of retailer, 180–184, 188; and coopera-
    tives, 189
Eggs, 10
Employment: problems of, 2–3, 8, 178; in
    food retailing, 18, 34; in food whole-
    saling, 51, 53–54; wages, 77, 88, 145–
    146, 166; impact of model on, 119–
    121; non-food retailing, 135–137; non-
    food wholesaling, 161–163; and manu-
    facturing, 172; and managers' attitudes,
    175. *See also* Personnel
Equipment: of self-service stores, 34–35;
    value, 86, 87; wholesale, 106
Exports, 111

Fajardo, 77, 146
Federal Trade Commission, 195
Field study, of food retailing, 14–17, 28
Fishing, 129
Food, 2, 12, 13; total consumption, 9–10;
    imported, 11, 36
Food distribution: retail system, 2, 14–36;
    management of, 62–73, 79; problems
    of operating, 70, 74–77, 114–116; model
    retail system, 81, 82–83, 86–104, 110–
    124; wholesale system, 36–61; model

wholesale system, 79–84, 105–109; im-
    proving, 177–198
Food stores, miscellaneous, 14
Fruit, 10, 12, 14, 15, 19, 27, 40, 112
Full-line stores, 19, 22–23, 24, 29, 32, 33; in
    model, 77, 78
Furniture, 10–11, 13, 180; retail distribution,
    126–127, 129, 130, 134, 135, 136, 140,
    141, 144–147, 148, 149–150, 151, 152,
    153, 156; wholesale distribution, 157,
    158, 159, 160, 161, 162, 163, 164–165,
    166–167, 169, 170–171, 172

General Supplies Administration, 60, 112
George-Deen Act, 179–180
Government, Puerto Rican: as contributor
    to income, 6–8; direct intervention to
    improve marketing system, 197–198
Grocery. *See* Food distribution
Guayama, 77, 146

Hardware: retail distribution, 129, 133, 135,
    136, 137, 141, 143, 144, 147, 148, 151,
    153; wholesale distribution, 157, 158,
    159, 161, 162, 163, 164, 166, 169, 170–
    171
Hardware Retailer, 142
High schools, home economics in, 178
Home Economics Department (University
    of Puerto Rico), 178
Home Economics Division, Department of
    Education, 178
Hotels, 41, 112, 113
Household equipment, 10, 126
Humacao, 77, 146

Imports, 11, 110, 111, 156
Income: of Puerto Ricans, 2, 5–9; and food
    distribution, 17, 86–87, 186–187; and
    non-food distribution, 125–128, 137
Industry, 129
Institutional purchases, 113
Insular Board for Vocational Education,
    181, 182
Insurance expense, 87, 105
Integration, possibilities for, 123
Inventory: self-service store evaluation, 35;
    scarcity of, 63; turnover rate, 89; in
    wholesaling, 106
Investment: in food retailing, 22–23, 88;
    in food wholesaling, 49–50, 51–52; in
    non-food retailing, 139–143; in non-
    food wholesaling, 164–165
Island Food Bills, 110–121, 122, 123
Isolated rural market area: markups, 90–
    93; and model food bill, 117, 118, 120,
    121; minimum stores necessary, 118–
    119

Junta de Salario Mínimo, survey of food wholesale gross profits, 59–60

Labor, 2, 3, 8; costs, 77, 106–107. *See also* Employment
Lard, 10, 11, 32, 40, 114
Lechoneras, 15
Licenses, restricting, 197
Limited-line stores, 32
Lorenz curves, applied to non-food retailing, 132

Management: organization, 62–64, 66–67; personnel policies, 64–65, 71–72; capital, 66, 67; attitudes, 67–68, 72–73; ethics, 68–69; need for better, 182. *See also* Retailer
Manatí, 77
Manufacturers: direct supply from, 48, 152, 154; agents, 158; as wholesalers, 172
Manufacturing and mining, 6–8
Margins: in food retailing, 28–35, 74–75, 79; in food wholesaling, 54–61, 74–75, 113, 121, 124; of consumer cooperatives, 190; controls, 193; and taxation, 196–197. *See also* Cost analyses; Mark-ups
Market areas. *See* Isolated rural; Market town; Metropolitan; Rural town
Market town market area, 77, 78, 85, 97–100; and model food bill, 117, 118, 121; non-food retailing, 129, 138–139, 152
Marketing system: problems of, 74–77, 114–116, 173–176; means for improvement, 177–198. *See also* Consumer; Food Distribution; Non-food Products; Retailing; Wholesaling
Markups, 60–61, 74; model retail system, 83–85, 90–93, 94, 96, 97–100, 101–104, 177; model wholesale systems, 106–109, 115; non-food retailing, 131, 148, 149–150; non-food wholesaling, 169; and chain stores, 187
Mayaguez: food retailing, 23, 27; food wholesaling, 38, 40, 41, 77; non-food distribution, 129, 130, 133, 146, 148, 152; educational opportunities, 181; chain stores, 187
Meat, 10, 19, 23, 27, 40, 44, 76, 112, 123; in model system, 77, 78
Metropolitan market area, 76, 77, 78, 85, 100–103, 117; and island food bill, 117, 118, 120; and taxation, 196. *See also* Mayaguez; Ponce; San Juan
Milk, 10, 12, 32, 40; dealers, 14, 115
Mintz, Sidney W., 63n
Model food distribution system: retail, 76–80, 82–83, 86–104; wholesale, 79–84,

105–109; alternatives C, CD, LS, 80, 85, 106, 108, 109, 117–122; and island food bill, 110–121; savings possible, 121–124

Nieves, Maximino Velez, 182n
Non-food products, 12–13, 40, 62, 69, 70; distribution, 125–127; survey of, 128–131; retailing, 132–156; wholesaling, 157–172. *See also* Appliances; Clothing; Drugs; Furniture; Hardware; Shoes

Office of Price Administration, 59, 60, 131, 148
Office of Scientific Assessment, 140, 147; program, 82, 86, 87
Onions, 40

Peas, 40
Peddlers, 74; importance of, 127–128, 133, 137; suppliers to, 137
Personnel: retail policies, 64–66, 71–72; untrained, 173; lack of for chain stores, 187. *See also* Employment
Pineapple, 129
Ponce: food retailing, 23, 27; food wholesaling, 38, 40, 41, 77; non-food distribution, 129, 130, 133, 146, 147, 152; educational opportunities in, 179, 181; chain stores, 187
Pork, dry salt, 10, 11, 40, 114
Potatoes, 40
Price: competition, 72–73, 174, 175; consciousness, 179, 180; controls, 193
Produce, 77, 78, 123. *See also* Fruits; Vegetables
Profit: food retailing, 31–32, 73, 87; food wholesaling, 54–61, 107; non-food retailing, 147; non-food wholesaling, 165–168. *See also* Cost analyses
Puerto Rico Agriculture Development Company (Praco), 197–198
Puerto Rico Census of Business, *1949,* 74, 84, 115, 116–117, 119, 125, 127, 129, 145, 157, 161, 177n
Puerto Rico Census of Distribution, 14, 15, 31, 36
Puerto Rico, University of, 178, 182
Purchasing, through chain stores, 187, 189

Quality, consciousness of, 179, 180

Refrigeration, 17, 78, 176
Reposterias, 15
Restaurants, 41, 112, 113
Retailer: attitudes and practices of, 3, 62–73, 174; -wholesaler buying, 108–109; and island food bills, 113–116; educa-

tion of, 180–184; and cooperatives, 185–186; and advertising, 192
Retailing, 3, 6–8, 73; food, 2, 12, 14–36; model food, 81–83, 86–104, 116, 119; non-food, 128–156; possibility of government-owned outlets, 197–198
Rice, 10, 11, 32, 39, 114
Rio Piedras, 77, 129, 146
Rochdale Principle, 190
Rural food stores, 20–21, 23, 24, 28, 76, 77, 87
Rural town market area, 77, 79, 85, 93–96; and model food bill, 117, 118, 121; non-food retailing, 129, 133, 139, 141, 142, 146, 151, 156; successful cooperatives in, 189, 190–191; and taxation, 196

Salaries: retailers', 88, 89; wholesalers', 105
Sales volume: food distribution system, 16–17, 18–23, 28, 30–32, 35–39, 40, 48, 49–50; model food system, 82–83, 85, 88, 92, 93, 96, 98–100, 115; non-food distribution system, 132–137, 142, 143–147, 149–150, 152, 155, 159, 160–168; measures to increase, 177
Salesmen, 39, 53–54, 137
San Germán, 179
San Juan: food retailing, 23, 27; food wholesaling, 38, 40, 41, 44–48, 50, 60, 113, 119; non-food retailing, 129, 130, 133, 146, 147, 148, 151, 152; non-food wholesaling, 158, 159; educational opportunities in, 181; shopping centers, 186, 187; proposed central warehouse facilities, 191–192
Santurce, 77, 119, 179
Savings, possible, 79, 121–124
Self-service stores, 33–35, 77; in market town areas, 97; in metropolitan areas, 100; as possibility, 187, 198
Shipping, costs, 112–113
Shoes: retail distribution, 129, 130, 134, 135, 136, 138, 141, 142, 143–147, 149–150, 151; wholesale distribution, 152, 153, 160, 170–171

Staples, 19, 23, 24, 29, 32, 39, 40, 76
Sugar, 40, 111–112, 173

Taxation: of non-food property owners, 147; for controlling entry, 196; zoning, 197
Tobacco, 115, 129
Tomato paste, 40
Tomato sauce, 10, 11, 32
Trade journals, 183
Transportation, 49–50, 76, 106, 116, 137, 156, 191
Truckers, 23, 27, 49–50
Truck farms, 129

United States: economy compared, 5–9, 173; food retailing compared, 20–21, 33; food wholesaling compared, 56; non-food retailing compared, 132, 136; non-food wholesaling compared, 161, 168, 170
United States Census of Business, *1948*, 74, 159, 160, 161
Urban food stores, 20, 21, 23, 24, 28, 76, 77

Vegetables, 10, 12, 14, 15, 19, 27, 40, 112
Vianda, 10
Vieques, 38

Wages, 77, 88, 145–146, 166; minimum wage zones, 146
Warehouses, 187, 188, 191
Weight, ratio to value, 116
Wheat, imports, 111
Wholesaler: management attitudes. of, 62; connections with retailers, 69, 77, 108–109; and island food bills, 110–113; as agent, 194–195
Wholesaling, 6–8, 173, 174; food, 23–27, 36–61, 157; model food, 79, 83–84, 105–109, 115; non-food, 137, 152, 157–172
Women, as part of labor force, 8

Yard goods. *See* Clothing

Zoning: wage, 146; taxation, 197